Eddie and Ev.

who gave it to me
to have two copies!

Waterloo
Messenger

Waterloo Messenger

*The Life of Henry Percy,
Peninsular Soldier and
French Prisoner of War*

Sir William Mahon

Pen & Sword
MILITARY

First published in Great Britain in 2017 by
PEN & SWORD MILITARY
An imprint of
Pen & Sword Books Ltd
47 Church Street
Barnsley
South Yorkshire
S70 2AS

ISBN 978-1-47387-050-5

Typeset by Concept, Huddersfield, West Yorkshire, HD4 5JL.
Printed and bound in Malta by Gutenberg Press Ltd.

Pen & Sword Books Ltd incorporates the imprints of Pen & Sword Archaeology, Atlas, Aviation, Battleground, Discovery, Family History, History, Maritime, Military, Naval, Politics, Railways, Select, Social History, Transport, True Crime, and Claymore Press, Frontline Books, Leo Cooper, Praetorian Press, Remember When, Seaforth Publishing and Wharncliffe.

For a complete list of Pen & Sword titles please contact
PEN & SWORD BOOKS LIMITED
47 Church Street, Barnsley, South Yorkshire, S70 2AS, England
E-mail: enquiries@pen-and-sword.co.uk
Website: www.pen-and-sword.co.uk

Contents

List of Plates

The fortress of Elvas – statue of a Seven Years War British grenadier.

Serjeant John Spencer Cooper, who made excellent 'Rough Notes of Seven Campaigns'.

Moulins in the Auvergne, where the Earl of Beverley and his son Algernon were paroled from 1808.

Les Perrots, Coulandon. The Durands were *vignerons* who lived in an annexe of this big house.

'Summoned to Waterloo' by Robert Alexander Hillingford (1898).

The sword used by Henry Percy at Waterloo, which he forced into the chest of a mounted French officer.

The clasp of Napoleon's cloak.

Sketch by Henry Percy of La Belle Alliance, where he was with Wellington when they met Blücher after the battle.

On 21 June 2015, the 200th anniversary of the event, the arrival of Henry Percy with the Waterloo Dispatch at Mrs Boehm's house in St James's Square was re-enacted. It is now the East India Club.

The Prince Regent's apology – replica French eagle.

Breguet pocket watch given by the Duke of Wellington to Henry Percy for taking the Waterloo Dispatch to London.

Henry Percy, painted at Moulins as a prisoner of war by Delatour Fontanet in 1811. It was in the possession of Marion Durand, then her son Henry Marion the general.

A newly discovered miniature depicting Major General Sir Henry Marion Durand, KCSI, CB (1812–1870). Son of Henry Percy and Marion Durand of Moulins.

Introduction

This book is a *life* of Henry Percy because he had an unusual life, but information being incomplete, it would be pretentious to call it a biography. Lurking in attics or archives somewhere there must be more facts to discover.

My interest in Henry Percy's life began in about 1968, when a formidable maiden great-aunt, great-grand-daughter of the Earl of Uxbridge, was given Reginald Colby's booklet about the Waterloo Dispatch for her 'eighty something-th' birthday.

She lived alone in faded splendour in an enormous draughty Georgian Irish house in Galway, changing nightly for her chilly candlelit dinner, alone in the vast dining room, as if the nineteenth century had never left us. Surrounded by memories and loneliness, and perishing cold, her isolation was not splendid at all. The senior family members were always interested in Waterloo because of 'One Leg' Uxbridge, as he was known. They spoke of the Boer War as though it were just the other day, and 'the last war' was the recent one in 1914.

It was almost impossible to find a birthday present for her. No politics (it was safer not to dabble in politics in the south of Ireland after 1916); no sport nor showbiz; no racy novels, with – perish the thought! – smut!

So Waterloo, with Colby's exciting story of the dispatch, was perfect. She was enthralled. I was privileged to be lent, and eventually bequeathed, the booklet. She also left me a copy of the guest list of the Duchess of Richmond's ball, and several contemporary scraps, to fire the imagination.

My two years at the Royal Naval Staff College, Greenwich included inherited responsibility for conducting the European tour, including visits to NATO headquarters, and a morning at Supreme Headquarters Allied Forces Europe (SHAPE) at Mons. At each puzzling establishment, the naval students suffered lengthy monologues in incomprehensible NATO-speak by earnest senior officers of allied nations, experts perhaps, but not at inspiring sailors. The RN antidote after NATO Headquarters was a good run ashore, with consequent hangover; not ideal preparation for next morning's lectures at SHAPE.

The cure for the malaise was a blustery afternoon at Waterloo. Before departure, Waterloo had been gently studied and discussed, the film shown. Away blew the cobwebs, and the interest awoke. They asked surprising, penetrating questions, even the French *Capitaine de Frégate* joined in. So Waterloo became more than just a curiosity. So did Wellington; you can't have one without the other.

This prompted a carefully manipulated final posting to Madrid, to allow a proper study of the Peninsular War. The discovery that Henry Percy had been at Corunna and later Oporto and Talavera was an eye-opener. Talavera was the nearest battlefield. When motorway construction disturbed a Talavera battlefield grave, the then Duke of Wellington, the Chief of the General Staff and the Spanish Duke of Albuquerque all agreed to come to Spain in 1990 and unveil a modern special memorial, with representatives of all the successor regiments of the opposing sides. The Spaniards very kindly paid. Julian Paget, who knows the Peninsula like the back of his hand, helped with the battlefield tour at Talavera and his clear maps of the battlefields are used in this book with warm thanks.

Percy was taken prisoner in Portugal a year or so after Talavera. Then it emerged that General Lefèbvre-Desnouettes, who had been captured at Benavente, would have met Henry Percy, then ADC to his beloved Sir John Moore. Afterwards Lefèbvre-Desnouettes lived on parole at Cheltenham. Henry, as a prisoner himself, also lived on parole, in France. There were even abortive attempts at exchanging Lefèbvre-Desnouettes for Henry's father, who had been detained in France. Lots of coincidences. All this was before Henry became famous with the Waterloo dispatch.

There seemed to be a story worth researching. Brian Cathcart's splendid book on Henry Percy's journey was well timed to surf the wave of the bicentenary. He is a good friend, we share discoveries openly and enthusiastically, from which both draw pleasure: another bonus of this strange odyssey. Tim Cooke, a Trustee of the Waterloo Association, not only co-chaired the magnificent Waterloo200 commemorations, but has also been a more than kind host who spotted Brian Cathcart and introduced Algernon Percy.

The French side of the story is certainly incomplete. Finding and handling the original letter signed by the Chief of Staff of Masséna's Army of Portugal to the Minister of War advising of Henry Percy's journey from Portugal to Bayonne was just one happy moment of many. If only that sheet of paper signed by General Fririon could tell us what he said that cold January morning at Villa Nova. It was there, in his hand.

Piecing it together has been a labour of love. Without encouragement and interest from friends old and new, the jigsaw could never have been attempted.

There have been sublime events, such as the eventual discovery in a village *Mairie* of the original birth certificate of Henry's son, born in 1812 to his French girlfriend, Marion Durand. It is also a sad story; Henry and his younger soldier brother Francis both died young; so did his second son James. We don't even know what happened to the boys' mother, Jeanne, after Henry's death. He called her Marion; they never married, and she stayed in France.

More cheerfully, we do know of the great success of the elder son and his Durand descendants, who rose to prominence and were great men in India. The Durand Line (named after Henry's grandson, Surveyor General of India) still describes the old porous frontier between the former India and Afghanistan.

It has been possible to make contact with the descendants of Henry's surviving son. The Reverend Stella, Lady Durand has been kind and supportive and with her son, Sir Edward, has solved the mystery of Henry's second boy's name: James. Sadly, that is nearly all we know of him.

Catherine Willson of the Hereford Archives helped with the portrait of Henry Symons, the parson who conducted the burial of Sir John Moore at Corunna, with Henry as a bearer. His prayer book from that service is in the National Army Museum. The saga of the capture of Lefèbvre-Desnouettes is enlivened by the kindness of Majors Oliver Howard and Peter Perowne of the King's Royal Hussars, for the Regiment has provided the image of Levi Grisdale's unique medal and the picture of Lefèbvre-Desnouettes at Benavente. I am very grateful for their willing help. Stephen Lewis and Janet and David Bromley, likewise, were very helpful with information on Grisdale's family.

At Alnwick Castle the archives have been a rich source of information, with patient interest and help from Clare Baxter, Christopher Hunwick, Eve Reverchon as translator, and Lisa Little, new to the chase, but a terrier. She discovered an unexpected comprehensive medical report on Henry at the eleventh hour, from which, unhesitatingly, Michael Crumplin has expertly produced a possible diagnosis of Henry's recurring malaise.

Without the Alnwick team, and Algernon Percy, who has been a constant encouragement and generous host, the project would not have worked. Algernon has been a great source of introductions, helping, with Libby Dineley, to solve the mystery of the unrecognized Mr Davison and Nelson's Purse, leading to Martyn Downer and his spectacular Nelson discoveries. Algernon also introduced Hoare's Bank, where Pamela Hunter found nuggets from Henry's bank account. Algernon also checked for family howlers, to which authors on the Percy family are vulnerable.

The Duke of Northumberland has been kind enough to allow the project to proceed unfettered. I am most grateful for the use of images and material. At Kew the National Archives yielded unexpected treasures, thanks to Tina Hampson, a canny researcher and example to all.

In France, while investigating Percy's time as a prisoner, by chance we stayed with Edith and Hubert de Contenson at Bresolles near Moulins. Hubert, it transpires, is descended from General Foy, and Edith is an enthusiastic former '*archiviste*'. What an amazing stroke of luck! When we told Edith of the newly discovered 1812 birth certificate, we were introduced to the family where Marion, Henry's girlfriend, had lived with her family. 'And the child became a British *Général*? *Vraiment*?' Such kind help makes it worthwhile. Edith has also spent much time finding treasures about the Percy family from the archives at Moulins. Our gratitude is unbounded.

At Vincennes Monsieur André Rakoto and Monsieur Bertrand Fonck, pre-warned of my mission, patiently watched my astonishment at the Henry Percy folder which had been dusted off from their prisoner of war archives.

In Paris, at the Musée de l'Armée, Madame Emilié Robbe spent a whole morning giving us a superb private tour explaining every detail in brilliant English. Then four years later she kindly helped greatly over the portraits of General Lefèbvre-Desnouettes and General Junot.

The Bagot family of Levens Hall, descended from Henry's brother and executor, Josceline Percy, have generously allowed photographs of Henry's Breguet watch and the Imperial Bees from Napoleon's cloak to be used in the book. The photograph of the eagle given to Mrs Boehm by the Prince Regent as an apology after he ruined her party is used with permission of the generous owner. It took twenty-five years' searching to locate it.

The wonderful, soon to be beautifully refurbished, National Army Museum has been a source of constant help. I thank the Director General, Janice Murray, and several of her predecessors for unfailing interest, as well as all the staff who are superb. This book would never have seen the light of day were it not for the incredible patience of my wife Rosie, who has trailed the archives of Europe with a resigned smile. Somehow she has maintained home catering standards at a dizzy height, notwithstanding the many Percy distractions.

Jamie Glover-Wilson oiled the wheels at Pen & Sword, for which I am greatly indebted. There were two key Pen & Sword influences, Rupert Harding the Commissioning Editor, whose Peninsular knowledge and encouragement gave great pleasure, and Sarah Cook. Her eye for detail and her cheerful enthusiasm while multi-tasking with other more learned books are an example to any author. From them all I have gleaned much wisdom, and enjoyed the experience greatly.

Any mistakes are mine alone.

Finally, here it is, imperfect and incomplete, but published, in the hope that some of the gaps can be filled by its readers.

Family of Algernon, 1st Earl of Beverley 1750–1830
Second son of Hugh Percy, 2nd Duke of Northumberland

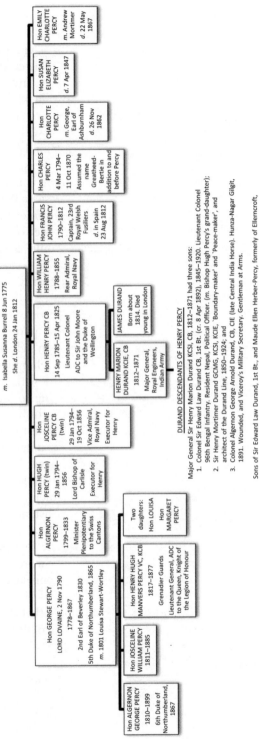

ALGERNON PERCY
1st EARL OF BEVERLEY
1750–1830
m. Isabella Susanna Burrell 8 Jun 1775
She *d.* London 24 Jan 1812

Hon GEORGE PERCY
LORD LOVAINE, 2 Nov 1790
1778–1867
2nd Earl of Beverley 1830
5th Duke of Northumberland, 1865
m. 1801 Louisa Stewart-Wortley

Hon ALGERNON PERCY
1799–1833
Minister Plenipotentiary to the Swiss Cantons

Hon HUGH PERCY (twin)
29 Jan 1794–1856
Lord Bishop of Carlisle
Executor for Henry

Hon JOSCELINE PERCY (twin)
29 Jan 1794–19 Oct 1856
Vice Admiral, Royal Navy
Executor for Henry

Hon HENRY PERCY CB
14 Sep 1785–15 Apr 1825
Lieutenant Colonel
ADC to Sir John Moore and the Duke of Wellington

Hon WILLIAM HENRY PERCY
1788–1855
Rear Admiral, Royal Navy

Hon FRANCIS JOHN PERCY
1790–1812
Captain, 23rd Royal Welsh Fusiliers
d. in Spain 23 Aug 1812

Hon CHARLES PERCY
4 Mar 1794–11 Oct 1870
Assumed the name Greatheed-Bertie in addition to and before Percy

Hon CHARLOTTE PERCY
m. George, Earl of Ashburnham
d. 26 Nov 1862

Hon SUSAN ELIZABETH PERCY
d. 7 Apr 1847

Hon EMILY CHARLOTTE PERCY
m. Andrew Mortimer
d. 22 May 1867

Hon ALGERNON GEORGE PERCY
1810–1899
6th Duke of Northumberland, 1867

Hon JOSCELINE WILLIAM PERCY
1811–1885

Hon HENRY HUGH MANVERS PERCY VC, KCB
1817–1877
Grenadier Guards
Lieutenant General, ADC to the Queen, Knight of the Legion of Honour

Two daughters:
Hon LOUISA PERCY
Hon MARGARET PERCY

HENRY MARION DURAND KCIE, CB
1812–1871
Major General, Royal Engineers, Indian Army

JAMES DURAND
Born about 1814. Died young in London

DURAND DESCENDANTS OF HENRY PERCY

Major General Sir Henry Marion Durand KCSI, CB, 1812–1871 had three sons:

1. Colonel Sir Edward Law Durand CB, 1st Bt. (cr. 8 Apr 1892), 1845–1920. Lieutenant Colonel 96th Bengal Infantry. Resident Nepal, Political Officer. (*m.* Bishop Hugh Percy's grand-daughter);
2. Sir Henry Mortimer Durand GCMG, KCSI, KCIE, 'Boundary-maker' and 'Peace-maker', and architect of the Durand Line, 1850–1924; and
3. Colonel Algernon George Arnold Durand, CB, CIE (late Central India Horse). Hunza-Nagar Gilgit, 1891. Wounded, and Viceroy's Military Secretary. Gentleman at Arms.

Sons of Sir Edward Law Durand, 1st Bt., and Maude Ellen Herber-Percy, formerly of Ellerncroft, Wotton-under-Edge:

1. Sir Edward Percy Marion Durand, 2nd Bt., 1884–1955; and
2. Brigadier Alan Algernon Marion Durand, MC. Royal Artillery. 3rd Bt., 1893–1971.

The baronetcy passed via the late Lieutenant Commander Mortimer Henry Marion Durand RN, 1898–1969 (son of Colonel Sir Edward Law Durand, 1st Bt.) to his son, Revd Sir Henry Mortimer Dickon Marion St George Durand, 4th Bt., 1934–1992.
Sir Edward Alan Christopher Percy Durand, 5th Bt., 21 Feb 1974.

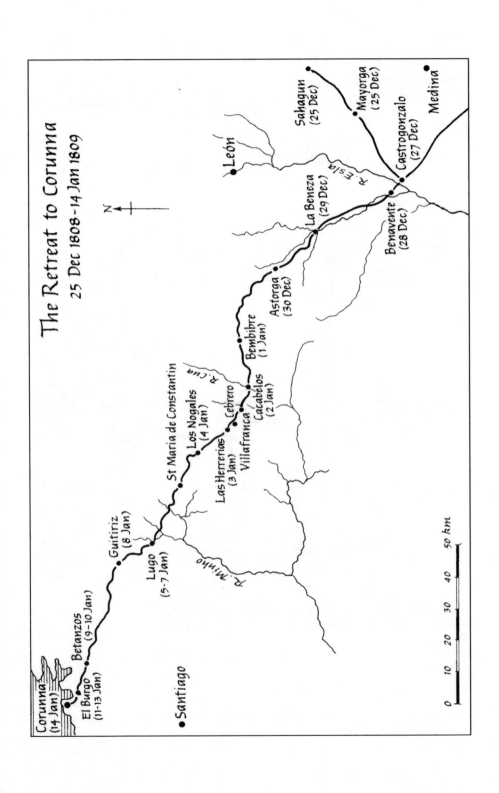

The Retreat to Corunna
25 Dec 1808 - 14 Jan 1809

Corunna (14 Jan)
El Burgo (11-13 Jan)
Betanzos (9-10 Jan)
Guitiriz (8 Jan)
Lugo (5-7 Jan)
St Maria de Constantin
Los Nogales (4 Jan)
Cebrero (4 Jan)
Las Herrerias (3 Jan)
Villafranca
Cacabelos (2 Jan)
Bembibre (1 Jan)
Astorga (30 Dec)
La Baneza (29 Dec)
Benavente (28 Dec)
Castrogonzalo (27 Dec)
León
Sahagun (25 Dec)
Mayorga (25 Dec)
Medina

Santiago

R. Minho
R. Cua
R. Esla

N

0   10   20   30   40   50 km

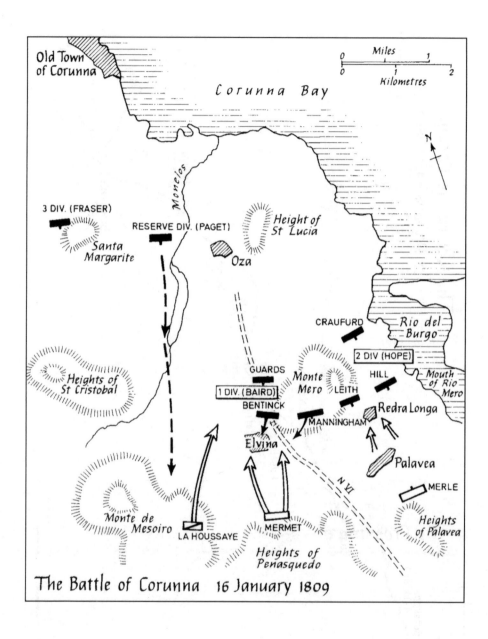

The Battle of Corunna   16 January 1809

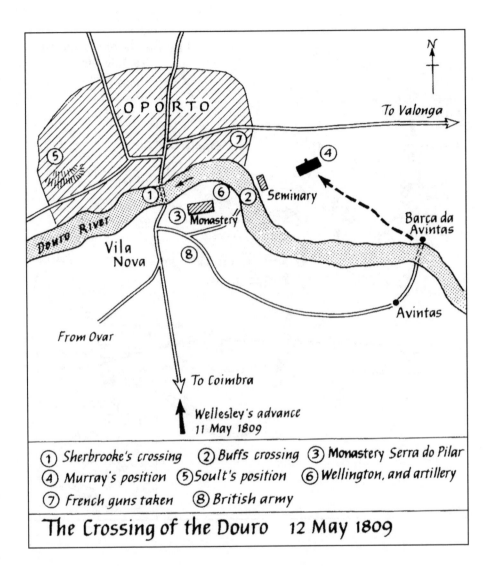

The Crossing of the Douro   12 May 1809

① Sherbrooke's crossing   ② Buffs crossing   ③ Monastery Serra do Pilar
④ Murray's position   ⑤ Soult's position   ⑥ Wellington, and artillery
⑦ French guns taken   ⑧ British army

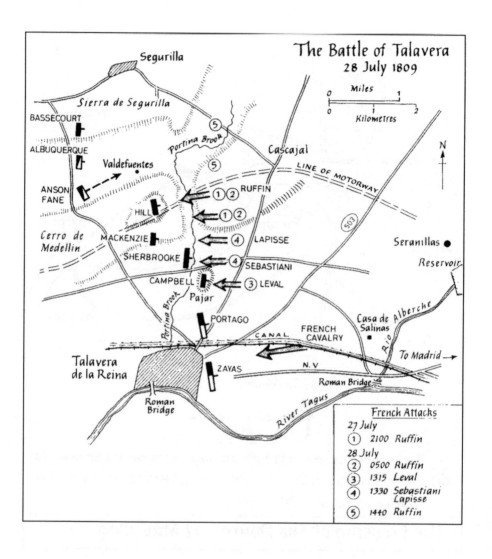

The Battle of Talavera
28 July 1809

French Attacks

27 July
① 2100 Ruffin

28 July
② 0500 Ruffin
③ 1315 Leval
④ 1330 Sebastiani Lapisse
⑤ 1440 Ruffin

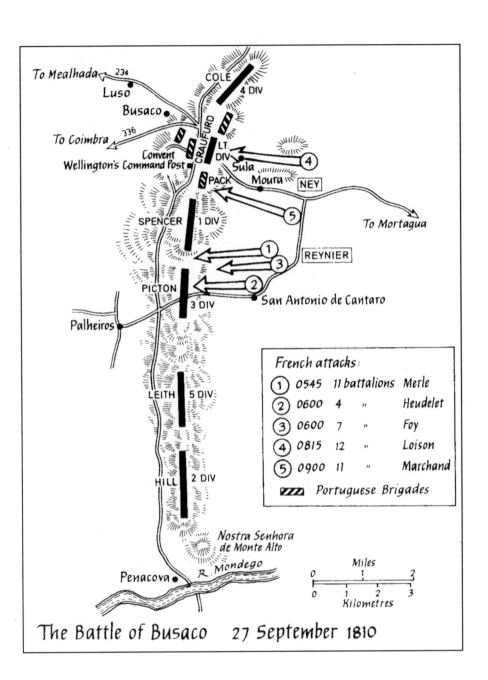

The Battle of Busaco   27 September 1810

French attacks:

①	0545	11 battalions	Merle
②	0600	4 "	Heudelet
③	0600	7 "	Foy
④	0815	12 "	Loison
⑤	0900	11 "	Marchand

▨▨▨ Portuguese Brigades

Chapter 1

Early Days
(1785–1808)

In England the harvest was awful again. The price of grain had become ridiculous, unrest was just below the surface; Europe was in turmoil. In fact, 1785 was a difficult year everywhere. In America, perhaps as an act of defiance, the dollar replaced the pound as a new currency for every state. France was bubbling angrily towards revolution, and two young men were, unknowingly, on the threshold of greatness.

At the Military Academy in Paris a 16-year-old Corsican artillery cadet named Bonaparte completed his course, and graduated on 28 September, forty-second in a class of fifty-one. This was much better than it appeared; he had completed the two-and-a-half-year course in just one year, while well under age. He was commissioned a *sous-lieutenant* in the La Fère Artillery Regiment at Valence in the Rhone-Alpes region of southeastern France. Officially he served in it until 1790, but for most of the time he was on leave in Corsica, leading a battalion of Republican volunteers under the direction of Pascal Paoli,[1] the leading Corsican nationalist who eventually escaped to England. Thinking that Napoleon was a confirmed nationalist, Paoli later offered to secure a British commission for him so that he might oppose the French. Napoleon was nothing if not pragmatic. He understood Corsica could never survive on its own, so he opted for France, and fell out acrimoniously with Paoli.

Arthur Wesley,[2] a shy boy from Ireland, attended the local Diocesan School at Trim in County Meath and then, after a short period at school in Chelsea, went to Eton. Other than taking on a boy called Smith, brother of the canon of St Paul's, in a successful bare-knuckled fight, and losing another in which he was thrashed, young Wesley stressed himself neither academically nor sportingly at Eton. When he left in 1784 he went to study for a year with the vicar of fashionable Brighton, the Reverend Henry Michell, father of sixteen children.

Arthur's parents, being uncertain of his direction in life, next sent him to Brussels to another tutor, Monsieur Louis Goubert. His mother, a somewhat forbidding lady, accompanied him. After almost a year in Brussels, it was decided that the boy was best suited for the army; there being no military academy in England, Wesley went, aged 16, to the Royal Military Academy at Angers, on the edge of the Loire Valley, for almost a year. The Academy, which catered for civilians as well as soldiers, was run by a celebrated military engineer, the Marquis Marcel de Pignerolle, whose brother supervised an excellent stable for the young gentlemen's riding tuition. Of 334 students at the Academy, 116 were British. Wesley took lessons in fencing, basic mathematics and dancing, as well as perfecting his French, which it is said he spoke '*bravement*' after Angers. In their distinctive scarlet uniforms with sky blue facings and gilt buttons, the students were a diversion for the local Dukes of Praslin and Brissac and their ladies. Young Arthur met and liked the Duchesse of Sabran, and met her again with delight in Paris twenty-eight years later. The young gentlemen learnt much about French attitudes and manners. The storming of the Bastille was still three years ahead, but some of the Angers gentry, including the Duke of Brissac and the Marquis de Pignerolle, became victims of the guillotine. Arthur is said by his fellow student mentor, later General Mackenzie, not to have been very attentive to his studies, but much occupied with his little terrier called Vick, which followed him everywhere. One result of his time at Angers was his lifelong admiration for France, but not her politics.

Our third principal character, Henry Percy, left a smaller mark in history in his short but colourful life. Known in his family as Harry, to us hereafter he will be Henry. The Percys had been the most powerful noble family in northern England since the early Middle Ages. Through the centuries they have had a turbulent history, and immense influence. In every generation there had been charismatic characters. The best remembered personality is perhaps Harry Hotspur, but for his part in the Rebellion of the Northern Earls in 1559 the 9th Earl of Northumberland was beheaded. Our Henry's nephew, another Hon. Henry Percy (later Lord Henry Percy), won a very early Victoria Cross in the Crimea. This ancient family numbers seventeen knights of the Garter, among whom are four Henrys and three Hughs, an untypically small repetition of names. Generations of the Percys tended to be large, and to complicate matters several Christian names recur many times through the centuries. Henry, Algernon, Josceline, George and Hugh are names that repeat enough to create a maze, cultivated, it might seem, to confuse the genealogist.

Into this dynasty was born on 14 September 1785 a fifth son, styled simply the Honourable Henry Percy. This was just a fortnight before the brilliant young Bonaparte passed out of the Military Academy, unnoticed in England, and while Wesley was enjoying dancing waltzes and walking little Vick at Angers.

For centuries the Percy family seat has been Alnwick Castle in Northumberland, the fulcrum of its influence, towering over the surrounding countryside. Syon House at Twickenham is an outpost, the last surviving ducal country house and estate in Greater London. At the western end of the Strand in London stood the Jacobean Northumberland House, the Percy family's original London residence, immortalized by Canaletto. It originally overlooked the old Royal Mews, which was replaced by the newly built Trafalgar Square, over which it looked out quizzically until the great house was demolished in 1874.

The term landed gentry does no justice to the Percys. Like most ducal families their interests have been perhaps even more extensive than their land holdings. Politics, dynastic marriages, estate management and service to the country were all high on the list of activities. The family's politics were vexed, with Henry's father and his grandfather vehemently opposed to one another's political views.

Henry's father was Algernon Percy, second son of the 1st Duke of Northumberland (1714–1786). When the old Duke died, a year after Henry's birth, Algernon became 2nd Lord Lovaine, and ceased, after twelve years, to be Tory MP for Northumberland. He was created 1st Earl of Beverley in November 1790. During the period of this story Henry's father was known as the Earl of Beverley, and Henry's eldest brother George as Lord Lovaine.

At his birth Henry had four elder brothers, named simply George (Lovaine), Algernon, and the twins, Hugh and Josceline. These boys were followed by three more: William Henry, Francis John and Charles John, each with two names. Their three sisters were Charlotte, Susan Elizabeth and Emily Charlotte. The happy family was close-knit.

Henry's childhood years passed in a world in which war, revolution, turbulence and terror were very real. The violent French Revolution and the Reign of Terror were watched with growing anxiety. The French King, Louis XVI, and his Queen, Marie Antoinette, were shockingly demeaned and insulted by the mob, and then publicly murdered by the guillotine. The French invaded Ireland in 1798, hoping to provoke a popular uprising. They were defeated through their own incompetence and a speedy British reaction, thanks in part to General John Moore. The rebellion was brutally suppressed. Many Irish 'Ascendancy' families became well-to-do temporary refugees in England, particularly at Bath.

Elsewhere, some civilized progress was being made; Mozart was entrancing the world of music with dazzling new compositions. The industrial revolution was gathering pace; steam was beginning to supplant water power in mills and factories. Machine tools were working metal more easily with newly invented powered lathes. Steel was cheap, and industry boomed. The economic impact was sensational: Britain became rich as never before. In 1800 the controversial Act of Union united the Parliaments of Great Britain and Ireland, by absorbing the Irish Parliament into Westminster, in the misplaced hope of preventing further unrest in Ireland. This was the dramatic backdrop to Henry's childhood, a period of forgotten anxieties.

Henry's education is not well recorded. There was a family tutor, Monsieur Dutens, a French gentleman refugee from the revolution. Eventually, like many of his family over the centuries, Henry went to Eton. The Eton records do not tell us his tutor's name, but he is shown as arriving there on 28 January 1800. He is listed as Mr Percy mi, following the Etonian tradition of referring to the son of a peer as Mr, and using the Latin suffix mi (minor) to indicate the presence in the school of an elder brother, suffixed as ma (major). Henry arrived when his elder brother Hugh (Mr Percy ma), later a distinguished cleric, had been at Eton for a year. By 1802 Henry was in the Fifth Form, Upper Division. The curriculum focused on the classics, although modern languages, music, art, dancing, fencing and arithmetic could be studied as extras. As these subjects were paid for separately, directly to the tutor, the school has no record of Henry's choice, and his reports, if any, do not survive. However, we know he was proficient in French, and that as a 'wet bob' he rowed, in preference to cricket.

In 1802 the war with France stopped. Englishmen poured over to Paris and the continent during the interlude of the Peace of Amiens signed in March 1802. Everyone was curious after ten years of revolution and hostilities. Among them were Algernon, Earl of Beverley, with his wife Isabella Susannah, and many soldiers, sailors, philosophers, scholars, artists and merchants, all eager to see the extraordinary young Corsican who had apparently accomplished so much, and might perhaps achieve much more. Beverley's family travelled to France and on to Italy through Switzerland. On their way home in 1803, when they had reached Switzerland, Napoleon suddenly lost patience and instructed the Governor of Paris, General Junot, to order all British citizens visiting France and Switzerland, which was under effective French occupation, to be registered within 24 hours. Non-combatants were to be detained on the spurious pretext of their potential liability for British militia service. They were detained, in some cases, for eleven years. The Beverleys were caught in this net. The Earl of Beverley, together with his wife, two sons and three daughters, was held at Geneva, and then Algernon, the most likely candidate for militia service if repatriated, was sent alone to Verdun, on parole. In February 1804 Algernon wrote directly to Napoleon from Verdun, explaining that his elderly father, suffering from gout at Geneva, needed somebody to look after his family. Amazingly, after some delay for police reliability checks, upon which Napoleon, with extraordinary attention to the minutiae of such things, personally gave instructions, Algernon was allowed to join the family at Geneva.

In London in February 1804 Monsieur Dutens wrote to Lord Lovaine explaining that Beverley's idea of asking General Paoli to contact his former colleague, now arch-enemy, Napoleon to negotiate the release of Beverley and the family was a non-starter. Dutens mentioned that a friend had told him Mr Henry was going to work for Mr Davidson (*sic.*), and felt it would be thought very odd if he were going as a clerk. The inference was that Henry was too young to be a partner in a bank, so was it sensible for him to work for Davison? Alexander Davison was a self-made banker, merchant and prize agent to Lord Nelson. A social climber, he must have been one of the finest networkers of his day, shamelessly using contacts with a close-to-the-wind dexterity which eventually landed him in trouble. Davison[3] was born near Alnwick in Northumberland and throughout his career traded on the powerful Percy interest. He nurtured an important relationship with Hugh Percy, the 2nd Duke of Northumberland, Henry's uncle, which even survived Davison's later disgrace and imprisonment for fraud. Davison supplied weapons and uniforms for the Percy Tenantry Volunteer Corps (of which George Lovaine was Colonel) and may even have occasionally loaned money to the family. Although not formally educated himself, Davison sent his twin sons Percy (what else?) and William to Eton. Before he was interned, the Earl of Beverley had dined at Davison's grand house in St James's Square, in company with the Prince of Wales and a dazzling social galaxy such as Davison liked to cultivate. Thus the contact was in place for Henry to have a short 'gap-year' attachment to the bank in Pall Mall, although Davison's influence with Henry does not seem to have continued.[4] After the short banking interlude, Henry joined the army. By this time young Cadet Bonaparte, with lightning progress, had become Emperor of France.

A lieutenant's commission was purchased for Henry in the 7th Regiment of Foot, The Royal Fusiliers, on 16 August 1804. Their Depot was at Maidstone, and the 1st Battalion was serving in North America. By 9 October 1806 Henry had become a captain at the age of 21. A second battalion was raised in 1804 and went to Ireland. Henry did not go to Canada, so the probability is that he went to Maidstone when he first joined. In 1808 his younger brother Francis John joined the regiment as a lieutenant, but Henry was already away with General Moore when Francis joined. In any case, Francis transferred early the following year to the 23rd Royal Welsh Fusiliers.

If Henry did go to Ireland after Maidstone, he did not spend very long there. His parents were acquainted with Lieutenant General Sir John Moore, an officer of highest repute, who on being knighted in November 1804 was so admired by his officers that they presented him with a diamond-encrusted star of the Order of the Bath worth 350 guineas (about £29,000 in 2016 money).

The appointment of Aide-de-Camp (ADC) was usually made through personal influence, and this undoubtedly applied to Henry, probably through his Northumberland grandfather, a retired general, who is likely to have known Moore. He joined Moore in Sicily, where he had been since June

1806, serving as second-in-command under General Henry Edward Fox, of the Mediterranean command, accredited as ambassador to the court of Palermo. When Fox returned home in ill-health, Moore held the Mediterranean command, but not the diplomatic portfolio. It was a period of intense intrigues in the Neapolitan court, which Moore disliked. He believed his diplomatic colleagues had been dazzled by the tawdry social life of the court, in which he thought the Queen exerted a malevolent influence, whilst affecting to be powerless. It was also the time of the unhappy expedition to Egypt under the command of Major General Alexander Mackenzie Fraser. Henry Percy was loaned by Moore to Mackenzie Fraser as aide-de-camp, and was present at the battles of Alexandria and Rosetta in 1807. His meticulous notes of the battle statistics bear out the widely held view that the expedition was not a military success, even if it achieved its aim of distracting the French by engaging the Turks' attention to events in Egypt. Moore's diary makes it clear that the excursion was worse, a military disaster, but not one of Mackenzie Fraser's doing.

In September 1807 Moore received orders from home to leave the command in Sicily to General John Sherbrooke, and to hasten to Gibraltar with 7,000 troops to help Portugal against the French invasion under Junot. The Portuguese royal family declined his assistance and withdrew to Brazil, so Moore, as instructed, took the troops home to England without landing in Portugal.

Henry Percy returned to England after the Alexandria expedition, and having spent two months with his battalion, the 2/7th Royal Fusiliers, in Clonmel, the next thing we know he was on his way to Sweden with Sir John Moore at the end of May.[5] While at Clonmel he was painted by the fashionable miniaturist, Frederick Buck, in Cork. The miniature contains a lock of hair, but to whom it was given is a mystery. Significantly, he would not have needed his ADC uniform in Ireland and would therefore probably have collected it from home in London on his way to join Sir John.

Chapter 2

Sweden
(1808)

In May 1808 Sir John Moore was sent to Sweden with an expeditionary force of 12,000 men to assist the 30-year-old King Gustavus IV, who was threatened by France, Russia and Denmark. No archival correspondence has been found showing Henry being formally part of Moore's staff during this extraordinary expedition. However, one small piece of evidence shows that he was there as ADC. After Waterloo in 1815 Henry Percy was required to submit a record of service on his admission to the Order of the Bath. A somewhat vague copy survives at Alnwick; in many cases he could not remember dates, and left them blank. But luckily he included the entry: 'In Sweden Aide De Camp to HE Lt Genl Sir John Moore.' So for completeness we must include a quick summary of what went on.

It was plain from Moore's conversation with Lord Castlereagh, Secretary of State for War and the Colonies, that the Government had no specific plan and had reached no determination beyond that of sending 10,000 men to Gothenburg, to be ready to act 'if occasion offered'. Two of his generals, Mackenzie Fraser and Edward Paget, were well-tried friends, and the third, John Murray, he had known in Egypt. Thomas Graham, an elderly and very distinguished soldier who had raised the Perthshire Volunteers at his own expense, was grudgingly allowed to accompany Sir John, as aide-de-camp to the Chief. Moore arrived at Gothenburg in HMS *Mars* on 17 May. He realized he was going to *terra incognita*, and that when he reached his destination he would soon know more than those who had sent him, since they had received no communication from Stockholm since 23 February. He was not allowed to land his troops, but was summoned to Stockholm to confer with the eccentric King Gustavus, whom he found to be only interested in amazing schemes of conquest. The apparently deluded king proposed that the British, with some Swedish troops, should seize Zealand, and that afterwards the British should go to Finland to fight the Russians. Moore politely objected that his force was too small for such operations. The king became excited. 'You may tell your country, you may tell your Government that I am not in need of its alliance. That I have the attachment of my People, and relying on Providence, I do not seek the assistance of Foreign Powers.' An impossible situation arose, in which it became clear that the King was faced by a bigger threat than he could confront, whilst utterly unprepared to be helped. He had quarrelled with the *Rikstag* on which he depended for money, and consequently was subsidized by Great Britain. The British troops, to the delight of the curious local people, were landed at an island off Gothenburg to alleviate the boredom of waiting, to bathe and play sports, and take part in amphibious landing exercises. They remained accommodated by the fleet in preparation for any eventuality.

Things came to a head at a further meeting with the King. Gustavus promptly ordered Sir John, who it seems was alone, not to leave the capital. Realizing that the situation was unmanageable, Moore made his escape in the guise of a peasant. On arrival at Gothenburg by night, he found a small boat, and to the surprise of the waiting staff officers, presumably including Percy, clambered aboard the flagship, HMS *Victory*, still dressed as a peasant. The excursion was abandoned and all returned to England. Nothing, it was felt, had been achieved. Not surprisingly, Moore thought that he had been sent on a wild goose chase, and in a private letter he referred to the service as the most painful on which he had been employed. While at sea on the way home orders were received to go to the Downs (the south coast anchorage) rather than Yarmouth. Moore was summoned to London, while the troops and horses remained on board. In his absence the ships were replenished and moved on to Portsmouth.

The meeting with Castlereagh was not an easy one. After the fiasco of the unnecessary Swedish expedition had been discussed, Moore was ordered to Portugal. There had been much concern about the expedition to Portugal, and while Moore was safely out of the way in Sweden the decision had been taken to employ the more junior Sir Arthur Wellesley, whose successful experience in India was valued. (The orthographic complications of the family name need not concern us, other than to understand that as a schoolboy and while in India Arthur Wesley used the name Wesley. Changes in family usage at varying times necessitated a change to Wellesley, which he used thereafter.) Now Moore had returned unexpectedly soon, creating an awkward command predicament. Therefore two senior, if inexperienced, generals, Dalrymple and Burrard, were ordered to Portugal. They would outrank both Moore and Wellesley.

In a letter from Portsmouth on 28 July 1808 Moore wrote: 'I understood from Gordon[1] and from others that there had been much intriguing about the command. Ministers had done everything in their power to give it to Sir Arthur Wellesley; but he was so young a lieutenant-general that the Duke[2] objected to it, and afraid of disgusting the army and the nation by such an appointment, they had given it up. Disappointed in their favourite object, they were determined it should not be given to me, and to prevent the possibility of it falling to me, Sir Harry Burrard was named as second.'

Aware of the difficulties in which Castlereagh found himself, Moore was displeased to be told he was to serve under Sir Hew Dalrymple and Sir Harry Burrard. Having held chief commands in Sicily and Sweden, he was being ordered to serve, without any discussion or justification, under other officers, one of whom had never been employed as a general in the field. He expressed himself very strongly to Lord Castlereagh at this treatment:

> Had I been an ensign it would hardly have been possible to treat me with less ceremony. It is only by inference at this moment that I know that I am to be employed, for your Lordship has never told me in plain terms that I was appointed to serve in the army under Sir Hew Dalrymple as a lieutenant-general, and coming from a chief command, if it was intended to employ me in an inferior station I was to expect something would be said to me. You have told me that my conduct in Sweden was approved, but by your actions I should have concluded it was the reverse. I am at a loss to conceive the cause; for if there is an officer in the service who has steered a straight course, who without intrigue or detracting from the merit of others has endeavoured by his own exertions to establish his reputation, I think it is myself.
>
> Why I should be the object of such obloquy I cannot guess; but, my Lord, I have been treated unworthily and in a manner which no part of my conduct could justify. His Majesty's Ministers have a right to employ what officers they please, and had they on this occasion given the command to the youngest General in the army I should neither have felt or expressed the feeling that the least injury was done to me. But I have a right in common with all officers who have served zealously and well to expect to be treated with attention, and when employment is offered to me, that some regard should be had of my former services.

Moore noted that when he had finished what he had to say, he 'rose abruptly and retired'. Ever one to do his duty for his country, having stated his case, Sir John returned to Portsmouth, handed over the troops to Burrard, and sailed for Portugal in HMS *Audacious* as second-in-command with him, at the end of July 1808.

Chapter 3

Portugal and Spain
(1808)

Henry Percy accompanied Sir John to Portugal in the role of ADC for the fourth time. From a frigate off Finisterre they learned that Sir Arthur Wellesley had landed in Mondego Bay, north of Lisbon. Burrard pushed on to Oporto, leaving Moore with the troops off Vigo in the north, whence he moved south to Mondego Bay and prepared to land.

Wellesley had landed on 1 August 1808, in fine but blustery weather, at Mondego Bay, near the fort of Figuera da Foz, which was secured by Royal Marines. He marched south to the picturesque little town of Obidos, which he reached on 16 August without making any contact with the French. Ever precise in his preparation, he undertook his customary thorough reconnaissance and discovered that the French under General Delaborde had taken up a defensive position a little further south at Roliça. For his first engagement Wellesley was on the offensive. He had 16,000 men and eighteen guns, the French 4,400 men and five guns. The French occupied a horseshoe of steep hills with the open side to the north facing Obidos. Wellesley divided his force into three columns to encircle the French. A Portuguese column of 1,350 men under Colonel Nicholas Trant[1] was sent round behind the hills to the west, while on the eastern side he deployed General Ferguson with 4,500 British infantry and six guns. This force was stronger so as to guard the eastern flank from the threat of French interference by troops under Loison from Abrantes. The third element of the pincer was Wellesley's 9,000-strong, three-brigade centre column, including a weak Portuguese battalion of Caçadores (Light Infantry) and twelve guns. He sent Fane's Brigade to his left to fill the gap between Ferguson and himself. They formed up shortly after dawn with admirable precision opposite the centre of the French position, and then advanced deliberately across the open plain towards Roliça. Delaborde was no novice. His detachment to the east, watching for reinforcements from Abrantes, reported Ferguson's column, and Delaborde recognized Wellesley's pincer trap. He stayed put until the last minute and then skilfully withdrew to a stronger position a short distance from Roliça on a steep ridge divided by four gullies which could only be attacked frontally. Neither was Wellesley a novice. He reacted calmly to the change. After taking time to regroup, Wellesley again pushed forward, intending his centre to assault the heights once Trant and Ferguson were in a position to provide support on both flanks. A crisis arose when, with great gallantry, the 1/29th (Worcestershire Regiment) commanded by Lieutenant Colonel George Lake, instead of skirmishing until the trap was closed, without waiting pushed vigorously ahead through the centre gully in the hillside. Despite coming under fire from three sides, they were able to reach the brow of the hill before being broken by a French charge. The gallant, if unwise, Lake was killed and six officers with other ranks were captured. The survivors of the 29th fell back down the hillside into the ranks of the supporting 9th (East Norfolk) Regiment. By now, Wellesley had ordered the 5th, 9th, 82nd and 45th Regiments into his intended frontal attack against the heights. After two hours of bitter fighting, during which the French threw back three assaults, the British finally gained firm footholds along the crest. The French fought hard and from very good defensive positions, playing for time in the expectation of Loison's reinforcements arriving from the east.

Delaborde, realizing his right flank was now under threat from Ferguson, managed to disengage from the battle of Roliça[2] and withdraw behind a screen of cavalry. To withdraw in contact has never been easy, and this fine example showed Delaborde's skill and experience. French losses amounted to 600 men killed or wounded and three guns lost; of the 474 British and Portuguese killed, wounded or taken prisoner, nearly half were from the 29th Regiment. Colonel George Lake's grave and monument remain at the top of the hill to this day.[3] Wellesley did not follow up for want of cavalry and because of the likelihood of Loison, reportedly only 5 miles away by now, intervening on the eastern flank. Furthermore, Wellesley had heard that Acland's and Anstruther's Brigades from England were waiting to land. So he moved south to Vimeiro, near the mouth of the Maceira river, to secure a suitable landing area nearby.

The next contact with the French was the first full-scale engagement of the Peninsular War, this time a defensive battle: the Battle of Vimeiro[4] on 21 August 1808. It had several special novel elements to it. Wellesley expected the French to attack him from the south to disrupt the landings. Accordingly, he took up positions facing south. The French under General Junot tried to push him back. Wellesley, seeing the French approach from the southeast, realized at once that they were in danger of outflanking him. He made a characteristically decisive redeployment of his defences with his flawless eye for detail and speedy understanding of what he saw. His mastery of ground played a key part. The battle which followed consisted of a series of attacks by columns of French infantry, all of which were repulsed without difficulty. The battle illustrated the superiority of the tactics that had been developed by the British Army in the period leading up to 1808. There were many innovations.

It was Wellesley's first major European battle, and he gained surprise by use of dead-ground, and sheltering infantry from artillery fire, concealed on the reverse slope. That day saw the first European use of Captain Henry Shrapnel's new spherical case exploding shell.[5] Another surprise for the French was the use of strong British skirmishing lines. The battle went according to Wellesley's plan once he had redeployed,[6] ending by noon with a clear British victory. The French lost 1,800 men killed, wounded or missing.

But then the command difficulty intervened. Junot sent his skilled 38-year-old negotiator, cavalry general François Étienne de Kellermann,[7] to Sir Arthur Wellesley's headquarters to ask for an armistice. He appeared no more than two hours after the arrival of Dalrymple. By this time Wellesley had been superseded as commander first by Sir Harry Burrard and then by Sir Hew Dalrymple. Dalrymple would not permit a pursuit. The striking victory was not exploited.[8] Neither Burrard nor Dalrymple felt the need to destroy the French, believing that by negotiation the enemy could be removed from Portugal without loss to either side. So the French were allowed to withdraw from Vimeiro unmolested, and negotiations followed.

The idea of a pursuit of the defeated French had been stopped on the spurious grounds that they would have a strong defensive position at Torres Vedras. Not so: the British forces were sufficiently numerous to bypass the position.

The first despatches from Wellesley, carried by Colin Campbell (later the general), spoke of a great victory over the whole of Junot's army. Bells pealed and cannons fired. The *Morning Post* of 2 September announced: 'Most Glorious News from Portugal, Complete Defeat of General Junot and Proposals for the Surrender of His Army.'

Under the provisions of the Convention of Cintra, the 25,747 French (of whom 20,900 were under arms throughout Portugal) were transported home in English ships with their plunder. When the terms of the Convention of Cintra arrived in England, the Government tried to put the best face on the bad news and again church bells were rung and the cannons thundered. The public was not taken in, and there was an outcry. Why allow them to go back to France and bother us again? Surely they should have been destroyed or made prisoners?

General Andoche Junot, Napoleon's former personal Secretary as a serjeant, was now the French Commander-in-Chief, ennobled by Napoleon after the invasion of Portugal as Duke of Abrantes. He was transported with his staff and plunder to the French naval base at La Rochelle in HMS *Nymphe*,[9] a captured French ship. He landed there on 11 October 1808, apparently with his two mistresses on his arms.[10] He had become a good friend of *Nymphe*'s very courteous captain, Commander the Hon. Josceline Percy RN, Henry's elder brother. On arrival at La Rochelle, Josceline was invited to dine by the Port Admiral. He declined politely on the grounds that while he was flattered to be invited and did not doubt his host's integrity, he realized that the Admiral would be obliged to obey should an order come from Paris to detain him and his ship. Charles Stanhope of the 50th Foot (Royal West Kent Regiment), and brother of Hester Stanhope, Moore's great friend, wrote to his sister from Camp Monte Santo on 26 October 1808:

> the frigate that took General Junot to France and is commanded by Captain Percy [he means Commander], brother to my friend [Henry], returned yesterday and I heard one of our officers say that he had been with some of the lieutenants who liked Junot very much and said he was the best fellow they ever saw, that he had given every man on board half a guinea and made the captain a present of a very valuable box of jewels and some cases of French wine. Now this appears to me to be damned shabby, I do not think [it] is the custom of the service.

The folly of the Convention of Cintra is illustrated by the fact that Junot's men were, indeed, back in Spain, fighting to subdue the Spanish uprising, by early December 1808. On 13 December elements of Delaborde's division entered Vitoria in the northeast of the country. Although Napoleon was unhappy with ex-Serjeant Junot's performance as Commander-in-Chief, a court martial was not convened. Napoleon eventually wrote to Junot: 'You have done nothing dishonourable; you have returned my troops, my eagles and my cannons, but I certainly hoped you would do better ... you have won this convention by your courage, not by your dispositions; and it is with reason that the English complain that their generals signed it.'

The Convention of Cintra was signed at the Palace of Queluz, a beautiful baroque palace outside Lisbon, sometimes known as the Versailles of Portugal. The British signatories were Burrard,[11] Dalrymple and, reluctantly, Wellesley. Wellesley and his two elderly superiors (nicknamed by the troops, who regarded them as two well-bred old ladies, 'the Dowager Dalrymple and Betty Burrard') returned to England to answer for the Convention of Cintra. Moore was lucky not to be involved in it.

Sir John Moore was appointed Commander of the Forces in Portugal and moved into Junot's headquarters buildings at Queluz. The staff, including Henry Percy, worked at the palace.

On 7 August 1808 Beverley's eldest son, Lord Lovaine, a salaried Lord of the Treasury at the time, was on his way to Portugal as an unpaid volunteer with Brigadier General Charles Stewart (Lord Castlereagh's half-brother), who was going out to assume command of the cavalry brigade. Lovaine's timing was inept from a family angle, as he was leaving behind a pregnant wife and three young children. Stewart departed for Portugal on that date, so his volunteer militia colonel, George Lovaine, conformed, to the irritation of his parliamentary superiors. As luck would have it, the military timing was convenient. On arrival at Lisbon the Convention of Cintra was being implemented. Wellesley was still there, as was Sir John Moore, with his ADC, Henry. Even more fortunate was the presence of brother Josceline, captain of HMS *Nymphe*, chosen by Admiral Sir George Berkeley to convey General Junot back to France. Through this lucky coincidence, leading to valuable introductions, Lovaine made key contacts whom he later approached when trying to secure Beverley's release. Lovaine toured and sketched extensively, helpfully dating and identifying his sketches.

Wellesley was a great admirer of Moore and visited him at Queluz before leaving for England. An unusual interview followed. Wellesley, the junior lieutenant general, after some clearing of the throat, made the surprising offer to intercede on Moore's behalf with the Government, realizing the indignity to which Moore had been put by Castlereagh. Wellesley had always got on well with Castlereagh. Moore, furthermore, would shortly have Charles Stewart, Castlereagh's half-brother, commanding his cavalry brigade. Ever the upright soldier, Moore did not wish to be involved in intrigues (as he described such things) but understood and appreciated Wellesley's kindness. After some hesitation, he gratefully accepted the offer.

While at Queluz, Junot, who relished the palatial life, had planted mulberry trees and redecorated the palace for Eugene Beauharnais, Napoleon's intended King of Portugal. Major General the Hon. Edward Paget was one among the many who visited Moore at Queluz.[12] He must have met Moore's young ADC, Henry Percy, that day and they got to know one another well during the Corunna campaign and the following year at Oporto. Later they met as prisoners of war in France. Paget's visit to Queluz is of no particular significance, but his letter of 19 September 1808 to his mother, Jane, Lady Uxbridge, describing Queluz, is nice:

> Some of the rooms he [Junot] had finished, and they are completely beautiful. The paintings on some of the ceilings are highly entertaining. – Imperial eagles trampling upon crowns and broken sceptres and spreading their wide wings over the representation of the Globe. Each eagle with an 'N' and Imperial crown etc. As he was deprived by us of his palace, he was determined at least to have everything movable that was valuable, and accordingly has stolen all the plate.[13]

The Convention of Cintra Inquiry was held from 14 November to 27 December 1808 in the Great Hall at the Royal Hospital Chelsea.[14] The Inquiry, with General Sir David Dundas as President, was immensely senior. The three generals were exonerated, but Burrard and Dalrymple never received another field command. The Government issued a formal denunciation of Dalrymple. Wellesley alone was voted the thanks of Parliament on 27 January 1809 for his victory at Vimeiro.

The French had been expelled from Portugal, and the Russian naval squadron, no longer guarded at Lisbon by the Royal Navy, departed for England. Spain was supposedly in a state of rebellion against the French, and the British Army was concentrated around Queluz, with Lisbon itself under the command of the Portuguese-speaking General Beresford.

On 8 October a frigate arrived bearing the following instruction for Moore from Downing Street:

> Sir,
>
> His Majesty having determined to deploy a corps of his troops, of not less than 30,000 infantry and 5,000 cavalry, in the North of Spain, to co-operate with the Spanish armies in the expulsion of the French from that kingdom, has been graciously pleased to entrust to you the Command in Chief of this Force.

Sir John Moore knew of the Spanish uprising against Napoleon, but intelligence was limited. He determined to head for Almeida and then cross into Spain via Ciudad Rodrigo, which had been recommended by the Spaniards through Brigadier Lord William Bentinck, who had been sent (with Moore's friend Colonel Thomas Graham) to liaise with the Spanish Supreme Junta at Aranjuez near Madrid. He decided that Salamanca would make a suitably central location, from which he could deploy in any direction, depending on the situation when his force was assembled there. He also knew that Galicia in the north of Spain had been garrisoned by Spanish soldiers for some time and that supplies would probably be inadequate for his army were he to go by sea to Corunna and enter Spain from there. In any case, a further 10,000 men had been sent from Falmouth under General Sir David Baird to reinforce him in Spain, and they were heading for Corunna. He believed it would be better therefore to march inland, and not go round by sea. The most important thing was to get the British troops out of Portugal before the weather broke. The condition of the routes into Spain was far from clear. Moore issued a General Order on 9 October. Troops were to be prepared to move at short notice; heavy baggage would be left at Lisbon, behaviour was to improve (intemperance is mentioned) and women and children were to be encouraged to return to England. The order was immediately put into effect, save the last condition, for which little response was achieved. The army was seized with enthusiasm under the leadership of Sir John, and soon the three difficult routes into Spain were crowded with advancing troops. The general, in modern terms, took a tactical headquarters, with his ADC Henry Percy, two principal staff officers, his Military Secretary, and a small escort of dragoons.

They left Lisbon on 27 October. Henry Percy's meticulous little red leather journal[15] tells the story, sadly with little detail.

> From the time the army marching by several corps left Lisbon we had nothing but weather and the irregular supply of provisions for the troops to contend with. The latter owing to the inactivity of the Contractor, who it appeared was perfectly unfit for the execution of the agreement which he had made, and the arduous task he had undertaken. When the command of the army was given over to Sir Jno. Moore no one particle of equipment was provided or any preparations even undertaken to allow the army to move. It was requisite therefore that all arrangements of this nature should, with all expedition be established so as to enable the several Corps to be put in motion, which was executed so promptly that tho' the dispatches [i.e. orders] only arrived on the morning of the 7th Oct, and 10th the first Regt marched. From this time by different routes corps were put in motion. Marching on Almeida [were] General Hope's and General Paget's divisions with all the Cavalry and Artillery but one Brigade of the latter crossed the Tagus, and by Elvas[16] proceeded by the great road towards Madrid[17]. These divisions had relieved the garrison of Elvas, the French troops which before the convention had been placed there by General Junot.

At the beginning the roads were paved and acceptable, but after Abrantes they deteriorated and were 'very fatiguing for horses'. On 3 November they crossed the Tagus at Villa Velha, where the sight of three brown eagles perched on a rock caused George Murray to ask Sir John if he thought they were a good omen. The journey was long and arduous, and the need to divide the army into three for want of road capacity worried Moore. He received intelligence from Madrid from Brigadier Lord William Bentinck first, near Alpedrinha. The French had, it appeared, received a reinforcement of 10,000 men, and General Castaños of the Spanish Army of Andalucia was making movements likely to cause an action. Moore sent a message to General Hope on the southern route to avoid entering Madrid.

The headquarters crossed the wide Agueda river over the long Roman bridge and entered Ciudad Rodrigo in early November, en route for Salamanca. The Spanish Governor welcomed them formally, and they must have spent the night there. The Governor lived in the castle, and doubtless the small staff accompanied their general there too. Little did Henry know the circumstances when next he would cross that bridge, on an overcast freezing cold late January day two years later, a prisoner, with an escort of 1,000 French soldiers, heading for the Bayonne reception centre.

Chapter 4

Salamanca, Sahagún and Benavente (1808)

General Sir David Baird sailed from Falmouth with reinforcements for Spain. In all, 150 transports carrying 13,000 men, in convoy with HM Ships *Louie*, *Amelia* and *Champion* as escorts, arrived at Corunna on 13 October 1808. Moore was still at Lisbon, static and struggling with administrative and logistic difficulties before moving inland.

Henry Percy's journal continues the story, dismissing the considerable difficulties of the journey by several different routes with appalling roads into Spain:

> The General left Lisbon on 27th [October] from which time nothing happened until we arrived at Salamanca. At this place the first intelligence respecting the enemy was that they had pushed forward a patrole [*sic.*] as far as Valladolid and the adjacent towns and villages.
>
> The situation he was now placed in was as disagreeable as it was unexpected. The various accounts of the Enthusiasm, the Zeal and even the successes of the Spaniards sent by those Officers who were employed by our Government to forward every intelligence from Spain, gave everyone such very different Hopes that this came so much more heavily against the Genl.
>
> It had always been his intention to collect his force at Ciudad Rodrigo and his orders to Genl Anstruther [of Paget's Reserve Division] were not to go any further than Salamanca. In hesitating, he lost no time, but ordered the whole to halt at Ciudad Rodrigo, but upon the following day from further intelligence he again ordered them to join him at Salamanca.

In addition to this account, the news of the defeat of the Extremaduran Army as well as that of Blake[1] had already arrived. This was on 17 November.

Moore arrived at Salamanca on 13 November and made his headquarters in the beautiful sixteenth-century renaissance Palace of San Boal.[2] Life at Salamanca had all the appearances of a sunny Salamantine autumn: the honey-coloured stone of the ancient university buildings, the bright autumn days with the beginning of a chill east wind, and the bustle of the local people chattering volubly in their classic cut-glass Castilian. There was anxiety in the air, and the locals could feel it, but there was also the curious ability of Spaniards to ignore impending problems. So life seemed to go on much as before. Moore's role was to support the Spanish uprising. He could do nothing till his force had reunited. Then, with intelligence and information, he must use it to best effect. Information was seriously lacking.

The summer of 1808 had been worrying. Salamanca, hot as ever, shimmered in the heat haze. Dust-devils whirled across the rolling *Meseta*, and the news was bad enough to make even the Spaniards anxious as seldom before. The invading French had occupied Madrid in March, and had brutally suppressed the patriotic uprising at the beginning of May with murderous ferocity. The cry '*Dos de Mayo*' ('Second of May') had become a rallying cry for those who dared to resist the rigours of the French suppression.

In June the French reorganized themselves into 'flying' columns to subjugate Spain's most active areas of resistance. Between June and August the French had tried to starve Saragossa, the proud capital of Aragon, into submission. In the early part of June Marshal Bessières of II Corps (succeeded by Soult in November 1808) sent a young general, Charles Lefèbvre-Desnouettes, to pacify Aragon. His 5,000 infantry and 1,000 cavalry, supported by two batteries of artillery, were too weak. The French embarked on a bloody siege against the recalcitrant Saragossa. This was undertaken with Lefèbvre-Desnouettes' customary energy; he was slightly wounded for the first time. Reinforced by a further 3,000 men after a fortnight, Lefèbvre-Desnouettes was then outranked by General Verdier, the incoming commander. The Spanish general, Palafox, remains to this day a heroic figure throughout Spain. The hungry Aragonese people defended their holy Cathedral city with astonishing bravery, while the rest of Spain watched in growing admiration.

Then on Thursday, 14 July, while Saragossa's agony was still stuttering away, the Spanish Army of Galicia made a muddled effort at cutting the French lines of communication with Madrid. Hope rose in the patriots' hearts. The Spanish chain of command was complicated. General Joaquín Blake's Army of Galicia was jointly commanded by Blake and the proud and difficult General Gregorio de la Cuesta. Joint command in Spain is vulnerable to clashes between strong personalities. The Spaniards were soundly defeated by Marshal Bessières' corps in a muddled, if stubborn, fight only 85 miles from Salamanca, at Medina del Rioseco ('The Mosque of the Dried-up River'). The adroit Bessières exploited the weak coordination between Blake and Cuesta and defeated the Spaniards piecemeal. French communications with Madrid remained open.

Despite their success at Medina de Rioseco, the French did not seize the country's major cities nor pacify its rebellious provinces. Only eight days later there was an unexpected boost for Spanish morale. On Friday, 22 July the French were soundly defeated in a spectacular Spanish victory. The Army of Andalucía, successfully commanded jointly by Generals Castaños and von Reding, defeated the French Army's II Corps under General Dupont in an uncharacteristically well executed succession of outflanking and enveloping manoeuvres at Bailén. Never had the shocked French experienced such mastery of the battlefield by an Iberian enemy. The Spaniards' tactics, perfectly executed, forced the French into a trap between the two wings of the Spanish Army. Three desperate French charges failed and Dupont, realizing that he was unable to escape, sought an armistice.

Spanish morale soared; the French were horrified. The news set panic into the French military headquarters in Madrid, leading to a general French retreat northwards to the Ebro river. Much of Spain was abandoned to the insurgents. France's enemies in Spain and throughout Europe rejoiced at this first check to the Imperial armies. Spanish heroism inspired Austria, setting in motion the rise of a new Coalition against France.

In Napoleon's eyes Spain was by now out of control; it was an affront to the Empire. Why was Spain in such a muddle? France had almost conquered Spain. Now the army stood with its back to the Pyrenees, struggling to retain control of Navarre and Catalonia. France had 75,000 soldiers in Spain. There were 86,000 Spanish troops, some, apparently, much better than expected. There were also some 35,000 British somewhere, whose interfering role was unclear.

Napoleon thought the French had lost their nerve at Bailén. It needed his personal dynamism, his decisiveness, speed and overwhelming numbers to get things moving again. He personally took command of the Spanish theatre and thundered over the Pyrenees at the beginning of November at the head of an avalanche of 100,000 fresh troops of the Grande Armée, with its marshals. Now the Spaniards would see that the French meant business. The Spanish rebels were divided on almost every question, while opinionated Spanish society was crippled by social and political tensions.

Napoleon's lightning offensive entailed a huge double envelopment of the Spanish armies. The Convention of Cintra had even enabled Junot's men, now in the Grande Armée, to deploy back to Spain by early December 1808.

Madrid, its church bells clanging, fell to the French on a cold wet Sunday, 4 December 1808. The Spanish Government, and Mr Frere, the British Minister, scuttled off westwards to Talavera de la Reina.

Rumours were rife in Salamanca. Napoleon was no longer revered in holy Salamanca since his excommunication by the Pope, and now some even said Madrid had fallen. What were all these English soldiers doing sitting here? Had they not been sent to help the insurrection? Should they not have gone off to fight the French? Yes, the red coats were decorative, and it was reassuring to see them in Spain, but – and the questions began. Just as Moore arrived there, tasked to support the Spanish uprising, it appeared that the French were threatening to dominate the country. The situation was fast-moving but information was fragmentary. Moore's force was still split. General Hope's column, still en route from Lisbon because of the bad roads, was 70 miles further east, towards Madrid. Crucially, it contained all Moore's cavalry and artillery. Baird was still to the northwest between Corunna and Salamanca, so Moore's force was seriously unbalanced. How best to use his force to support the Spaniards was very questionable.

At Salamanca Moore rose well before dawn each morning, and worked till mid-morning. Having dealt with his copious correspondence and the orders for the day, he rode out before dinner. Accompanied by an ADC, sometimes Henry, and his great friend Colonel Paul Anderson, whom Henry knew well from Sicily and Sweden, he visited the local hierarchy and the invaluable source of information that was Father Patrick Curtis of the Irish College. Not for nothing was a general's personal staff referred to as his family. It soon became evident that the advance of the French seemed to have had no effect amongst most of the inhabitants of Salamanca. They now seemed to have no particular anxiety, to be enjoying themselves and going about their normal business. The British troops were in good spirits, and pleased that Napoleon was in Spain.

Moore had originally arranged with Baird that they should join forces at Salamanca. The Spaniards, however, seemed indifferent to Baird's needs for supplies (or more likely unable to help but unwilling to say so), so some of the pre-positioned depots, intended for use by Moore's army of 30,000, had to be consumed. He was anxious that there should be stores in place in the event of a withdrawal, an eventuality that seemed daily more probable. He therefore instructed Baird to halt. To Moore's relief, General Hope's detachment joined him at Salamanca on 3 December, an event which coincided with information of several Spanish defeats. Hope had escaped being caught by the advancing French. The confused situation was not helped by conflicting advice and intelligence.

At this stage Henry Percy became witness to Moore's difficulties and the loneliness of command. The episode involved a former French officer, Colonel Venault de Charmilly, who lived as an émigré in England and was married to Lady Dufferin's daughter, whose nephew Captain Blackwood was in Moore's regiment. Moore, an astute judge of character, had strong reservations about de Charmilly's reliability. He was sensitive since it seemed that there were many 'friends of the French' in Spain who had probably been supplying false information and confusion. De Charmilly arrived at Salamanca offering to raise a regiment of cavalry for the British cause. Moore, suspicious of de Charmilly, was at pains to be polite. Moore's hunch was right:

de Charmilly's history was indeed chequered. Implicated in the St Domingo massacre of 1794 under General Rochambeau (who was at this time a prisoner of war in Wincanton), de Charmilly had been a coal merchant in England, then a distiller, a money lender, and eventually a bankrupt. Moore allowed de Charmilly to be aware that he knew about St Domingo. He had felt it necessary to see the man, since he claimed to bring dispatches from Baird. These dispatches, victims of the courier system, had apparently been found by de Charmilly at Zamora. Moore diplomatically asked de Charmilly to dine with him, and invited him to the parade[3] the following morning. After the parade the Chief asked de Charmilly to come and see him for a few minutes. By this time Moore knew from his 'family' (i.e. his personal staff of ADCs and senior staff officers) that de Charmilly had letters of introduction to no fewer than twenty-five eminent military and naval officers in the Peninsula, including Mr Frere, the newly appointed British Minister at Madrid. Moore declined to accept de Charmilly's offer to be a volunteer, and likewise was unable to 'countenance' the raising of a regiment of cavalry. Perhaps, suggested Sir John, His Royal Highness (the Duke of York) might name him, in which case, presumably, the matter would be different. De Charmilly declined a further invitation to dine, since he was already expected with General Fraser, and the following day with General Beresford. Moore was less than impressed and commented with some asperity at the recommendations the colonel had. He did not need de Charmilly to be the bearer of letters to Mr Frere, thank you very much, nor did he need the offered map of Spain. De Charmilly left for Madrid on Saturday, 26 November, leaving a strong negative impression on Sir John and his family. Unbeknown to de Charmilly, Moore had already decided on the need to withdraw. He was troubled by the letters he received from Mr Frere, from whom he had requested advice on the political implications of his entirely logical military decision. Frere, however, whose advice was sought solely on the political implications of military options, wished Moore to advance to the relief of Madrid, and disagreed with his decision to withdraw northwards (which was not what he was being asked). Frere even recommended two senior Spanish officers, who pressed the case, ineffectually. Much information and contradiction continued for the next few days, culminating in an extraordinary episode on Monday, 5 December. Colonel Charles Stewart (Lovaine's friend), half-brother of Lord Castlereagh, arrived from General Hope's division. Moore showed him the correspondence which had passed between Castlereagh and himself, explaining his intention to withdraw. Stewart, we now know, wrote to Castlereagh saying that Moore's decision was fatal but that he was decided. He said he wished they had the hero of Vimeiro at their head now (instead of Moore). Meanwhile, in London, the Cintra Inquiry was ploughing on laboriously in the Royal Hospital.

That evening, unexpectedly, de Charmilly appeared once more, explaining importantly that he was the bearer of a letter for the Chief from Mr Frere. He was told that the general was too much engaged to see him, but he refused to hand the letter to anybody else, insisting he had given his word to deliver it to the hand of the general himself. After ten minutes he was received coolly by Sir John. The letter from Frere, after stressing the importance of Sir John's decision, referred him to the bearer for details of what was happening at Madrid. Colonel de Charmilly explained there was an important new development: the Duke of Infantado was the President of a new Junta for the defence of Madrid. The Duke, whom de Charmilly had seen, wished Sir John to assume the chief command of all the Spanish forces. Mr Frere had been astonished when he heard of this development from Colonel de Charmilly at Talavera.

The next morning Colonel de Charmilly arrived at 11.00am. The ADC on duty was Henry Percy. Henry explained that the Chief had gone straight to his room to write letters, and could not be disturbed. He advised the colonel to return at about one o'clock, when the general usually rode out. Meanwhile, he would try to mention his call. De Charmilly spent the morning trying unsuccessfully to see other general officers whom he knew. He visited the Plaza Mayor and conversed with several people, civilian and military, all of whom disapproved of retreat. He returned to the palace at 1.30pm, and Percy said there was no news. The general was still working because a King's Messenger was leaving for London that night, and it looked as if Moore was finishing his dispatches before the messenger left. De Charmilly became desperate, so Percy agreed to speak to the Military Secretary, Major Colborne, whose office adjoined the Chief's. Neither of the two officers wished to disturb the general. After a time, Colborne gingerly entered, and returned saying de Charmilly might go in. Moore was furious not to have been given the letter from Mr Frere the previous evening. De Charmilly explained that Mr Frere had asked that he should not produce the second letter unless it was necessary. The letter was seized from de Charmilly, who tried to explain further. Moore told him to stand by the fire and allow him to read the letter.

The letter from Frere was explosive. In effect it said that if Moore were determined to withdraw, Mr Frere asked that Colonel de Charmilly, whose intelligence had already been referred to, should be examined by a Council of War.

It is said that Moore strode towards de Charmilly and asked if he knew the contents of the letter. De Charmilly did. Moore was furious. It was not solely the inappropriate message from Frere, erosive of his authority. It was his seemingly inept choice of confidant and messenger. Moore appears to have felt that Frere had been duped by de Charmilly, and had fallen for a doubtful story which was strongly to the advantage of the French.

De Charmilly, desperate to escape the Chief's rage, was eventually allowed to leave the room. Sir John at once wrote to Frere. He explained that he wished to continue a cordial and proper footing with the Minister. The choice of Colonel de Charmilly was, however, unacceptable and inappropriate, even if he were a friend: 'I have prejudices against all that class, and it is impossible for me to put any trust in him. I shall, therefore, thank you not to employ him any more in any communication with me.'[4]

It became evident, after the de Charmilly incident at Salamanca, that Moore's position was perilous. Whilst Frere was anxious for Moore to intervene in support of Madrid, it had become clear that the size and strength of the likely opposition, and indeed the distances involved, would mean that he would be ineffective and would hazard his force in a manner which he knew was unjustifiable. Regardless of minor details, and the unrealistic political views from Madrid, he recognized the danger of being trapped in one of the Emperor's pincer movements. Should Napoleon decide to advance from the south, the presence of Marshal Soult's[5] corps on the Carrión to the north was a serious trap.

Suddenly, by great luck, vital intelligence arrived. An intercepted French dispatch from Berthier (the Emperor's Chief of Staff) to Soult dated 10 December gave accurate and timely details. Madrid, said Berthier, was calm and occupied by the French. Moore now knew for certain that he was right not to go south towards Madrid. Obligingly, Berthier, in a classic breach of security, included the precise breakdown of Soult's force (to the north of Moore), a helpful detail. The Emperor was of the opinion that the British were in full retreat. There seemed to Berthier no reason why the French should not now occupy the whole of the Kingdom of León (on the edge of which Moore was positioned). Finally a summary of the expected French deployment routes for the army was helpfully included. Of the authenticity of this document there was no doubt. Just in time, realities were firm.

Moore decided at once that he must not march northeast on Valladolid, even though he now knew it had been evacuated; instead, he wheeled half-left to the north, because he realized that he had an opportunity to take a 'wipe' at Soult, whose strength, he knew, was less than his. This, he calculated, was worth doing. It remained vital to watch the south to know in time if the Emperor were to deploy and try to trap him.

By now the weather was becoming distinctly wintery; snow and freezing winds had set in. Moore moved his headquarters from Salamanca north to Mayorga. Ahead of him ranged two cavalry regiments[6] from the brigades under Lord Paget.[7]

On the bitterly cold, snowy night of Tuesday, 20 December 1808, Paget ordered the 10th Hussars to move through the town of Sahagún, occupied by a French cavalry force of about 600, whilst he made a sweep around Sahagún with the 15th Hussars so that the French might be trapped. General John Slade was slow in moving off with the 10th Hussars. The French cavalry became aware of the British cavalry and moved hastily out of the town to the east, unmolested. In the dawn light next morning, however, the French regiments, catching sight of the 15th Light Dragoons to the south, formed up in two lines with the 1st Provisional Chasseurs (commanded by Colonel Tascher[8]) in front and the 8th Dragoons behind them. They had mistaken the 15th Hussars for a Spanish cavalry force: this was too good to be true! They were on the point of attacking when they were themselves charged. Surprised, the French cavalry were unable to advance and received the charge of what shockingly turned out to be British hussars whilst stationary. Their attempts at stopping the charging British with carbine fire were ineffective. The 15th charged, unharmed, through the snow, covering about 400 yards of snowy, frozen ground, shouting "Emsdorf and Victory!"[9] It was so cold the soldiers were wearing their pelisses, rather than having them slung over their shoulders, and many wore cloaks as well. Eyewitnesses wrote of numbed hands hardly able to grasp reins and sabres. The clash when the British crashed into the line of chasseurs was ferocious, and it was recorded that horses and men were overthrown and shrieks of terror, intermixed with oaths, groans and prayers for mercy, issued from the whole extent of their front.

The impetus of the British cavalry carried them through the ranks of the chasseurs and into those of the dragoons behind. The French broke, and fled eastwards with the British in pursuit. Many French cavalrymen (the chasseurs were largely of German origin) were made prisoners at very little cost to the 15th Hussars.[10]

The 15th Hussars' charge at Sahagún taught the French to be wary of British hussars. The simple presence of cavalry in the Rear Guard deterred French cavalry from making harassing attacks for the remainder of the retreat to Corunna. The French 1st Provisional Chasseurs were so depleted by their losses[11] at Sahagún that the survivors were absorbed into other units.

Paget having successfully made the desired 'wipe' at Soult's cavalry, Moore began to withdraw. The cavalry protected his rear during the parts of the withdrawal when the ground was suitable.

About the time of Sahagún, Moore, conscious of the danger to his south, received definite intelligence that Napoleon was indeed leading his army of some 80,000 men towards him. There was now a distinct danger of the British force being trapped between the two French forces: the classic 'hammer and anvil' tactic. Moore realized that the only practical option open to him was to avoid the trap by withdrawal. On Christmas Day the retreat started when

Moore's force crossed the river Esla at Castro Gonzalo, near Benavente, and began to move northwest in the direction of Astorga on the route to Corunna. The troops were decidedly unhappy at not having a chance to fight the French. There was a distance of over 300 miles to cover, much of it through steep wild mountainous country, with appalling roads, often little more than mule tracks used by local farm or peasant traffic.

Luckily for Moore, Napoleon did not realize the need to hurry to catch him. After forced marches from Madrid, he rested and regrouped his troops for a critical 24 hours at Tordesillas, 50 miles to the south of Benavente. Napoleon thought Moore was still at Sahagún. That day's delay enabled Moore to escape the trap.

As Moore's force withdrew, he left a Rear Guard behind under Brigadier General Robert Craufurd. At Castro Gonzalo the wide river Esla flows northwards, creating an obstacle. The (then) only bridge was a long Roman bridge, over which the British withdrew. It was prepared for demolition, and careful instructions were given as to when it should be blown. (In modern military parlance it was a reserve demolition.) Craufurd's admirable Light Division troops formed the close defence of the bridge, and after the last British units had crossed successfully, they blew the two centre arches and withdrew tactically.

Two sentries of the 43rd (Monmouthshire) Light Infantry were left behind to warn of the approach of the French, who were, indeed, in pursuit. Private Richard Jackson ran back, as arranged, to give the warning, receiving numerous sabre cuts from the Frenchmen as he dashed away, leaving his companion, John Walton, to face the enemy alone. The gallant Walton bravely stood his ground and astonishingly beat the French off. He escaped unhurt, although his uniform and equipment, it is said, were cut by sabres in over twenty places. His bayonet was badly bent and heavily notched from parrying sabres.[12] It is said that Napoleon himself approached the high ground on the enemy bank to look at the bridge. Anxious to drive in the withdrawing British Rear Guard, the French leading elements, a cavalry group of 600 chasseurs of the Imperial Guard commanded by Major General Count Charles Lefèbvre-Desnouettes (the protégé of Napoleon who had besieged Saragossa) pushed on fast. Finding the bridge destroyed, they looked for a ford. The river was deep. There was pressure to catch up, and the Emperor's eyes were on them. Get on! One can imagine the pressure, as ever, to push on. Keep moving! Get over by the ford: if necessary, SWIM!

Without checking the western bank, Lefèbvre-Desnouettes led his mounted troops into the deep, fast-flowing and nearly freezing Esla. Paget's cavalry, mostly concealed, watched and waited. A thin screen of cavalry outlying pickets found by the 18th Hussars was visible to Lefèbvre-Desnouettes; no problem to his large numbers. He did not recognize it for what it was: a screen ready to withdraw to a stronger inlying picket, springing an ambush. According to one British witness, the French crossed the river and fired their carbines at the outlying picket, driving them slowly back. They were un-affected by the carbine fire. When the moment was right, Major Loftus Otway of the 18th charged with the inlying picket, despite being heavily outnumbered. The French cavalry proved too strong, however, and drove Otway back for 2 miles towards Benavente. In an area where their flanks were protected from attack by walls, the British, now reinforced by a number of the 3rd Hussars, King's German Legion (from Charles Stewart's Brigade), rallied and then counter-attacked.

The French were temporarily driven back, but their superior numbers told, and they forced the British hussars to retreat almost as far as Benavente. Stewart drew the pursuing French towards General Paget, who had substan-tial numbers of British cavalry reserves. The French were preparing a final charge when Paget intervened. He had led the 10th Hussars, with squadrons of the 18th in support, round by the southern outskirts of Benavente, and had managed to hide his squadrons from view until he could surprise the French on their left flank. The fighting of mounted swordsmen is always vicious, and in this case the wounds were very severe. One witness saw the arms of French troopers cut off cleanly 'like Berlin sausages'. Other French soldiers were killed by savage blows to the head – blows which divided the head down to the chin.[13] The French withdrew pell-mell back to the river, their squadrons broken. A scrappy running fight ensued. The chasseurs were forced into the river, while those who were left on the western bank were either cut down or made prisoner.

General Charles Lefèbvre-Desnouettes' horse was wounded and he could not cross the river. A Westphalian private soldier, Johann Bergmann of the 3rd Hussars, King's German Legion (KGL) saw a French officer mounted on a dripping horse, which appeared to be wounded. The officer seemed to have a slight wound on his forehead, but it might have been his horse's blood. In any event, Bergmann managed to capture the officer. Some accounts say the officer had a broken sword, while another theory is that he had lost his sword in the river: not so. Other versions suggest he was disarmed by Bergmann. Again, not true. At that moment an alert private soldier of the 10th Hussars, who was part of the mixed pursuit party, intervened. Levi Grisdale of Penrith realized that the youthful Bergmann did not recognize the officer as impor-tant, and probably could not cope. So he cleverly relieved Bergmann of a potentially difficult prisoner. Bergmann, unperturbed, returned to his regi-ment, unaware that the prisoner he had handed to Grisdale was General Count Charles Lefèbvre-Desnouettes himself (of whom, of course, he had never heard). As the chasseurs swam their horses back across the river, the British troopers fired on them with their carbines and pistols. The French cavalry re-formed on the east side of the river and opened carbine fire on the British, but they were smartly dispersed by the fire of the Royal Horse Artillery.

The story of the general's capture is full of contradictions, and a great many eyewitness accounts: the 10th Hussars believed Grisdale's story that he had captured Lefèbvre-Desnouettes. Bergmann never stated his part in the action until many years later.[14] Grisdale was credited with capturing Lefèbvre-Desnouettes, and remains a regimental hero. Such was the regiment's pride in his feat, the officers of the 10th Hussars presented Grisdale with a fine silver medal for his good work.[15]

Grisdale was interviewed after the regiment returned to England. His discovery of Lefèbvre-Desnouettes is explained as follows:

> Grisdale noticed the French commander, accompanied by two trumpeters, hurrying from the field of action, followed by two privates of the 3rd Hussars KGL, in hot pursuit. The French general's horse outstripped those of the trumpeters, and Grisdale passed the two privates of the KGL. As the general lost his companions of his flight, Grisdale pursued him single-handed.
>
> The General fled along the serpentine margin of the river, and thereby lost much ground, of which Grisdale took advantage, and by cutting across from angle to angle, he at length, after a rapid chase of two miles, succeeded in getting in his front. The General now, from necessity, checked his horse; but betraying symptoms of resistance, Grisdale instantly levelled, and discharged his carbine, the ball of which slightly wounded his adversary on the cheek. Grisdale was preparing to defend himself with his sword (his pistols having been previously discharged) when, to his surprise, he beheld Lefèbvre throw his sword away, as a token of surrender. This gave Grisdale time to re-load his carbine, which having done, he advanced to the General, took the pistols from his holsters, the sash from about his waist, and having dismounted, snatched up the cast away sword; then re-seating himself in the saddle, he turned the rein of the General's bridle over the horse's head, and so conducted him to the British army: the main body of which, at that time, was coming up.

The interviewer stated that Grisdale had too much honest pride to demand the General's watch and money, but a private of the 3rd, who was less scrupulous and exalted in his ideas, did the General that favour before he reached the British lines.[16] Grisdale gave the sash, sword[17] and pistols to his Colonel (Leigh), who, on returning to England, presented the sword to the Prince of Wales. It joined the Prince Regent's collection at Carlton House. It is recorded as belonging to Lefèbvre-Desnouettes. Its decorated blade shows it to have originally been from the 1st Hussars. The sword belongs to the Royal Collection and is on permanent loan to the Royal Armouries at Leeds. The 1809 interviewer continues:

> Grisdale has recently been raised to the rank of corporal, as the first step only of more considerable promotion. He is an exceedingly well made, well looking man: his countenance is ruddy and expressive, and strongly indicates that he possesses that intrepid spirit which should, at all times, distinguish the Briton and the soldier. He is a native of Gracestock [*sic*.], in Cumberland; his age is twenty-four. He has a mother living, to whom he is most affectionately attached; and where filial piety exists, we seldom look for human courage in vain.

Any continuing mystery, however, seems to be cleared away by later witness statements made by Private Bergmann himself. His statement is corroborated by several other German Hussars who had taken part in the action, and by letters from German officers who were present. Bergmann's extensive testimony, taken at an Inquiry at Osterholtz on 8 March 1830, is recorded in the third person. It states that there were:

> three charges that day ... at the third charge, or in reality the pursuit, he came upon the officer whom he made prisoner. He was one of the first in the pursuit, and as he came up with this officer, who rode close in the rear of the enemy, the officer made a thrust at him with a long straight sword. After, however, he had parried the thrust, the officer called out 'pardon'. He did not trouble himself further about the man, but continued the pursuit; an English Hussar, however, who had come up to the officer at the same time with him, led the officer back.

Bergmann went on to say that he had not known the officer was Lefèbvre-Desnouettes until after the action, when he was told he should 'have held fast the man'. He added that he was young and 'did not trouble' himself about the matter. All he remembered was that the officer 'wore a dark green frock, a hat with a feather, and a long straight sword'. All the other German witnesses and letters confirm Bergmann's story, but we also learn that the General fired a pistol at Bergmann 'which failing in its aim, he offered him his sword and made known his wish to be taken to General Stewart'. But Bergmann didn't know General Stewart personally, and while he was enquiring where the general was to be found, a Hussar of the 10th English joined him, and led away the prisoner. So this it seems is the truth of the matter: Lefèbvre-Desnouettes was surrounded by a German troop and captured by Private Johann Bergmann. Levi Grisdale, with the 10th Hussars, might have arrived at the scene at the same time as Bergmann or very slightly after; opinions differ. Lefèbvre-Desnouettes asked to be taken to General Stewart and so

Bergmann, not knowing General Stewart personally, handed him over to Private Grisdale, who led the prisoner away. As a result of the Inquiry the King's German Legion awarded Bergmann a pension in recognition of his part in the action.

Lefèbvre-Desnouettes, shivering in a sopping wet uniform, was delivered under escort to Sir John Moore's headquarters at Benavente, where he was properly looked after by the ADCs. Henry Percy was there, and probably involved. Under flag of truce, a fresh horse and clean uniforms were brought forward (how the river was crossed is not explained), so that General Lefèbvre-Desnouettes was properly dressed for dinner with Sir John Moore. He was even given fresh linen (underwear) belonging to the general. Moore met him and, speaking French, kindly asked how he was. Lefèbvre-Desnouettes looked dejectedly at his empty sword slings. His dignity seemed affronted. Sir John Moore unbuckled his own, fine presentation East India pattern sword (given to him by his officers after the Egyptian Campaign) and gave it to Lefèbvre-Desnouettes, who gratefully fastened it to his slings.[18] Dinner was necessarily frugal, with Moore's loyal French *valet de chambre* François presumably remaining quietly in the background. Lefèbvre-Desnouettes was downcast, saying that the Emperor was unforgiving of those who did not succeed.[19]

Henry Percy noted some years later:

> All had marched but the Cavalry, who remained to protect our rear. The precautions of blowing up the bridge and Picquets at the several fords were taken, and at 8 o'clock the latter were driven back by a strong body of the Imperial Guards commanded by Lt Genl [*sic.*] Lefevre [*sic.*]. General Stewart collected them as soon as he found the 7th and 10th forming up in his rear, charged and routed the whole consisting of at least 600 men, his being to the amount only of 150. Among the taken was Genl Lefevre, two captains and many prisoners. The remainder took to flight and crossed the river where they formed again and fired upon our men. But a gun of the Horse Artillery after two shots dispersed the remaining part of the Corps.

Chapter 5

The Retreat to Corunna
(1808–1809)

On Saturday, 31 December 1808, the village of Bembibre was reached. The soldiers, short of food, soaked to the skin and very cold, found the wine vaults. These were breached, and the drunken stupor that resulted, although a disgrace, was but a mere hint of the excesses that were to follow during the retreat as discipline disintegrated. Conditions were terrible; boots and shoes were falling to pieces, and the baggage animals could not drag the waggons for want of forage.

Henry continues:

> Upon the 31st Lefevre was sent home with an Aid de Camp [*sic.*] of the General's from Astorga[1] where we arrived the day before, finding the Marquis of Romana and the boasted army of 25,000 men running in all directions from León.

The ADC chosen as escort to England from Astorga was Capt Henry Wyndham[2] of the Coldstream Guards. Henry Percy was present throughout the retreat and was involved in the goings-on of the general's family.

The retreat was becoming very difficult indeed, and a combination of appalling cold weather and almost no rations was provoking a breakdown in discipline in some quarters. This was in part because the infantry soldiers' morale was undermined by what they perceived as a reluctance by the commanders to stand and fight. Retreats sap morale. The constant cold, with rain turning to snow, coupled with occasional unrestrained access to rough drink, with hardly any food or shelter, provoked serious trouble. The Rear Guard and the Foot Guards kept their discipline, and in consequence lost fewer stragglers and preserved their fighting ability and morale. Henry Percy describes, in a matter of fact style, a 'melancholy' incident on 3 January, which is much quoted by others in more graphic detail.

> Our advanced posts were beyond Cacabellos [*sic.*] about one league from Villa Franca. Here we were, from the irregularity of our men, obliged to have the dreadful task of shooting one of our men.[3] At the moment they

were prepared for this melancholy event, reports from the outposts warned us of the force opposite. General Moore went, however, to where the men paraded and told them how sorry he was, but how determined to punish with this rigour any of his army. He was now going to take up a Position against the Enemy, but with how much more confidence would he have gone out to oppose them had their behaviour been more correct. The sentence was obeyed, and we then went in time to witness our Cavalry retreating with the greatest order covered by our flanker sharp shooters and light troops. We were in time for the General to give all necessary directions, and having withdrawn them, the Enemy charged into the Village and were so near to the General that he was obliged to push on to get away in time. Our guns and Riflemen did some execution, and deserters since have mentioned General Colberg [sic] having fallen at the head of the (French) Cavalry.[4] From about 2 pm till night we were engaged, but few men were lost. One Captain of the Rifle Corps was wounded and is since dead.[5] This evening the General ordered the whole [force] to make a night march and his post was always in the rear with the reserve, the Cavalry having passed through the infantry to get forward to Lugo, the country affording no opportunity for that force to act.

Conditions deteriorated, and the journal hints at the horrors of the retreat:

Until the 5th nothing occurred except the most fatiguing marches and the sad sight of Soldiers and their Wives lying dead with fatigue and cold upon the mountains above Nogares[6] [sic.]. Indeed, the march of the army might have been traced by the dead animals lying on the road from this latter place. We were constantly followed by the enemy who, being close upon our rear, and until we pointed a gun they followed us firing continually on our Rear Guard. They had also passed a bridge which our Engineers had ill destroyed ... we this evening took up our position at Constantina,[7] a very small village, but the ground very favourable to us here. We had some firing, and a few of our stragglers fell into the hands of the Enemy. We killed a few also of the French.

This night we stole a march upon them, for only General Paget's Division formed the Rear Guard, and arrived at Lugo early in the morning [of 7 January]. They [the French] came up with us this evening and fired with two Spanish small guns taken on the road.[8]

At about 12 o'clock on the 7th we saw a Column of the Enemy moving towards our left and centre. We were shortly after attacked and we succeeded in completely repulsing them, killing about 50 and taking 25 prisoners. Our loss was one or two men only. The General was now convinced that the following morning would now have shown us a battle.

But they declined tho' we waited for them the whole day and at night marched for [Guitiriz].

The prospect of a battle had produced an immediate improvement in morale. The soldiers were much looking forward to the chance to get their own back on the French, on whom, in part, they blamed their misery. They were disappointed this time. The same effect on morale was noticed a few days later at Corunna.

It is said that the night of 8 January was the worst of the whole retreat. There was a thick fog and freezing rain. Navigation became very difficult, and several regiments lost their way. The French cavalry managed, with admirable stamina and discipline, to close in and seize almost 500 prisoners. The survivors struggled on. Henry's journal, missing the detail of that awful night, simply says: 'They again came up with us, but only, I think, a few horsemen, and the following night [9 January] we arrived at Betanzos.'

The retreat was nearly over, and the army was beginning to descend from the mountains. On 10 January they could see ahead the coastal plain with villages and habitation. The Atlantic could be clearly seen in the sunshine. Spirits rose. On 11 January they struggled into Corunna. The General had ordered the ships to move round from Vigo to Corunna to evacuate the army, but the transports had not yet arrived. In any case, it would be necessary to secure the port and hold off the French while the evacuation took place. Accordingly, preparations began to put Corunna into a state of defence. In Corunna there was ample ammunition, thousands of new British muskets, originally intended for the Spaniards, and huge quantities of uniforms and food. This was all speedily put to good use, and the new muskets issued.

On the 11th we quitted this and made another bad attempt at blowing up the bridge. The Cavalry of the Enemy pushed on and were received by our Rear Guard, repulsed and so far checked that we saw little of them until the following day when they appeared with their Riflemen in the house on the further side of the river where we had succeeded in destroying the Bridge. Captain Stewart,[9] ex-ADC to General Paget was wounded, not badly.

As Sir John Moore watched the survivors of his demoralized and ragged army plodding down the slope towards the town there occurred one of those incidents that establishes a lasting tradition. The great author Sir John Fortescue himself says: 'One brigade caught the General's eye, for they were marching like soldiers. "Those must be the Guards," he said, and presently the two battalions of the First Guards, each of them still 800 strong, strode by in column of sections, with drums beating, the drum major twirling his staff at their head, and the men keeping step as if in their own barrack yard. The senior regiment of the British Infantry had set an example to the whole army.'[10]

On the night of 11 January 1809 the divisions of Generals Hope, Baird and Fraser reached Corunna. General Paget's distinguished Rear Guard waited at El Burgo outside the town, where the tidal river Mero was crossed by a substantial stone bridge.[11] They destroyed this bridge successfully, with an explosion which was heard throughout Corunna. If this difficult demolition could be successful, it poses the question why so many other bridge demolitions during the retreat had failed. This was only the second successful demolition of the retreat (Castro Gonzalo being the other). One contributory reason was the need for entrenching tools, especially picks, to prepare the strongly built stone bridges for the charges. Entrenching tools had been deliberately abandoned after Benavente to lighten the soldiers' load when retreating in the mountains. The Rear Guard held back the frustrated, bickering but wary French, who were unable to cross the Mero for at least two crucial days.

Chapter 6

The Battle of Corunna and the Death of Sir John Moore (January 1809)

Corunna, at last. The weather was better, a brisk gusting wind blowing in from the sea. There were ships in the harbour, but neither the transports nor their escorts had arrived. Moore's chief responsibility was to save his army, which was obviously more important than fighting a battle. In consequence, he arranged the defence of Corunna to cover the embarkation when the ships arrived. It was essential to revive the army, restore its cohesion and morale, feed it, rest it and issue boots, uniforms, new muskets and every necessity available from the pre-positioned stores. Much of the British stock in Corunna had been originally intended for support of the Spanish army, but that plan had been overtaken by events.

As soon as the main body of the army arrived, individuals were re-equipped as quickly and completely as possible. Rest, good hot food, new muskets, replacement uniforms and new boots improved everything, especially the spirit of the soldiers. The army became a fighting force once more. Morale surged at the prospect of fighting the French. Before the battle took place they had been transformed by four days of good food. While the Rear Guard held Soult back, Moore deployed his reinvigorated army.

Huge quantities of surplus stores were destroyed, rather than have them fall into enemy hands after the evacuation. One spectacular event was the destruction of the magazine, which contained 4,000 barrels of powder. The resulting gigantic explosion blew in most of the windows in Corunna, and even caused a small tidal wave.

During the afternoon of Saturday, 14 January, to everybody's relief, the transports began to arrive. The sick and wounded, the cavalry and the fifty heavy cannon were quickly embarked. Many of the horses were not worth taking to England and over 2,000 were slaughtered on the beach. The cavalry and artillery were embarked, their numbers having only slightly reduced in the retreat. They had led the way without interference after Cacabelos during the retreat's most demanding stages.

By the time the sick, and those left out of battle had been embarked, and the contingent from Vigo had been deducted from the main force, Moore was left with about 15,000 fit men to face the French. Of this number, the majority were infantrymen, but some 200 were gunners, with enough horses left to draw the nine light 6-pounder guns needed for the defence. Moore's deployment was not ideal because his numbers were too small to allow him to occupy the outer ring of hills – the Heights of Penasquedo – which he would have preferred. He had no option but to choose the inner ring of slightly lower hills, which centred on Monte Mero. This shorter length of line enabled Moore to keep a stronger reserve.

Marshal Soult, with 20,000 men, had three infantry divisions, three cavalry divisions and forty guns. (The French did not organize by fixed brigades, but had larger regiments, which they grouped as required by the situation.)

Preliminary French moves in the late afternoon of 15 January resulted in the British picquets forward of the main positions being driven back. The French quickly established two batteries of ten guns on the western hills whence they could fire on Bentinck's[1] Brigade. Positions were also set up facing both Hope's and Baird's positions. Meanwhile, Moore was trying to ginger up the embarkation process. The winter darkness came before any serious attack took place but he knew the real battle would surely start at dawn.

*   *   *

Dawn came, but no French attack. The morning dragged on with manoeuvring, but no French aggression. A favourable wind meant the chance of a clean break from the French was improving. Moore wanted an engagement; his soldiers longed to get even with the French, and he hoped to improve his reputation and negate the impact of some of his retreat decisions which had inflamed his critics. It was a dilemma; of course a clean break would preserve the army, if it could really be achieved. On the other hand, his army was itching for a fight, and to deprive the men again would invite trouble on all sides. There had even been suggestions from some of Moore's senior officers that he should negotiate with Soult, to allow a peaceful withdrawal, but, aware of the opprobrium arising from the Convention of Cintra, he dismissed such suggestions.

Moore concluded that Soult might have decided to wait and avoid a main engagement. Why, after all, risk lots of lives when it was clear that the British were on the point of evacuation? Perhaps Soult did not want a battle. Moore took a calculated risk. He instructed General Edward Paget to move quickly to the harbour; the other brigades would follow at dusk, and the whole British force should embark that night.

Paget had just begun to move when the two batteries of French guns opened fire on Bentinck's positions at Elviña. The village itself has narrow little streets, with stone walls and very limited fields of view. Soon after this the French began to attack Hope's positions.

Moore himself moved quickly to Elviña, arriving just as the front of a French column, preceded by a cloud of *voltigeurs*,[2] began forcing the skirmishers of the 50th (West Kent) Regiment out of the village. Further to the right Moore saw another column, with cavalry support, manoeuvring to outflank the British.

He ordered Mackenzie Fraser to deploy forward from Corunna, and be prepared to link with Paget to engage the outflanking force to the west. The attacks to the east by Generals Merle and Delaborde were less vigorous, and Moore recognized that the main effort was on his right (as he expected, and for which eventuality Mackenzie Fraser and Paget had been specifically positioned).

When he reached Bentinck's Brigade he told Lieutenant Colonel James Wynch[3] of the 4th (King's Own) to 'throw back' their right wing to cover the flanking move by Mermet's 47e Infantry. Complimenting Wynch on the tidy execution of this move, Moore returned to the hillock above Elviña so that he could see what was happening. On arrival there he was told that Bentinck had been wounded.

Moore remained with Bentinck's Brigade to direct operations, since this was clearly the main attack. He ordered the 42nd (Black Watch) to retake the village from the 31e Léger, shouting 'My brave Highlanders, remember Egypt! Think of Scotland.'

With the 4th (King's Own) holding the right flank, the Black Watch, supported by the 50th (West Kent), began fierce close-quarter fighting in the narrow old streets of Elviña near the church. They could not make much progress and fell back, suffering numerous casualties in the close fighting. Moore was watching from the cross-roads at the northwest corner of Elviña. Alert French gunners of the grand battery on the high ground above Penasquedo had noticed groups of senior officers gathering at this point from time to time.

Moore realized he needed reinforcements and sent for the divisional reserve: Warde's two battalions of the First Foot Guards, each 800 strong. Henry Percy recorded his involvement:

> We went to the outposts as usual, and only returned for breakfast at 9.00 a.m. We arrived on the ground as the first gun was fired by the Enemy who opened Batteries on our two flanks. After a cannonade of half an hour we found ourselves pretty warmly engaged and withdrew the skirmishers. Our Picquets were driven in, and my General led the 42nd up to the support of the Front, who received the enemy so well that they took to flight and we killed and took many prisoners.

The 50th on the right were very forward in dispossessing the Enemy of a Village [Elviña] in their front which they completely succeeded in with the loss of their two Majors and a great proportion of officers and men.

The 4th [King's Own] now came up on the right, while on their Right the 95th [Rifle Corps] and 52nd [Oxfordshire Light Infantry] drove them [the French] back from our Right Flank and the General sent me to bring up the Guards to the support of the 42nd and General Paget's Division to that (i.e. support) of the 4th.

Most accounts sent to Sir John Moore's brother for his biography, including Henry Hardinge's own, state that Henry Hardinge was sent to summon the Guards. Percy's claim, however, is not unreasonable, since the need for a back-up messenger was always important once casualties began to mount. Likewise, it is possible that Henry Percy's account, which was written much later, confuses this with another errand on which he may have been sent by Moore. Similarly, the tall George Napier of the 52nd, aged 24, also an ADC, had been sent to summon the Guards to support Bentinck's Brigade. He saw Moore's horse rear, and Henry Hardinge dismount to catch him in his arms. He continued and found Colonel Warde and gave him the message. On his return he found Sir John dreadfully wounded. What is certain is that Moore had been waiting near the cross-roads with Colonel Thomas Graham and Captain John Woodford of the 1st Guards (both on Moore's staff) when Hardinge returned. Hardinge's account says Percy was already there. Percy says: 'When I returned there was no difficulty in finding the General. Where the fire was hottest, there he was animating and encouraging his troops in the most spirited manner. But I found him that instant wounded most dreadfully by a cannon shot' (from the Grand Battery).

Moore fell at Graham's feet. Helped by Henry Percy, Graham lifted Moore and laid him against a bank. Thomas Graham wrote in his diary: 'He fell at my horse's feet, but such was the invariable firmness of his mind that he bore this pain without an alerted feature. I scarcely thought him wounded till I saw the state of his arm. We lifted him against a bank. I sent Percy for a surgeon, though it seemed quite a hopeless case, and by [the wounded] Lord William Bentinck's advice I rode to tell General Hope that the command had developed on him, Sir David Baird having left the field early in consequence of a wound in his arm.' Percy, who was sent to find the surgeon, wrote: 'I turned my poor horse, who was so tired as scarce to be able to stir, to get a surgeon. But he [the General] was carried off before I could return.'

Surgeon McGill of the Royal Scots, who was not far away, with his 'impedimenta behind a large rock', attended Moore in the field. (Poor McGill died two weeks later, probably of dysentery.) The general's left shoulder was shattered, the arm hanging by a piece of skin, the ribs over the heart were broken and bared of flesh, and the muscles of the breast were torn into strips. McGill removed a piece of lapel with two buttons which had been driven into to the wound. Moore thanked him, but told him, 'My good man, you can do me no good; it is too high up.' He was moved in a blanket by six men of the 42nd and the Guards, with Hardinge's sash supporting him in the 'easiest possible posture'. As they lifted him his sword got between his legs and the hilt entered the wound. Hardinge made to unbuckle the belt, but was stopped: 'It is as well as it is. I had rather it should go out of the field with me.'

Moore told Hardinge that he need not go with him. 'Report to General Hope that I am wounded and carried to the Rear.' Percy continues:

> I now, with the rest of the Staff, attached myself to General Hope who commanded, Sir David Baird[4] having been wounded early in the action. And remained till it was quite dark. On our right it was necessary to gain a Village which the Enemy had possessed themselves of, which the 14th [Buckinghamshire] Regiment did in a brisk attack.

It was a ghastly afternoon for Moore's 'family'. Their beloved Chief had been hideously struck down. George Napier's brother Charles, commanding the 50th, had been seen charging at their head into Elviña, with Charles Stanhope, his second-in-command. George had heard that Elviña had been taken, and that the attackers had been repulsed. His friend and fellow ADC, young James Stanhope,[5] was equally involved and anxious. Before joining General Hope they went quickly to find out how their brothers had fared. George Napier saw with horror some soldiers carrying a blanket with the body of an officer shot through the heart. He leapt from his horse, acutely worried, and lifted the handkerchief covering the face of the corpse. The ghastly pale face was Charles Stanhope. At that moment his friend James Stanhope shouted that they must hurry and join General Hope. So they left the scene, and George Napier broke the news as kindly as he could. James, he said, bore it as a soldier should. He did go back for a last look at his poor brother. George himself had a close shave when the officer in front of him was wounded in the foot, and then young Burrard (the old general's son), who was following him, was hit by grapeshot in the chest. He died two days later on board ship.

George Napier stayed with General Hope as he toured his brigades, encouraging and directing them in the heavy fighting. As they approached the 50th, which was still in close action, a senior captain of the regiment reported to General Hope. 'Sir, our commanding officer, Major Napier is killed. We have no field officer left. Our ammunition is expended. What are we to do?'

Moore's call for the deployment of the Reserve of Fraser and Paget had been exactly right. It was beautifully handled by General Edward Paget, so as darkness fell he was enveloping the Grand Battery. By 5pm the fighting was beginning to die down. The French drums began to beat retreat at 6pm. Soult had no wish to continue with a battle which it was evident was achieving nothing at great cost.

At this stage Sir David Baird, Moore's wounded second-in-command, was having his right arm amputated at the shoulder on HMS *Ville de Paris* in the port. General Hope, seeing the battle slowing, went quickly to Corunna to consult with the naval officers and to superintend the embarkation. He, like so many, was horrified at the loss of the Chief, their friend, Sir John Moore.

General Hope released George Napier from looking after him as he had heard from some officers of the 50th that his brother Charles was merely wounded, not killed as he had feared. He might still be lying out there. By the light of a flaming resin torch, Napier spent a long time examining the body of every fallen officer he could find on the battlefield. After that he searched the hospitals; sadly, some of the wounded men there said they had seen Charles killed. With a heavy heart George turned to go to the Cantón Grande,[6] Moore's headquarters house.

From the windows of many of the houses in Corunna it was possible to see the battlefield. More people had watched from the heights of St Lucia. They saw the battle ebb and flow, heard the roar of gun fire, and the volleys of musketry; saw the smoke drifting over the valleys, and heard the cheering as the red-coated and tartan-clad British drove back the French columns at the point of the bayonet. Then, as dusk fell in the evening afterglow, six soldiers and a small escort were seen carrying a wounded man back to the town in a blood-soaked blanket, slung between two poles. They were followed by some staff officers and a surgeon, the black feathers of his cocked hat streaming in the wind, walking anxiously on either side of the litter. It had taken almost an hour to reach the town. Several times the general, ignoring the agony of his wound, asked the soldiers carrying him to turn so that he could see the progress of the battle.

The news that a cannon-shot had shattered the shoulder of General Moore had brought a mixed crowd of Spaniards and British soldiers to the door of his lodging in the Cantón Grande. A tall dark clergyman, aged 28 and very correct, entered the British headquarters after the little *cortège*, without hesitation. Mr Henry John Symons,[7] Chaplain to the Brigade of Guards, had been instructed that his services were likely to be called for.

François David,[8] Sir John's loyal French valet, had been upstairs finishing his packing. He came down with a candle and met the stretcher-party. This was the third time he had seen his master borne wounded from the field, but this time, observing all the men bearing him in tears, and a clergyman following, he became speechless with horror. The General smiled at François and murmured in French, 'My friend, this is nothing.'

Assistant-Surgeon John Maling and another doctor attended but, perceiving the patient much agitated, withdrew. Moore told Paul Anderson[9] that this was the way he wanted to die. Anderson, a close friend and companion, had saved Moore's life in St Lucia. He made detailed notes in a small notebook.

'I have made my will, and have remembered my servants, Colborne has my will. And all my papers.' Major Colborne then came into the room. He spoke most kindly to him, and then said to me 'Anderson, remember you go to ... [Willoughby Gordon[10]], and tell him it is my request, and that I expect he will give Major Colborne a lieutenant colonelcy. He has long been with me, and I know him most worthy of it.'

Of everyone who entered the room he asked 'Are the French beaten?'

When Graham and General Paget arrived he could not remember having asked for them, and seemed surprised they had arrived.

Anderson noted one kind remark of Moore's: 'Everything François says is right. I have the greatest reliance on him.' In spite of his dreadful wounds, Moore remained conscious and dictated several messages recommending promotion for officers who had been distinguished in the battle. He repeatedly said that he was dying in the way he had always wished. He was, nonetheless, worried about public opinion at home as a result of the horrors of the retreat. 'I hope the people of England will be satisfied,' he said; 'I hope my country will do me justice.'

Percy continues:

after this I received the orders of the General [Hope] to return to my General [Moore] and give him the news of our proceedings. [I] found him, with some of his friends, on a bed on the floor. The sight was too dreadful. He smiled as I entered and said 'How are you, my good fellow? Have they beat the French?' I answered in the affirmative. 'Thank God' he exclaimed, 'that is enough.' And then [he] enquired if all his Aides de Camp were safe.[11] Answered also in the affirmative, and he begged to be remembered to his friends. [He] said placidly, though in the most horrid tortures, 'I find myself too strong. I fear I shall not die for a long time.' He settled everything with his friends and told them where to find his will, and died an hour after I arrived, in the arms of his staff.

The loss was too great to be borne without the most bitter sorrow. His left breast and arm were torn from his body and his ribs forced into his Lungs. With all this, a few minutes after his death his face resumed the most calm and almost smiling appearance; the consciousness of his Virtues secured him this Quiet, and may God have preserved his soul.

A short time before the end Moore said to James Stanhope, 'Remember me to your sister.'[12] These were his last words. A few minutes later he pressed

Anderson's hand closer to his body, in an effort to pull up his long martial frame. The surgeons noticed the familiar symptom and moved again. Just then the eight o'clock gun sounded from the Admiral's flag-ship. The surgeons came forward as Anderson removed his right hand and stood up. At that moment the exhausted George Napier entered the room. He noticed that the 'high-spirited, guileless Harry Percy was pouring forth in convulsive sobs the overflowing of his warm and generous heart, and poor James Stanhope completely struck down by the double loss of his brother and his friend.[13] Although last in this imperfect sketch, not least absorbed in the deep anguish of despair stood his faithful and devoted servant, François, bending over his master's mangled body, his hands clasped in speechless agony, his face as pale as the calm countenance he wildly gazed upon.'

Henry Percy left no account of the burial of Sir John Moore, at which he was present. Luckily there are a number of eyewitness accounts of the event which later became one of the landmarks of British history with the publication of the Reverend Charles Wolfe's[14] epic (if factually inaccurate) poem, 'The Burial of Sir John Moore'.

Moore had let it be known that he wished to be buried where he fell, but it was impossible for him to be buried at Elviña. Early the next morning, Tuesday, 17 January 1809, the Reverend Henry Symes arrived at the headquarters house on the quayside. The body of Sir John Moore had been removed after midnight by the officers of his staff to the quarters of his friend Colonel Thomas Graham of Balgowan,[15] up in the citadel. The staff discussed whether the general's body should be buried at Corunna or taken back to England. Mr Symons had felt it better to withdraw the previous evening, since the 'family' seemed so overwhelmed by their loss. He decided not to embark with the troops, whose progress towards the fleet had been going on all night, but to wait and see what decision had been reached about the general. As he made his way up the steep narrow little streets to the Citadel, dawn was just breaking.

In the small quarters of Colonel Graham, Mr Symons found the officers of Moore's 'family' waiting outside the room in which the general had been laid. They looked drawn, tired and pallid. Colonel Graham said he had spent the night in the room with the general's body, and he had even slept for some hours. Graham had been appointed to General Hope's headquarters, and together with George Napier he headed off there at once, to help with the evacuation. Napier and Graham were back in time for the burial.

During the night a working party of soldiers from Captain William Gomm's[16] company of the 9th (East Norfolk) Regiment had been digging for some hours by lantern light. The aides, Henry Percy included, had taken turns to attend the preparation of the grave. There are suggestions that Moore, who greatly admired Brigadier General Robert Anstruther,[17] who had died of an illness the day before the battle, had said that he wished to be buried beside his friend. Luckily there had been no rain for several days and the working party had, with some difficulty, managed to dig down to a sufficient depth.

It was a grey blustery morning; a strong southwesterly gale was making white horses in the Bay of Biscay. From the landward bastion the watch-fires could still be seen flickering but the battlefield was empty. The last picquets were pulling back, leaving the ramparts and town covered by Hill's Brigade. The French, discovering that the main positions had been quietly evacuated overnight, pushed towards Santa Margarita Heights. At about 8am they fired a few shots. The burial party in the citadel had to hurry. There was no coffin. Sir John lay on his bier in uniform, wrapped in a soldier's blanket. Over that was his cloak.

The chaplain[18] opened his black leather-bound prayer-book, the pages fluttering in the wind, his black robes and preacher's white bibs blowing wildly. He had been warned that a serious attack might develop at any minute, and that the officers who might be ordered away were anxious to perform their last duties. The prayers chosen were few and short, but the burial was most properly carried out, with the chaplain raising his voice against the growing gale. Only six officers were present:[19] Colonel Thomas Graham, Colonel Paul Anderson, acting Adjutant General, Major George Napier, Major John Colborne,[20] Military Secretary, and Captains the Hon. Henry Percy and James Stanhope. When the chaplain's voice ceased, they stepped forward and Sir John Moore was lowered into the Spanish soil on the long crimson sashes of these four officers of his family.

By mid-day the French had brought six guns to the heights above the southern end of the bay, and opened fire upon the transports within range. After some initial chaos in the harbour, the Royal Navy restored order. Hill's Brigade embarked and put hastily to sea after some disruption which meant that a number of officers could not reach their own regiments' ships. Finally Beresford's Brigade embarked on 18 January, covered faithfully by the Spaniards who held off the French till embarkation was complete. The last formed body of troops to embark was Captain Gomm's[21] company of the 9th Regiment.

* * *

Henry Percy embarked on the huge HMS *Ville de Paris*[22] in the company of 22-year-old Captain Hon. Alexander Gordon, the wounded General Sir David Baird's nephew and ADC. Also on board was John Colborne. *Ville de Paris* was a magnificent Chatham-built first-rate ship of 110 guns, the flagship of Admiral Sir Samuel Hood, KB. She replaced the French flagship, *Ville de Paris*, financed by the citizens of Paris, which had been captured at the Battle of the Saints in 1782 and foundered in a hurricane whilst being towed to England as a prize. The new *Ville de Paris*, the name proudly retained, an enormous ship of the line under Captain Carden,[23] sailed fast for home with a large number of officers and men on board, through a furious southwesterly storm[24] in the Bay of Biscay. Lieutenant General Sir David Baird, who had been wounded just before Sir John Moore, was 'doing well', in spite of the pitching and heeling of the great ship. Lieutenant General Sir John Hope, as we have seen, was in command from the moment Sir John Moore was wounded. Thus there arose the delicate matter of who should produce the dispatch.

Sir John Hope naturally thought he had been in command, so the responsibility should fall to him. But Sir David,[25] senior, and alive, insisted that Hope should report to him, and that the dispatch should originate from him as the senior officer. He ordered his nephew Alexander Gordon to carry the dispatch (which was really Hope's account with a brief left-handed covering letter from Baird) to London. Gordon, very properly, questioned this. His uncle replied, 'If you don't wish to go, I shall send [Captain] Baird.' It was a long-standing convention that an officer delivering a victory dispatch should, if qualified, be advanced one step on the promotion ladder, and Baird wished to help his nephew.

Baird's decision caused indignation among Moore's staff, who felt that the honour should go to them. George Napier wrote: 'So indelicate a thing was never done under similar circumstances.' The grudge lasted for years, and the Napier brothers felt (incorrectly) that Baird's choice of courier had cost George his promotion. Consequently, Alexander Gordon receives little credit from a Napier pen for his distinguished service throughout the remainder of the war. Such is the delicacy of choice of dispatch courier.

The news first reached London from Lord Paget, who had sailed earlier with the cavalry soldiers and avoided the worst of the storm. Paget, with his staff, had been aboard HMS *Endymion* (Captain Capel). Lord Castlereagh wrote to the King late on the evening of Sunday, 22 January to say that Lord Paget had arrived in London with the news. It was not till 2am that he was able to forward General Hope's dispatch, which he had just received from Gordon.

Colborne arrived in London a few hours later and went to see the Commander-in-Chief, the Duke of York. Colonel Willoughby Gordon, the Duke of York's Military Secretary, was a friend of Moore's, and Colborne was received with much kindness. They listened to the whole story, and seemingly drew their own conclusions. Colborne received his promotion immediately, while Alexander Gordon was still waiting anxiously three months later.[26]

Be the jealousy over the dispatch as it may, Henry Percy and Alexander Gordon, the two junior ADCs, travelled together. Alexander Gordon was an intelligent and friendly officer in the 3rd Foot Guards. During the tempestuous voyage through mountainous seas Henry and he became good friends. Alexander Gordon's letters to his brother in London, written during the retreat whilst he was serving as ADC to his uncle, Sir David Baird, reflect the drop in morale. He reported the events in a balanced way, but it is notable how his tone changed from one of support for Sir John Moore's decisions, understanding his dilemmas, to one which vehemently criticized the delays and his apparent reluctance to fight the French. Whether this was his uncle's influence or his own opinion is immaterial. He did not allow it to interfere in what grew into a close friendship with Henry Percy, who for the rest of his life admired Moore as a true role model, and wore a gold locket containing a lock of Moore's hair to his dying day.

The news from Corunna shocked England. Heroic Moore was much mourned. As at Dunkirk in 1940, thanks to the Royal Navy and civilian transports Britain's only continental army had been saved to fight another day. The public had had misgivings about the campaign, and domestic politics became fraught.

* * *

Sir John Moore is still revered in Corunna. There is a plaque on the Cantón Grande headquarters house, and his tomb is much venerated. Marshal Soult is often credited with having arranged the tomb. Indeed, he did make arrangements to ensure the grave was looked after, and the Soult monument to Moore is at the spot near Elviña where he fell. However, it was the Spanish general, the Marqués de la Romana, who took it upon himself, on behalf of Spain, once the French had evacuated Galicia, to arrange the erection of a temporary monument in the form of a broken shaft of a column, made of wood, painted to resemble stone. Above it was raised a pediment of real muskets and shells. On its completion, Romana attended in state and, in the presence of the civic authorities of the place and the whole garrison, unveiled the column, and wrote on it in black chalk, with his own hand:

> *A la Gloria del Excelentísimo Señor Don Juan Moore,*
> *General en Jefe del Exércitos Británicos,*
> *Y a sus Valientes Soldados,*
> *La España Agradecida,*
> *Batalla de Elviña, 16 Enero 1809.*[27]

After the war the Prince Regent, who had admired Moore, hearing of the temporary nature of the monument, ordered that a permanent memorial should be erected at Corunna. There is now an iron railing around a plain granite urn which is placed upon marble slabs. These slabs are inscribed in Latin, English and Spanish, but are difficult to read from behind the railing.

There is also a wall with the Charles Wolfe poem, and a fine new bust of Moore graces the San Carlos Gardens where he lies. Poor General Anstruther, by contrast, receives little attention.

There remains one of those historical curiosities which is at last resolved: the poetic lantern. The poem by Charles Wolfe stated that Moore had been buried at dead of night with a lantern dimly burning. The Reverend Henry Symons read the poem and wrote to the topical magazine, *Notes and Queries* in 1852, describing his attendance on Sir John Moore. Certain facts in the poem are laced with heavy poetic licence, and Symons sought to set the record straight.

All the eyewitness accounts agree that it was early daylight at Corunna when John Moore was taken from Graham's house up to the ramparts for the service. The Norfolk soldiers had dug the shallow grave overnight to the best of their ability, so the sods were not turned 'with our bayonets' during the funeral. Nor, come to that, was it performed by moonlight. It seemed probable that Wolfe's reference to the lantern was his romantic imagination.

The moving poem inspired several artists to produce paintings of varying quality, purporting to show the scene of Sir John's burial. Each depicts the famous 'lantern dimly burning'. In one it is held by a curiously effeminate kilted figure, who might be a poor artist's idea of a Black Watch soldier. In another the soldier is anonymous, and in yet another he might be in the Royal Artillery, although the uniform is a much later pattern. How odd it is, then, to discover that at Tynemouth Priory there is a grave to Alexander Rollo of the Royal Artillery, who died on 26 May 1856. The inscription states: 'CORPORAL ROLLO HELD THE LANTERN AT THE BURIAL OF SIR JOHN MOORE AT CORUNNA ON 17th JANUARY 1809.'

The original medal roll of the Military General Service Medal confirms that there was a Corporal Rollo (later wrongly transcribed as Rolls) who was awarded the clasp Corunna (in addition to Roleia and Vimiera). The rank of bombardier was reserved for those NCOs who served the guns till late in the nineteenth century. Other lance corporals and corporals, including Royal Artillery drivers, in the Royal Regiment were described as such.

Alexander Rollo's family and descendants have populated a flourishing blog[28] for several years. Their forebear certainly was at Corunna, and throughout the retreat. Whether he served with the nine light guns that fought at Corunna is unknown. Possibly he was one of the gunners who was to have been embarked, but was taken for fatigues instead. A useful young NCO, he might easily have been taken for duty by night while the grave was being dug, when lanterns and torches were needed. Who knows? The only thing that seems certain is that the lantern was not needed next morning at the burial service.

One other clue is that the internet has revealed the name of the corporal of the guard at the headquarters house on the evening of 16 January. He was one Joseph Mills, but his regiment has not been discovered. If, as seems possible, he came from the same company of Norfolk soldiers as the grave diggers, he did not survive long enough to submit a claim for the Military General Service Medal in 1847. The only Mills claimant in the 9th Regiment was not at Corunna. Likewise, there is no Royal Artillery soldier who received the Corunna clasp named Joseph Mills.

In one of a series of coincidences, Colonel Maximilien Sébastien Foy, whose brigade had been fighting Hope's division at Piedralonga on the eastern side of the battle, recorded that he moved the following evening into Moore's house in the Cantón Grande.[29]

*   *   *

Now there only remains General Lefèbvre-Desnouettes, the peacock French prisoner, before we are clear of Henry Percy's involvement with Corunna and Moore.

General Charles Lefèbvre-Desnouettes, who was sent to England from Astorga with the ADC Captain Henry Wyndham and a servant, embarked at Corunna in HMS *Cheerful*, Lieutenant Carpenter's punchy new 68ft naval cutter with eight 18-pounder carronades and four 6-pounder guns. From Portsmouth Lefèbvre-Desnouettes was escorted to Portchester Castle, the reception centre for French prisoners of war. The sword lent to him by Sir John Moore was taken from him, probably by Wyndham, intending to return it to Sir John. It seems likely that Wyndham held on to it after Moore's death, since they almost certainly arrived at Portchester Castle before the news of the battle of Corunna and Moore's death had reached England.

The Wyndham memorial tablet in Petworth church states, confusingly, that he carried the dispatches after the battle of Corunna (16 January). He did, but not those describing the battle, for, as we have seen, they were written by General Hope with a covering note from General Baird. Wyndham brought back Moore's dispatch from Astorga (via Corunna) dated 31 December. In it, Moore concludes by stating: 'I send the French general Lefèbvre to Corunna, to be forwarded to England. He is a young Man, and I should suppose from the Station he held, a personal favourite of Buonaparte.'

Lefèbvre-Desnouettes was placed on parole. His detailed movements are not certain till 1810, when he was in Cheltenham, graciously accommodated in 1 The High Street, with Stéphanie his wife, a naval ADC, Lieutenant Armand Le Duc, and two Imperial Guardsmen as servants. More of that later.

*   *   *

Moore's Corunna deployment was as follows:

Left Flank, Lieutenant General Sir John Hope's 2nd Division protected by the Rio Mero. He had two brigades forward (Hill and Leith), and one brigade back (Catlin Craufurd).
- **Maj Gen Rowland Hill's Brigade (forward left)**
  2nd (Queen's), 5th (Northumberland Fusiliers), 2/14th (West Yorkshire Regt), 32nd (Duke of Cornwall's Light Infantry). Between Hill's and Leith's Brigades was a gun position of either five or four light 6-pdr guns.
- **Major General James Leith's Brigade (forward right)**
  51st (King's Own Yorkshire Light Infantry), 76th (2nd West Riding Regt, later Duke of Wellington's), 2/59th (East Lancashire Regt).
- **Major General Catlin Craufurd's Brigade (back)**
  36th (2nd Worcestershire Regt), 71st (Highland Light Infantry), 92nd (Gordon Highlanders).

Centre: Lieutenant General Sir David Baird's 1st Division, based on Monte Mero, consisted of three brigades.
- **Maj Gen Coote Manningham's[30] Brigade (forward left,
  on Leith's right)**
  3/1st Royals (3rd Bn, The Royal Scots), 26th (1st Bn, Cameronians, Scottish Rifles), 2/81st (2nd Bn, Loyal North Lancashire Regt). Between Manningham's and Bentinck's Brigades there was a gun position of either five or four light 6-pounder guns.
- **Maj Gen Lord William Bentinck's Brigade (forward right,
  in the village of Elviña)**
  4th (1st Bn, King's Own, Royal Lancaster Regt), the Right flank battalion of the British formed line; 42nd (1st Bn, Black Watch, Royal Highland Regt), 50th (1st Bn, Royal West Kent Regt).
- **Brig Gen Henry Warde's[31] (Guards) Brigade (rear)**
  1/1st Foot Guards (1st Bn, Grenadier Guards), 2/1st Foot Guards (2nd Bn, Grenadier Guards).

Right Flank. This was more open and exposed, so Moore placed a larger proportion of his force there, in two elements.
- **Lieutenant General Alexander Mackenzie Fraser's 3rd Division**
  Five battalions (2,600 men), not formed into brigades: 6th (1st Bn, Royal Warwickshire Regt), 9th (1st Bn, Norfolk Regt), 23rd (1st Bn, Royal Welsh Fusiliers), 79th (1st Bn, Queen's Own Cameron Highlanders), 82nd (2nd Bn, The Prince of Wales's Volunteers, South Lancashire Regt).
- **(Reserve) Major General Sir Edward Paget**
  The former Rear Guard. Five battalions (1,500 men), not formed into brigades: 20th (1st Bn, Lancashire Fusiliers), 28th (1st Bn, Gloucestershire

Regt), 1/52nd (2nd Bn, Oxfordshire & Buckinghamshire Light Infantry), 91st (1st Bn, Argyll & Sutherland Highlanders), 1/95th (1st Bn, Rifle Brigade). Four of Moore's nine light 6-pounder guns were with the Reserve.

Soult's organization was as follows:

- Merle's 1st Infantry Division: 2e, 4e Léger, 15e, 36e Ligne.
- Mermet's 2nd Infantry Division: Brigadiers Gaulois and Jardon: 31e Léger, 47e, 122e Ligne, 2e and 3e Swiss (red uniforms).
- Delaborde's 3rd Infantry Division: 17e Léger, 70e, 86e Ligne, 4e Swiss (red uniforms).
- Lahoussaye's Cavalry Division: 17e, 18e, 19e, 27e Dragoons.
- Lorge's Cavalry Division: 13e, 15e, 22e, 25e Dragoons.
- Franceschi's Cavalry Division: 1e Hussars, 8e Dragoons, 22e Chasseurs, Hanoverian Chasseurs. (There remains controversy as to whether Franceschi was present.)

Chapter 7

England, Ireland and Back to the Peninsula (January–April 1809)

Henry Percy, exhausted and shivering, arrived off Plymouth in HMS *Ville de Paris* around 25 January 1809 after immense seas in the Bay of Biscay. The harbour was congested. The wind suddenly veered to the west so *Ville de Paris*, *Barfleur* and several other ships plunged on to Portsmouth. It was bitterly cold and blustery; then came heavy drifting snow. By the time Henry reached London after a miserable draughty journey, sooty snow blanketed the slushy streets.

There is little written evidence of Henry's movements before his return to the Peninsula in April. We know he went home to his parents' house, No. 8 Portman Square. As was noted in Chapter 1, Henry's parents, along with two of their sons (28-year-old Algernon and 14-year-old Charles) and their three young daughters Charlotte, Susan and Emily had all been detained by Napoleon on their way home from Italy in 1802 at the end of the short-lived Peace of Amiens. Initially they were held in Geneva, but in late 1805 Beverley and Algernon were sent to Moulins in the Auvergne and Lady Beverley and her girls came home.

Lady Beverley was determined to secure her husband's release, and a reply to her from the Foreign Secretary, Canning, of 18 August 1808,[1] survives, significantly addressed to her at Portman Square. So we know she was home when Henry reached England after Corunna.

We do not know for certain where Henry's eldest brother George, Lord Lovaine (1778–1867), was living. He had married in 1801, and was by now 31 years old. He and his wife Louisa may have been living in Grosvenor Square. Occasionally in 1812 they were in Beverley's house in Portman Square. Number 8 had been kept open before Lady Beverley and the girls arrived back from France, under the care of Mr John Deans, the Earl's confidential servant, who lived with his wife in nearby Connaught Terrace.

Henry's other brothers were busy. He had twin brothers a little older than himself: Hugh, with whom he had been at Eton, now rector of Bishopsbourne in Kent, and Josceline, whom we have already met evacuating General Junot from Portugal to France in HMS *Nymphe*. Henry's next younger brother William Henry, aged 21, was also serving in the Royal Navy. Francis John, the second youngest brother, aged only 19, was serving in the 23rd Foot (The Royal Welsh Fusiliers).[2] Charles, the youngest boy, was nearly 15, and it is not certain if he was with his parents on their unfortunate trip to Italy. If he was with them, he returned to England from Geneva with his mother and sisters, being ineligible for militia service. His curriculum vitae certainly makes no mention of any irregularity in his schooling.

Many years later Josceline's daughter, Sophy Louisa Percy Bagot, wrote a book of family reminiscences called *Links with the Past*. Her elderly memory was slightly adrift. Reflecting on the brothers' contributions to the war, she recounts a meeting which must have taken place, although some details are muddled and it is difficult to establish exactly where or when the meeting took place. She wrote:

> From 1808 to 1810, as captain of H.M.S. Nymph [*sic.*] he [her father, Josceline Percy] was employed in the blockade of the Tagus, until Lisbon was taken.[3] There he fell in with his brother, Captain William Percy, R.N., in command of a ship;[4] with his brother, Henry Percy, 14th Light Dragoons, A.D.C. to Sir John Moore;[5] with his brother Francis, a soldier under Sir John Moore's command, in which regiment I forget (Francis had overgrown his strength, and died of fatigue in the campaign); also with his eldest brother, Lord Lovaine, who, I believe, had volunteered on some general's staff[6] – a very unexpected and delightful meeting for all these brothers on active war service![7]

When Henry arrived in London that miserable late January day, the country was in shock. First there had been widespread disgust at the Convention of Cintra, and the hope to redeem some standing in the eyes of Europe by the intervention of Sir John Moore's army had proved groundless. The British Army had been sent to help the gallant Spanish insurrection, to help drive out the hated French from Spain. Instead, it had returned exhausted and in rags. Its commander, once held in the highest esteem, had been killed heroically. It seemed that nothing had been achieved at great cost and humbling loss of prestige.

The Government made positive statements in the *London Gazette*, praising the gallantry of the troops and the 'victory' of Corunna. And yet, the 26,000 ragged, filthy and exhausted soldiers who had come home seemed to tell a very different story of a chaotic retreat, rout and a complete breakdown of discipline until the battle. Yes, they had undoubtedly been through terrible times in frightful weather. But why? And what had been achieved? As to the losses incurred, how could they be justified?

The Spanish armies, of which so much had been expected, were apparently destined for one defeat after another. The public in England had seen and heard enough of Iberia, what with the disgraceful Convention of Cintra, and now this. It had been a disaster to become involved in Spain.

Lord Castlereagh had a tricky political time against such a surge of opinion. He made a chivalrous gesture in assuming all responsibility for the miscarriage of the campaign, defending Moore's reputation against that part of the press which attempted to shield the Government by blaming the general.

Meanwhile, there had been secret negotiations with Austria, under the terms of which she would provide 400,000 men against Napoleon in exchange for a two million pound lump sum and a hefty monthly subsidy. The British Government wished to embroil the French in Spain, if only to curtail French expansionist ambitions elsewhere. Furthermore, there was an immediate menace to England of invasion by French troops massing in the Netherlands. Planning began urgently at Horse Guards for a Walcheren expedition to counter this threat.

In February matters became clearer. Portugal, recently blooded by the French and relieved by the British, agreed to the British paying for, training and providing officers for her army. Castlereagh, no longer faced by the dilemma of choosing between Moore and Wellesley as commander, asked Sir Arthur to propose a scheme for the defence of Portugal, and gave him command of the force. Wellesley suggested a force of 30,000 regular Portuguese, backed by a militia of 40,000, and a force of 20,000 British troops. Sir Arthur found enough men in England to take his figure to 26,000, including 3,300 cavalry. No more were available for the time being because of the forthcoming Walcheren expedition. The transport fleets involved were enormous.

At the same time a scandal erupted over the Commander-in-Chief's conduct. A series of charges were brought against the Duke of York alleging corrupt employment of his patronage in the award of military appointments, commissions and promotions. His conduct had been less than upright. Mrs Mary Ann Clarke, a courtesan who was his mistress, was a dishonest schemer. By 1805 the Duke decided her conduct had gone far enough and paid her a pension from their separation in 1806. Pressed by her creditors and scorned by the Duke, her pension having inexplicably stopped, she warned him that unless the arrears of her pension were paid she would publish all his letters. Blackmail. No payment was made. So she kept her word and released a shower of embarrassing letters revealing individuals bribing her to advance their careers with the duke. Hell hath no fury ... It was, however, shown that the Duke had from the first fought manfully to resist all traffic in commissions. It was convincingly demonstrated that Mrs Clarke was an adept forger of the Duke's handwriting. Although acquitted by the House, the Duke, one of the very finest apolitical commanders-in-chief, did the only possible thing and resigned at this critical moment.

Against this confused and polarized background, difficult decisions were necessary. A sizeable force remained in Portugal. Its deployment or return needed resolution. On the evacuation of Sir John Moore's troops from Corunna, the remnants of his army in the Peninsula came under the command of Lieutenant General Sir John Cradock at Lisbon. A number of British outposts in Portugal had small British garrisons, such as at Elvas, where a battalion remained. For the immediate future it seemed that the threat to Portugal came from the north. In Galicia the French had driven off Sir John Moore's army, but had outrun themselves in the effort.

Unknown to the British, Napoleon had circulated among his generals his strategic plan for the subjugation of Spain and Portugal. He declared, imperiously, that the Iberian campaign was almost over, assuming his master plan was correctly implemented. In reality the French were facing continued resistance in Spain, and the huge French Army was deployed in widely separated local campaigns. Napoleon had hurriedly returned to Paris after Benavente, in theory to deal with Austrian threats, but perhaps to disassociate himself from the failure to bring Spain to heel after Moore's brilliant stratagem to divide his forces. Napoleon, more than the British public, understood Moore's strategic success in support of the Spaniards.

In the absence of clear instructions from home, or any intelligence from Spain, Sir John Cradock concentrated his forces, building a coherent force rather than having unsupported units scattered randomly at great distances from one another. He unilaterally abandoned the 'forward policy' by removing any garrisons, however small, from the Spanish border. Poor man, he could not win: to withdraw and consolidate was viewed as defeatist, and failing to help the Portuguese; to leave the scattered garrisons was to invite their destruction piecemeal.

A debate raged in Parliament, but decisions were reached. Bonaparte still showed unmistakable expansionist tendencies. French military strength was still the greatest threat to the free world. British support for the Spaniards would not be abandoned; withdrawal was not an option. Portugal, our oldest ally, must be supported, come what may.

While this political solution was developing, Henry Percy's career changed course. Without a friendly general as patron and employer, he returned to regimental duty. The 1st Battalion was busy in 1808 moving from Canada to the West Indies. In January 1809 it took part in the successful invasion of Martinique as the island was captured from the French in a masterly amphibious operation. At least British arms were successful somewhere against the French that January, even if the success were hardly commented upon in London. After this the battalion returned to Canada.

Second battalions were normally home-based, providing trained manpower for the overseas battalion. Ireland had a large garrison, a leftover from the

1798 Rebellion when the French had invaded, weakly supporting the ragtag, if ferocious, rising. General John Moore had been deeply involved with the force which dealt with this distraction.

Clonmel[8] in Tipperary, long a garrison town in an unruly area, had been home to the 2nd Battalion, The 7th Royal Fusiliers since 1808, and Henry arrived there that spring. It was not a popular station. Relations between the army and the locals were strained. The training role of the second battalions meant that they were often under the established strength of a thousand men. Recently, however, militia men had been permitted to transfer to regular battalions, and this had resulted in the battalion at Clonmel being at above 50 per cent strength. There was excitement when word came of a new expedition to Portugal to reinforce Cradock's now coherent force. Henry was given command of the Light Company in Lieutenant Colonel Sir William Myers' 576-strong battalion. They sailed from Cove[9] on Wednesday, 29 March 1809, arriving at Lisbon after a bracing ten-day voyage on Friday, 7 April 1809.

Chapter 8

The Peninsula: Oporto
(1809)

The contrast between Clonmel and Lisbon was marked. Henry, who knew Lisbon well, must have been pleased to be back. It was a fine warm spring day. The brigade from Ireland landed at Almada, just east of where the high motorway bridge[1] now crosses the Tagus. By the time they arrived, the Russian warships impounded at Lisbon the previous year had been escorted to England.

Their transit camp was temporary, ideal for a weekend of unloading and sorting out. The battalion moved on Tuesday, 11 April, in locally contracted boats up the Tagus to Villa Franca de Xira. It is a scenic journey even today. Olive, orange and lemon groves come down almost to the water's edge once the built-up area on the left bank has been passed. After a short pause at Villa Franca, during which they joined the 2,500-strong Brigade of Guards,[2] they marched northwards in stages for about 66 miles to reach Leiria on 15 April, and came under the command of General Sir John Cradock. At Leiria they heard with delight that Sir Arthur Wellesley had been sent to take command. He did so on 22 April.

General Cradock disappeared to Gibraltar. By now Marshal Soult's plundering French Army had occupied Oporto, 70 miles north of Coimbra, with extreme violence. For reasons of intrigue, which Wellesley soon discovered, Soult did not wish to advance towards Lisbon. Wellesley determined to drive the French out before Soult changed his mind. A success at the start of Wellesley's campaign would be politically and militarily helpful. It would enable him to liaise with the Spanish armies to set up a combined attack on Marshal Victor in Spain.

Wellesley did not hesitate to take the initiative. His approach to the Oporto operation was unorthodox. He left 12,000 men defending Lisbon. Then Beresford and his 6,000 Portuguese were sent off by a circuitous route to Lamego to cut off Soult's withdrawal route to Spain. The remainder waited near Coimbra until Beresford was in position. Wellesley personally took command of the main army at the delightful university city of Coimbra, which he reached on his 40th birthday, 1 May.

At the beginning of May Henry Percy and his battalion were on the march again, this time moving another 50 miles north to Coimbra. Arriving on 3 May, they saw the lavish processions on St John's Day in Coimbra, considered by the Protestant English as extravagantly profane, although an English regiment's band led the procession this time.

On operations, then as now, the expression 'careful timing' often means rush to wait, only to rush again. Wellesley co-ordinated his moves. The Fusiliers were in the rear of the main column marching from Coimbra to Oporto on a rough and narrow road. The last day's march is always hard going. Henry's Light Company had precious little water all day. Their heavy knapsacks, the clouds of dust and the need to move fast with sore feet[3] was exhausting. They felt knocked up, as the expression had it. After marching between 20 and 30 miles they had to double the last 4 miles to the action at Villa Nova on the south bank opposite Oporto. Imagine their disappointment to find that the enemy had already been beaten and had given them the slip. Their arrival had been on schedule; the French had been outmanoeuvred.

The Douro at Oporto is 325 yards wide. It was in flood. The river twists as it passes through Oporto. It is bordered in places by 200ft-high sheer cliffs which prevent those on the top from seeing the river directly below. Soult had destroyed his bridge of boats at 2am that morning, the explosion clearly heard, but not understood, by the British. All the local boats had been removed to the north bank. This was no surprise to Wellesley, who arrived at Villa Nova early on 12 May. He set up an observation post in the high Monastery de Serra de Pilar. The Bishop's seminary across the river to his right seemed to be unoccupied. He calculated it was invisible to the French in the main part of the town. It was also big enough to hold two battalions within its enclosed walls.

It was reported that there was a sunken ferry at Avintas, 2 miles upstream. It was being pumped out and could probably be salvaged. Wellesley immediately sent two King's German Legion battalions and some cavalry under Murray to cross there, which they successfully achieved.

Wellesley chose people well. He engaged Colonel John Waters, of the Portuguese service, as a scout. Waters knew the area and the local people intimately, having worked there for several years in the wine business. A character, fluent in Portuguese, Spanish and French, Waters appeared with a splendid Portuguese barber who had rowed across from the north in his own skiff. He announced that there were four serviceable and unguarded wine barges hidden on the river bank east of the city. Waters also confirmed that the seminary had been unoccupied thirty minutes before.

Wellesley ordered the barges to be seized. Waters promptly assembled a 'splendidly mixed party of the barber, a prior from Amarante and four peasants', who somehow managed successfully to bring the barges to the south bank. Wellesley was delighted. 'Well. Let the men cross.'

This was an immense risk. It was broad daylight, and the enemy force was at least equal in size. But the daring unorthodox approach worked. Each barge, he had been told, would take thirty men and its crew; the distance was 300 yards each way. That should mean 600 men over in an hour. The first officer across was a lieutenant in the 3rd Foot, the Old Buffs. No reaction; extraordinary.

The Buffs quickly occupied the seminary with Major James Wellington's[4] battalion company, while the Light Company of Captain Charles Cameron remained outside to disrupt enemy attacks forming up. The remainder prepared to defend, closing the iron gate onto the Vallongo Road and building a firestep around the wall. The boats returned for the next load. The next two boats arrived quickly, astonishingly without interference until the last one, which was carrying Lieutenant General Edward Paget, was just landing. Some 600 men were secure before the French woke up and began serious action. During the French attack on the seminary General Paget was badly wounded by a musket ball, which resulted in the loss of his right arm at the shoulder. He was replaced as divisional commander by Major General Rowland Hill.

The next two battalions, the 48th Northamptonshires and the 66th Berkshires, reinforced quickly. Soult, who was unwell, had been up most of the night writing orders and dispatches. He was struggling with difficulties among his generals, a fact of which Wellesley was well aware through a French captain who had become a secret informer.[5] Soult certainly had more on his mind than the defence of the Douro at that moment. He was still in bed at 11am. His staff had just had breakfast. He was not expecting problems from Wellesley that day, nor did his staff.

The alert General Maximilien Foy raised the alarm. Seeing boat-loads of soldiers in red coats crossing the river, he immediately summoned infantry and guns from his brigade and sent a messenger to Soult, who was informed that there were men in red coats on the home bank. Soult dismissed it as one of his Swiss[6] battalions going bathing.

After some delay Foy attacked the seminary with three battalions. The attack failed because the British defenders were protected by the perimeter wall. Wellesley had quietly placed eighteen guns on the Serra Heights near his observation post. They had a superb field of fire across the river. When the French began to manhandle their guns into position to support Foy's attack, Wellesley's guns engaged with instant effect. The first shot was a new shrapnel shell which burst precisely as planned, directly above the first French gun coming into action, killing or wounding all the gun numbers.

This was no bluff, so General Delaborde mounted a further attack on the seminary, which was also successfully repulsed with heavy casualties. It needs discipline to attack a well defended wall in close formation, under accurate artillery fire, especially when the previous two attempts have been savaged by the defenders' volleys and lethal shrapnel bursts.

At midday Soult mounted an *ad hoc* brigade attack. To find the manpower for this he called in the soldiers guarding the boats on the river bank. Seeing this, and understanding Wellesley's urgent need for boats to get his troops over the river, hundreds of local Portuguese rushed out and bravely took them over to the British.

This enabled Wellesley to launch his third crossing. General John Sherbrooke's 1st Division crossed in the area of Soult's former bridge of boats. Men began to feel success: all were keen to be involved. The Guards should have gone first, but the eager 29th Worcesters, already at the riverside, sent back word that they could not make way for the Guards in the narrow streets!

Sherbrooke's troops moved quickly into the town itself and broke up the enemy's third attack on the Seminary.

Soult's defensive plan had depended on keeping the river as an effective barrier. This was now compromised and Soult knew he was beaten. With difficulty, he distributed an order to withdraw eastwards. Murray, specifically placed for such an eventuality, should have cut him off, but, although he saw the French rushing past at close range and in no proper formation, he inexplicably failed to engage. Wellesley, seeing the French escaping unmolested, sent a staff officer to ginger up the British reaction. There followed a spirited charge by a squadron of the 14th Light Dragoons, which, at heavy cost to themselves, scattered the fleeing French and took 300 prisoners. Major Felton Bathurst Hervey[7] led the charge and was badly wounded, losing his right arm. The French rear guard disintegrated and an instant later the troopers were among them, hacking and slashing. Both general officers present were roughly handled; General Foy was cut down, while General Delaborde was bowled over. One unexpected difficulty experienced by the 14th was the Prussian eagle they wore in their helmets. The peasants in both Spain and Portugal mistook it for a French eagle and attacked them. The helmet with the eagle on the side was changed in 1812 to a shako. The Prussian eagle is worn to this day by the successor regiment, the King's Royal Hussars.

Percy's Light Company crossed the river and marched up the steep narrow streets. Every window, balcony and door was crowded with people crying '*Viva Ingleses!*', waving handkerchiefs and scattering roses on the passing troops. The company was quartered in a splendid mansion in the highest part of the city. 'In this palatial edifice our men did justice to a grand dinner which had been prepared for the French officers.'

Wellesley was pleased with the results of the day's work. He dined on Soult's dinner at the Palacio das Carrancas, and then sat down to write his dispatch, followed by a General Order dated 'Oporto 12 May 1809':

> The Commander of the Forces congratulates the troops upon the success which has attended their operations for the last four days, during which they have traversed above eighty miles of most difficult country, in which they have carried some formidable positions; have beaten the enemy repeatedly; and have ended by forcing the passage of the Douro, and defending the position so boldly taken up with a number far inferior to those by which they were attacked. In the course of this short expedition the Commander of the Forces has had repeated opportunities of witnessing and applauding the gallantry of the Officers and troops, &c, &c.

The dispatch left for London the next day with his ADC, Henry's friend, Captain Stanhope.[8]

The French retreated in disorder. There were several follow-up skirmishes, giving Soult sleepless nights and anxiety for two days before he retreated headlong north towards Spain. Wellesley followed for a short distance, his follow-up force including the 2/7th Royal Fusiliers.

After a day's rest the Fusiliers pursued the enemy for 32 miles to Braga. By now it was raining heavily and the roads were deteriorating. John Cooper takes up the tale:

> We reached Braga as the rear guard of the French was leaving it. Halted in the market place. Being very hungry I tried my hand at begging. A grocer gave me three loaves. Having a few *vintins*[9] I bought half a gallon of good wine, to which my comrade and I sat down in the main street and did justice. While feasting we were eyed by our Colonel Sir William Myers,[10] and Captain Percy, brother to the late Bishop of Carlisle.[11] One of them asked for a little bread. A loaf was handed.
>
> 'Have you any wine?' The canteen was given. 'Have you anything to drink out of?'
>
> 'O, yes,' and a splendid gilt china cup, fit for a king, was presented. Seating themselves on two stones at a little distance they regaled themselves freely, and returned the remainder with many thanks.

The British pursuit continued long after dark, stumbling among rocks and stones. The rain fell heavily and the men were silent and knocked up. Wax candles were lit and they marched by their light. Cooper was called forward by his company commander, who was mounted and ahead.

'Have you any bread?' said he.

'Yes, sir,' I replied, and gave him a loaf. When he had done eating he said, 'Should you ever be in want of my help, let me know.'

Captain Percy was greatly beloved by his company. As a man he was handsome; as an officer, kind; and as a soldier, brave and adventurous.[12]

Henry's company followed the French as far the village of Pinderia, up in the rough hilly country near the Spanish border. The French abandoned huge amounts of their stores and ammunition, and retreated by a single narrow, steep, twisting route over the mountains to Orense, entering Spain in a 'most wretched condition'. Cooper noticed the local peasants made wet weather cloaks of straw which, like thatch, 'turns' rain.

*   *   *

Soult had been decisively defeated. Wellesley had demonstrated his ability as an offensive commander, employing surprise and unconventional tactics to achieve rapid results. But this alone did not allow exploitation of his victory because his resources were inadequate. He had achieved his aim, cleared the French decisively, and demonstrated that they could be defeated by an offensive. The rain was awful, and the troops of both sides were exhausted. Lacking transport and supplies to move further forward into what might have been an over-exposed position, he consolidated, halting the rout in the wild country short of Orense.

In the engagement at Oporto Soult had lost 300 killed and wounded. Among them was General Foy, who received a nasty sabre cut.[13] Soult also lost 1,500 men taken prisoner, and the British captured seventy French guns.

British casualties were 123. The battle at Oporto, sometimes known as the Crossing of the Douro, demonstrated Wellesley's brilliance at reading ground, his willingness to take a risk, and his decisiveness. The risk he took, carefully calculated, was enormous, but his judgement that the French were not alert was correct.

Soult's retreat had been barred by Beresford, as planned. Defeated tactically and undermined politically by intrigue, Soult had no option but to flee north in disorder, destroying his guns and exploding his powder. The French became a disorganized rabble, leaving a trail of vengeful damage and destruction to Portuguese churches and property. The Portuguese peasants, in consequence, showed no mercy to the French; Commissary August Schumann of the 14th Light Dragoons recorded seeing a well dressed Portuguese at the head of a band of peasants offering an English sergeant 10 gold florins to give up some prisoners. The cruelties perpetrated by the Portuguese against the French soldiers who fell into their hands are indescribable. Naked and bloody corpses of French soldiers were to be seen lying in the road, shockingly mutilated.

Wellesley's aim had been achieved: Oporto had been relieved. The tempting prospect of catching Soult himself had become unrealistic. Wellesley had built confidence with a small but significant success. Now he had bigger things in mind: the Talavera campaign.

The British returned by stages to the Coimbra area, leaving Soult to struggle northwards to Orense in Galicia, devoid of guns, equipment, transport and ammunition. Any threat from Soult had been neutralized for the time being. By 24 May the British had returned to Oporto, where they were received with rapturous applause. On 14 June they moved to Abrantes, where they waited till the end of the month while preparations were made for the advance into Spain. During this time at Abrantes the Fusiliers had the misfortune to lose 'some men, murdered by the Portuguese'.[14]

* * *

The complication in understanding the Peninsular War at almost any stage is the fragmented concurrent operations in different parts of the Peninsula. The French had a single aim: to subdue Spain and Portugal. The British, likewise, aimed somehow to relieve these two countries of French occupation. Wellesley's arrival in Portugal coincided with six separate sub-campaigns being carried on simultaneously by the French against the Spaniards and Portuguese throughout Iberia.

Wellesley's brilliance lay in his clarity in identifying key objectives which were attainable, related to numbers, distance, and return on effort and administration. It is crucial to understand his numerical position. At Oporto he had a fighting strength of 16,400 British and 2,000 Portuguese troops. In the Peninsula as a whole the French under Soult, Victor, Sebastiani[15] and King Joseph Bonaparte had nearly 80,000 men. In addition, there were the relatively distant sub-campaigns of Ney and Mortier elsewhere in the Peninsula, each involving substantial numbers of French troops. To reduce the major elements of the French armies in Spain, Wellesley could either engage them one at a time, or try an allied offensive, depending on the numbers being opposed at any one time. His objectives had to be cost-effective, and of course must contribute to the overall aim. His line of last resort was to prevent Portugal from falling once more under French occupation. After the Oporto operation, Portugal was, he hoped, secure, at least for the moment.

Chapter 9

The Talavera Campaign (1809)

Oporto was clear of the French; Soult was ineffective in Spain. By the summer of 1809 Wellesley had begun to combine with the Spanish Armies of Extremadura and La Mancha for an allied march on Madrid. If successful, this would neutralize a key French corps, in the first attempt at an allied offensive, against Marshal Victor.

During May 1809 Wellesley reorganized his force at Abrantes, where the castle dominates the Tagus bridge. Before the Oporto operation, he had sent Major General John Mackenzie with 12,000 men[1] to Abrantes to prevent Marshal Victor from interfering in the south of Portugal during the Oporto operation. Mackenzie's task included guarding the key Roman bridge joining the two halves of Extremadura at Alcántara in Spain. This was the only all-year crossing place within 70 miles. During the latter stages of the Oporto pursuit,[2] when he was at Montealegre in the mountains, Wellesley heard from Mackenzie that the French had taken the important Alcántara bridge, defended by a Portuguese garrison. Victor must be concerned about Wellesley's intervention in Portugal, and might interpret it as preparation for an advance into Spain. Victor perhaps thought the presence of Mackenzie's force at Abrantes was an advance guard, not a containing force, since he had no idea Wellesley was 130 miles away, punishing Soult. Mackenzie worried that the French might move into Portugal behind Wellesley. With his uncanny ability to read the enemy's intentions, Wellesley replied[3] confidently:

Convent of S. Terso, 21st May, 1809
My dear Mackenzie,
I have received your letters to the 18th, and I observe that the enemy has carried the bridge at Alcantara, with 10,000 or 12,000 men, and has advanced as far as Castello Branco. I do not think it is clear, however, that a column will enter Portugal on the side of the Alentejo; but if one should enter and you have taken up the bridge at Abrantes and secured the boats on the Tagus, I do not see what you have to apprehend from it at this season of the year, more particularly after the late heavy fall of rain. I beg, therefore, that you will not be too ready to give credit to the

report that a column is invading Alentejo. Secondly, that if one should enter Alentejo, you will not be too ready to abandon your posts in the mountains towards Castello Branco, if you have taken up your bridge at Abrantes and have secured the boats.

If no column should enter by Alentejo, or if you should have reason to apprehend that it will be able to cross the Tagus, I must say that I consider your force, constituted as it is, fully equal to keep a corps of 12,000 French from entering by those passes.

You are in error in supposing that the Portuguese troops will not fight. One battalion has behaved remarkably well with me; and I know of no troops that could have behaved better than the Lusitanian Legion did at Alcántara the other day; and I must add that if the Idanha a Nova *militia* had not given way, they [the Lusitanian Legion] would have held their post.

If the enemy should turn the passes, and come by the Estrada Nova ['New Road'], you are equally able to defend the Zezere, till I shall come up to your assistance. The head of the army will cross the Mondego by the 25th, so that I shall not be long separated from you.

My opinion is that Victor cannot venture to invade Portugal with his whole force. It is probable that the corps which has crossed at Alcantara is a reconnoitreing [*sic.*] party, sent in for the purpose of ascertaining what has become of Soult, what our force is, &c.: and if this be true it will go from Castello Branco to Guarda. If it does so, it will run the risk of never getting out of Portugal again.

Believe me, &c.

Arthur Wellesley.

There follows a short administrative postscript which ends with an encouraging commander's exhortation:

I have just received your second letter of 18th, which pleases me much better than the first. Look at your instructions, my dear Mackenzie, act boldly upon them, and I will be responsible for all the arrangements.

AW

Wellesley had started to get ready for his Spanish advance. He determined to assemble his force and reorganize it in the area of Abrantes on the Tagus near the eastern border of Portugal. Accordingly all regiments, wherever situated, were set in motion to assemble, in a carefully coordinated plan. Henry and his company moved by gentle stages to Abrantes, arriving about the middle of June. Meanwhile, Wellesley was busy liaising with his fellow commander in the Spanish army.

On 27 May Wellesley sent a lengthy update to Captain General Don Gregorio de la Cuesta, proposing cooperation for a venture towards Madrid.[4] Wellesley's summary to Cuesta of his Oporto campaign exemplifies his succinct reporting:

> I did everything in my power to intercept the enemy; and although I did not succeed, I have pleasure to inform your Excellency, that since I attacked him in the Vonga on the 10th instant, he has lost one fourth of his army, and the whole of his artillery and equipments. The road between this [Oporto] and Montealegre is strewed with baggage, and the carcasses of men, horses and mules; and he is gone into Galicia, very little able to do mischief to anybody.

Thus, at end of May the threat from Soult to northern Portugal had been neutralized. The south was secured by Mackenzie. So now Wellesley could get on, into Spain. He wrote from Coimbra to Mr Villiers,[5] the British Minister at Lisbon, on 31 May:

> I shall soon be in Spain, and if Victor does not move across the Tagus, he will be in as big a scrape as Soult. I hope to receive from you, before long, some orders respecting my conduct, supposing I should drive Victor away from the frontiers of Portugal, and should be required by Cuesta or the Junta to pursue him.
>
> We are getting on well, and I hope the Government are satisfied with us.

Then, in a rare confidence, he tells his local superior an embarrassing home truth:

> The army behave terribly ill. They are a rabble who cannot bear success any more than Sir John Moore's army could bear failure. I am endeavouring to tame them; but if I should not succeed, I must make an official complaint of them, and send one or two corps home in disgrace. They plunder in all directions.
>
> I have sent Colonel Bourke[6] and Colonel Cadogan[7] to Cuesta, to arrange a plan of co-operation in an attack upon Victor.

Henry Percy's company occasionally plundered, and John Cooper recorded:

> At this period the English troops made sad work in Portugal by plundering the inhabitants. No sooner was the day's march ended, than the men turned out to steal pigs, poultry, wine, etc. One evening, after halting, a wine store was broken open, and much was carried off. The owner finding this out, ran and brought an officer of the 53rd, who caught one of our company, named Brown, in the act of handing out the

wine in camp kettles. Seizing Brown by the collar, the officer shouted, 'Come out you rascal, and give me your name.' Brown came out, gave his name [as] Brennan, then knocking the officer down, he made his escape, and was not found out.

During our march to Abrantes a Portuguese fingered an officer's cloak. Unfortunately for him he was caught, tied up, and well flogged. Under his torture he roared out at the top of his voice for Jesus, Mary, and Joseph, but nobody came to assist the rascal.[8]

Wellesley took personal control of the reorganization and administration, attending to every small detail. Preparing for the operation took almost three weeks. Wellesley combined the brigades into divisions, to which battalions always belonged thereafter unless detached. Four infantry divisions were formed for the campaign, with the 2/7th Royal Fusiliers and the 53rd (later King's Shropshire Light Infantry) remaining together as before, in Lieutenant General Alexander Campbell's[9] Brigade of the 4th Division. The general, unusually senior to command a brigade, was really the divisional commander, there being no colonel or major general for the brigade.

Finance was always difficult. Wellesley wrote to Lord Castlereagh on 11 June:

> I think it is proper to draw to your Lordship's attention the want of money in this army. The troops are nearly two months in arrear, and the army is in debt in Portugal a sum amounting to not less than 200,000*l*. The whole of this sum ought for some months at least, to be sent in specie from Great Britain, otherwise the operations of the army will be cramped for want of money.[10]

Wellesley's daily orders reflect his experience in India. He directed that marching should begin at daybreak and end as early as possible; that huts were to be constructed where possible, so the battalions should camp in woods where possible, and within practical reach of water, adding: 'The Commander of the Forces requests that olive and other fruit-trees may not be used by the troops in hutting, except in cases of evident necessity.'

The move forward began at the end of June under glorious blue skies, getting hotter every day. From Abrantes the route (familiar to Percy from his journey with Moore the previous October) followed the Tagus, crossing on a bridge of boats at Villa Velha de Rodão in a rocky gorge, where the deep river is fast-flowing, even in summer. The move was made in gentle stages, and the following evening Percy's company camped in a field of mown flax near Saranadas de Rodão. They made huts of flax sheaves and rested tolerably. The next morning some 'rascals' set fire to the flax, making a terrific blaze. Cooper adds, with soldierly wisdom 'of course nobody did it'.

They passed through Castello Branco,[11] where the general insisted both officers and men must wade through the river, regardless of a bridge within a hundred yards. (In January 1811 Henry crossed that bridge as a prisoner: no wading that day.) 'There were, of course, sad grumbling and sulky looks.' While the Fusiliers were grumbling in the heat at Castello Branco, Napoleon decisively defeated the Austrians at Wagram. It mattered, if not immediately, because the Austrians left the allied coalition, thereby releasing more troops for Napoleon's use.

Amid the sound of clanging church bells, the Fusiliers entered Plasencia,[12] a typical old Spanish cathedral city, on Sunday, 9 July. The officers preferred quarters in houses to escape the heat. Wellesley, whose mind was mostly on higher things, amplified his hutting orders for the officers' attention, thus:

1. All officers belonging to regiments which are in huts must be encamped with the men, excepting those whose health requires that they should remain in houses. Applications for quarters for those Officers must be made through the General Officer commanding the brigade or to the Officer of the Master General's department with the division.

John Cooper supported Wellesley's vigorous use of discipline:

It has frequently been stated that the Duke of Wellington was severe. In answer to this, I would say he could not be otherwise. His army was composed of the lowest orders. Many, if not most of them, were ignorant, idle, and drunken. It is true the troops were ill-supplied with provisions in the Peninsula; it is also true they plundered when an opportunity occurred. But could a general, so wise, just, and brave as Wellington was, suffer the people that he was sent to deliver from the tyrant Napoleon, to be robbed with impunity? No; he could not; he did not. By the discipline he enforced the British army to become more than a match, even at great odds, to the best of Napoleon's boasted legions.

Spain seemed cleaner and less primitive than Portugal. A temporary British hospital was set up in a convent at Plasencia for stragglers and the sick. Plasencia, renowned for its hatred of the French, changed hands by force eleven times, much damage being done to the fine medieval buildings. The locals delighted in a murderous crusade against the French.

Meanwhile, at Plasencia Wellesley received important information about enemy dispositions. The bruised Soult was now at Zamora, and might have been tasked to approach Braganza. Fine; doing that would present no threat to Wellesley's northern flank. But were Soult to hear that Wellesley was threatening Madrid, he might intervene. He was ten days' march away.

Useful intelligence also came from letters taken from the unfortunate General Franceschi[13] when the guerrilla leader El Capuchino captured him en route for Madrid with only two ADCs, Captains Bernard and Saint-Joseph, as escort. The valuable dispatches to King Joseph, giving Soult's situation and intentions, were sent to Seville to Mr Frere, who immediately sent them to Wellesley.

Wellesley also knew that Mortier's corps was near Valladolid. It too could intervene in ten or so days, should it realize his threat to Madrid. Time and Spanish effectiveness were becoming critical. So Wellesley rode 40 miles in searing heat to meet Cuesta near Almaraz on Monday, 10 July.

The Talavera approach march continued, and the 2/7th Fusiliers reached Oropesa, 19 miles west of Talavera, on Friday, 21 July.

Oropesa shimmered in the summer heat, even though snow was still visible on the Gredos Mountains to the north. Oropesa castle, now a luxury Spanish Parador, dominates the north side of the town. Percy's Light Company moved into a filthy convent. They were in an arched-over part of the building, close to the vault in which the dead friars were interred. Wood was very scarce for cooking, so Private John Clapham entered the vault and, throwing a friar from his coffin, he smashed it, 'cooked his mess, and dined like a respectable man'. Cooper relates how at dead of night there was a commotion and a terrible uproar which roused the whole convent, with cries of 'The French are coming!' This was attributed to the supposed anger of the ejected friar, and blamed on Clapham. The real cause was never established.

Cuesta linked up as planned with Wellesley at Oropesa. His army did not impress the British onlookers as it marched past Wellesley. Don Gregorio was not an easy man, and diplomacy was decidedly not his forte. Brave, over-confident and difficult to goad into action, he regarded Wellesley as a very junior partner in the campaign. He had a point. Cuesta was senior in age and rank, a very experienced Spanish general, operating in Spain. He commanded a force of forty-one battalions in six divisions, two cavalry divisions and thirty guns. He had 34,800 men to Wellesley's 20,600. It was a question of quality.

Cooper watched the Spaniards, and dismissed them scornfully: 'Here the Spanish army under General Cuesta, a worthless wretch, passed us to the front, boasting they would thrash the French. They numbered about 38,000, and were dressed in blue, green and yellow. A motley crew they were. Many of them had muskets without locks etc.'

Henry and his men did not know that Victor's 22,000-strong army had moved east and was behind the Alberche stream, just beyond Talavera. Victor, likewise, had no idea Wellesley was so close. Victor's army, marching from the Portuguese border area, was living off the land, with no commissariat rations, and the men were desperate for food. King Joseph Bonaparte (Napoleon's elder brother), with an army of 12,000, was at Madrid. To the south was Sebastiani's weak French IV Corps. The danger to Wellesley was that they might all unite. As luck would have it, Sebastiani was not inclined to move north on account of the nearby Spanish Army of General Venegas, an unplanned but useful deterrent.

Wellesley's anxiety centred on General Cuesta. He had been unimpressed by his visit to Cuesta at Almaraz. He was uncertain about the general's support for the Spanish Government, detecting a view among Spanish officers that Cuesta was contemplating toppling the government to take power. Wellesley's mind was on military matters with an engagement becoming daily more likely. He had anticipated a battle in the Talavera area several weeks before, writing to Castlereagh from Plasencia on 15 July:

> I went to General Cuesta's quarters at Almaraz on the 10th, and stayed there till the 12th, and I have arranged with that General a plan of operations upon the French army which we are to begin to carry into execution on the 18th, if the French should remain so long in their position.
>
> The Spanish army under General Cuesta consists of about 33,000 men (exclusive of Venegas's corps), of which 7,000 are cavalry. About 14,000 men are detached to the bridge of Arzobispo, and the remainder are in the camp under the Puerto de Mirabete.
>
> The troops were ill clothed but well-armed, and the officers appeared to take pains with their discipline. Some of the corps of infantry were certainly good, and the horses of the cavalry were in good condition.

If Cuesta's force were effective, and could manoeuvre satisfactorily, the relative strengths would suffice to take on Victor and any local reinforcements he might rally, so long as there was no delay for reinforcements to upset the numerical balance.

On Saturday, 22 July the army edged towards Talavera town. The advance guard clashed with a defensive screen of six dragoon regiments[14] deployed by Victor 9 miles west of Talavera. Seeing hesitation, Cuesta sent a whole infantry division[15] forward. It skirmished ineffectively for several hours. Eventually, Anson's British cavalry brigade approached in a business-like manner, and the French screen hastily withdrew east of Talavera. Victor's two infantry battalions in Talavera, seeing their cavalry withdraw, scuttled off too. By early afternoon the French were all behind the Alberche, a small river, in places a shallow, wide, tree-lined stream with a gravel bed, which ripples gently into the Tagus about 3 miles east of Talavera. A few yards north of Tagus a fine Roman bridge (much battered, destroyed and rebuilt over the centuries) spans the Alberche from east to west. The other water feature is the Portina brook, which trickles from north to south and enters the Tagus at Talavera. It is about 3 yards wide, and is usually almost dry in July. Its banks are scrubby and its main use was as a reference point, and the provision of a small amount of brackish water. About 800 yards west of the Portina, near the northern end of the British line, is a hill, the Cerro de Medellín. It seems unimportant from the low ground. From the top, now the site of a luxury bungalow, the view instantly shows that the Medellín is the key to the position. Wellesley recognized this on that Saturday afternoon. His layout had been predetermined; it was just a question of allotting areas to the divisions. East of the Medellín, beyond the Portina, is an open 300-yard slope towards a raised feature called the Cascajal (pronounced 'Caskarharl'). This became the centre of the French line. South of the Medellín the ground flattens out towards Talavera, with scrub, gnarled olive trees and short fields of fire. Halfway to Talavera lies an incomplete bastion, the Pajar de Vergara. This was the junction between the British to the north and the Spaniards to the south.

Having reconnoitred north of Talavera, Wellesley went towards the Alberche to identify the key features there. He discovered that Victor, east of the Alberche, would be constrained on his south by the Tagus if he were attacked from the north. Wellesley made up his mind. Victor must be attacked by being outflanked before he could be joined by King Joseph. Time was critical, and Wellesley was dubious about the Spaniards. So he deployed a strong screen along the Alberche, with Donkin's Brigade based on an enclosed farm complex, the Casa de Salinas. This fine building, with its chapel and towers, is nearly a mile west of the Alberche, offering good visibility. There is a large walled yard with a pair of high wooden doors (not unlike Hougoumont at Waterloo).

Next, Wellesley went to see Cuesta. He took ages to persuade but by midnight he had agreed to take part in a joint dawn assault. Cuesta would attack over the Roman bridge (at that stage passable) and local fords over the Alberche. The British would attack on the Spaniards' left.

Wellesley's doubts were correct, for Cuesta's army was even less agile than he thought. A dawn attack in July is very early. The thirteen British battalions, with efficient battle procedure, were under arms and ready among the olive groves by 3am. They advanced silently, and were then inexplicably halted. No Spaniards.

No cooking had been done, so they waited under arms for the Spaniards to appear. Silence. Wellesley rode off to see what was happening, and found Don Gregorio almost a mile from the bridge, seated unconcernedly on the cushions from his carriage (which was drawn by nine mules). His staff, according to Napier, had not woken till 7am. It transpired that Cuesta had decided not to attack that day. There are several versions of his excuses.[16] They do not matter, since the plan had not worked. Wellesley was most unhappy, and after an interminable negotiation he persuaded Cuesta to attack the next morning (Monday, 24 July) at dawn ... '*Sin falta*,' they agreed – without fail.

Later that Sunday morning news came that the French picquets were thinning out, suggesting a withdrawal towards Madrid. To Wellesley, this meant they should move fast to cut off Victor, so he went quickly to Cuesta and took him forward to observe, but seeing some outposts still in position he declined to attack. Wellesley was furious. The unfortunate British soldiers who had been waiting to attack since 3am were at last allowed to cook. Wellesley's fears about Don Gregorio were being confirmed. Now Cuesta had a sudden mood swing. By dawn the next day, when the joint attack was to have gone in, Victor had vanished eastwards. Cuesta became aggressive and keen to follow up Victor. It is easy to be aggressive when the enemy has disappeared.

Wellesley patiently explained that the agreement made with Cuesta earlier in the month, under which the Spaniards would supply carts and food, had not been honoured and that until it was, he, Wellesley was not moving beyond the Alberche in pursuit of Victor. In that case, Cuesta announced angrily, the Spanish army alone would pursue Victor.[17] Wellesley advised against it, and commented that Cuesta 'will get himself in a scrape' – a word he often used in his predictions.

So on that roasting Tuesday, 25 July the Spaniards lumbered over the Roman bridge in pursuit of Victor's rear guard. They followed for 30 miles as far as Torrijos, only 15 miles from Toledo, a big achievement in one day in that heat. Two cavalry squadrons of the King's German Legion went as far as Santa Olalla because Wellesley needed to know whether Victor had taken the road towards Madrid or headed for Toledo.

Victor then joined forces with King Joseph, gaining numerical advantage. It suited Victor that he had only been pursued by Cuesta's troops, and that the British, other than the few King's German Legion squadrons which had now returned to Wellesley, were nowhere to be seen. Similarly, Cuesta's ambitious urge to relieve Madrid ahead of Venegas suddenly evaporated when he realized he was now heavily outnumbered.

Change of plan – he must withdraw as quickly as possible to Talavera. This decision coincided with Victor's move to the offensive. Victor now chased Cuesta westwards, and cut up Cuesta's rear guard at Torrijos. After that, he did not follow Cuesta so keenly, allowing Cuesta to reach the Alberche without further bother. There Cuesta found Wellesley had deployed two divisions[18] to the east. To Wellesley's amazement, it seemed that Cuesta was going to halt his tired army and spend the night on the east (enemy) side of the Alberche, and not take up the agreed position north of the town, on the right of the British line. Sir Arthur rode to see Cuesta to urge him to conform on the west of the Alberche. But Cuesta was asleep, and his staff would not allow Sir Arthur to see him. An impasse followed, which eventually resulted in Cuesta agreeing to make a start early the next morning. Wellesley must have wondered about Cuesta and early starts, but he need not have worried.

Very early on Thursday, 27 July the Spaniards crossed the Roman bridge and the Alberche fords. They moved straight to their allotted positions, and were followed by Sherbrooke's 1st Division, which occupied its sector between the Medellín and the Pajar de Vergara. Mackenzie's 3rd Division, comprising six battalions, together with Anson's two cavalry regiments,[19] withdrew over the Alberche through the olive and cork oaks to the area of the Casa de Salinas, east of the main position.

The ground between the Alberche and the Casa de Salinas is flat and covered in scrub and low trees, giving short fields of fire. Observation was, and still is, limited. It seems likely that few if any observation posts were positioned near the Alberche. The British battalions[20] in this division were mostly inexperienced. The French under General Lapisse had little difficulty in outflanking them to the north.

During their withdrawal Mackenzie's soldiers had set fire to the practical straw 'huts' left on the bank of the Alberche by Victor's withdrawing French. These were simple structures, just a single straw roof on legs like a table, used to provide shelter from the sun and the early morning dew. There was a breath of easterly wind, and the smoke hung lazily over the poplar trees on the west bank of the Alberche in the scrub. The ford was screened. Wellesley was up the southern tower at the Casa de Salinas, observing by telescope, with some of his staff. The horses and escort were in the yard below, with the high wooden gates open. Unbeknown to the British, Lapisse's Division of thirteen battalions was approaching through the trees from the left, or northern, flank. There was suddenly sporadic fire from the forward picquets of the 5/60th as the French infantry were engaged at close range. It was sensible to have deployed such reliable and experienced soldiers as the picquets on the left. The British defenders on the right were surprised. Some men were sleeping; others were preparing their bivouacs: arms were piled along the line. Donkin's Brigade (87th and 88th, and Mackenzie's 31st) was broken and driven back in some disorder, losing about eighty men taken prisoner.

Wellesley clattered down the steep twisting staircase, mounted his horse and galloped from the yard just as the French approached. He rushed west across the open field to where the redoubtable Lieutenant Colonel William Guard and the steady 1/45th[21] stood firm by a treeline, and on them he reformed the 31st. A little further north towards the line of cork oaks and olives was the half-battalion of the 5/60th, and here Wellesley rallied the hastily withdrawing 87th and 88th. The firmness of the 45th and the 5/60th saved the day. Experience proved its worth.

In his haste to escape from the tower, Salinas family folklore says that Wellesley forgot his telescope. Family tradition[22] has it that his telescope was 'acquired' by a French officer. The lead French regiment was the 16é Léger.[23]

The withdrawal to the main British position, harassed by the French, was a costly experience. A fighting withdrawal is difficult, even for experienced troops. The battalions eventually extricated themselves with the help of Anson's cavalry, although they, too, were engaged by French horse artillery. The infantry took up their positions on the lower slopes of the Medellín, much agitated and bloodied by their experience. The 2/87th lost fourteen officers that day, of whom one, Ensign Nicholas La Serre, with less than a year's service, was killed and the remainder wounded.

The Casa de Salinas action resulted in 440 casualties, largely the result of inexperience.

The evening of Thursday, 27 July, was again oppressively hot. Once Donkin's Brigade had been extracted, the men rested and licked their wounds in their new position, incorrectly on the reverse slope of the Medellín. The allied line stretched almost 3 miles to the north of Talavera.

Henry Percy's Light Company of 2/7th Royal Fusiliers had not been involved in the Salinas affair, and were in Alexander Campbell's Brigade,[24] just north of the guns of Lawson's Company ('A' Battery of six light 3-pounder guns) at Pajar de Vergara.

While the Spaniards took up their positions in the morning, the gunners temporarily moved nearer the British troops. At about six o'clock in the evening the French drove in the advanced picquets in front of the Fusiliers, and appeared in masses in the vineyards and rough ground on the British right wing. The French cavalry came forward, scouting Wellesley's and Cuesta's layout. Unintentionally, they approached the junction between the Spaniards and the British. On the right end of the line, nearer the town, the Spaniards spotted them. The musket in use by the Spaniards had an effective volley range of about 150–250 yards.

Suddenly the French cavalry was greeted by a massive ragged volley of musketry from four Spanish battalions at a futile range of 1,000 yards. There were cries of 'Treason', and the four battalions took off, fleeing helter-skelter to the west. Wellesley, standing a short distance away as nearly 2,000 of them decamped, commented that they seemed to have been frightened by the sound of their own fire. Their officers went with them. As they went, they plundered the British baggage train, creating an indelibly bad opinion with Wellesley.

This incident prevented Wellesley from being able to position all his troops exactly as he had planned. Meanwhile, the French probing attack fizzled out.

That evening at 9pm Marshal Victor launched a surprise late dusk attack against the Medellín. Victor knew the ground from the previous week, and probably hoped that a night attack might secure the vital ground and avoid a major engagement the next morning. He was not far wrong. Night attacks are not a feature of the Peninsular War. Control was too difficult. In this case the French attack almost succeeded.

The two British brigades of Christopher Tilson[25] and Richard Stewart,[26] both of Rowland Hill's 2nd Division, tasked to defend the Medellín, were behind (west) of the summit, intending to take up their forward positions at daybreak. They had no observers forward.

The vital high ground of the Medellín feature was also defended by Donkin's, Lowe's and Langwerth's Brigades. Forward to the right on the low ground was Cameron's Brigade. There were five batteries of guns, from the north, carefully placed close to the flank of an infantry brigade for protection. In the low ground, northwest of the Medellín, the cavalry of Anson's Brigade were resting, with Fane and Cotton's Cavalry Brigades on their right.

General François Ruffin's 1st Division attacked in three columns[27] thirty men wide, each of three battalions. They approached in the rapidly fading light down the Cascajal slope, heading for the top of the Medellín. As they advanced they overran the forward picquet of the 7th Line Battalion, King's German Legion[28] and pushed on up the hill. Heavy firing broke out.

General Rowland Hill, who had been in Talavera, raced back and with the help of the brigade major of Tilson's Brigade managed to restore some cohesion. With great difficulty, much confusion and hand to hand fighting, the French were pushed off the feature and down the slope to the front. They withdrew, but it had been a serious incursion, almost resulting in the loss of the key feature of the Talavera position. The outcome of the whole war had hung in the balance.

The Salinas withdrawal during that afternoon meant that forward picquets were deployed on the right of the British line. Colonel Sir William Myers, an experienced officer, sent Henry and his Light Company forward with a company of German soldiers. Cooper mistakenly thought they were Brunswick Oels,[29] because many of the soldiers were German and the uniforms were 'black'. In fact they were the company of the 5/60th Royal American Regiment which was attached to his brigade. Many of these experienced soldiers were German. Their uniforms were dark green. They moved forward as a picquet into the vineyard some 300 yards in front of the brigade's main position. There they concealed themselves as best they could (the Fusiliers' red uniforms did not help), and lay down among the bushes. The night became suddenly very cold after the scorching day. While they were in the forward picquet position they heard the furious French attack on the Medellín, half a mile to their left. When the French withdrew, some passed through the vineyards to Henry's front, opening a sharp fire on the picquet, but in Cooper's words, 'repulse was their portion'.

The rest of the night was quiet in front of the Fusiliers. In the Medellín sector the layout of troops was reorganized by Hill, proper observation was arranged and casualties were evacuated.

Hill himself had a narrow escape. A French infantryman seized the bridle of his horse and captured him, but in the confusion he broke free. The brigade major of Richard Stewart's Brigade, Captain Daniel Gardiner,[30] with whom Hill had gone forward to rally the troops, was seriously wounded and died in hospital in Talavera the next day. Hill had two ADCs, his younger brother Clement,[31] who had been slightly wounded at Oporto but was now fit, and the recently appointed Captain Edward Currie[32] of the 90th. Both managed to escape in the mêlée. The French numbers, although overwhelming, were insufficient to capture and hold the hill. In a series of brave and confused counter-attacks the British infantry drove some 1,500 men of 9e Lèger off the Medellín.

* * *

Daylight comes early in July; tired hungry men, on edge, had spent the night trying to rest. Little parties from both sides had needed water and had crept forward down the hill to the Portina, where they tried to fill water bottles from the grubby pools of the almost dry stream. A strange degree of live and let live obtained, the simple comradeship of soldiers preventing any violence as they quietly refilled their bottles and returned to their own lines.

Wellesley ordered the infantry to retire quietly to the reverse slope before dawn to avoid the expected artillery barrage. Suddenly, in the clear light of the cool morning of what promised to be another July scorcher, a single French gun fired. That signal began an intense bombardment. It was countered by the British guns from the flanks, and an artillery duel began. Then the sinister regular massed drum-beat of the French advance, known to the British as 'old trousers', could be heard. The columns were approaching. Cooper in Percy's company says that Lawson's guns to the south fired along the front of the British line at the flanks of the advancing French columns. Intense fire and heavy casualties caused this attack to fail. There followed a pause of two hours while the French debated their next step. The wounded were evacuated, in the British case to a small farm building at the rear known as 'the blood hospital'.[33]

Two heavy attacks on the left of the British line had now failed and the vital Medellín remained firmly in British hands. After the pause, during which the temperature rose rapidly, the French resumed their attack, this time on the British right. Four dense French columns supported by eighty guns, following a cloud of light troops (*voltigeurs*) approached Campbell's Division. As the

French neared the picquets of Henry's Light Company they called to them in Spanish, temporarily deceiving them, but the Fusiliers ran back to raise the alarm and the main line stood up to receive the attack. The French opened volley fire and the Fusiliers' line wavered. Sir William Myers jumped off his horse and, snatching one of the colours, exhorted the men, 'Come on, Fusiliers!' This gave the men fresh heart and the officers were inspired to urge the men forward. The Fusiliers and the 53rd charged forward and delivered a rapid rolling fire, so that in a few minutes the enemy melted away. They left behind six cannons which they had not had time to discharge. French cannon were too small in calibre to be of any use to British gunners, so they were spiked.

The French, having failed twice on the left and once on the right, now hurled a stronger force under King Joseph[34] at the centre of the British line. Talavera had developed into a fierce two-day battle of attrition in extreme heat. Eyewitness accounts say that the fighting moved to and fro with continued intensity. Smoke obscured much of the battlefield and the battle was hard to read. The thunderous noise of artillery, the roll of musketry and the huzzas and screams of the men pushing back the masses echoed confusingly round the olive groves.

The British Guards were brought up and swept back the centre thrust, but pursued the retreating French too far and suffered heavily when the French rallied. Wellesley, watching from the top of the Medellín, saw the critical moment and quickly sent forward the 1/48th[35] under Lieutenant Colonel Charles Donnellan, who had two horses shot under him. Severely wounded, lying on the ground, Donnellan took off his hat and handed command to Major George Middlemore,[36] saying 'You will have the honour of leading the 48th to the charge.' Whereupon they charged so splendidly that the Guards were able to retire and reform behind them. Cooper reports that a serjeant of the Guards told him he thought that the Foot Guards had lost 600 men.[37]

Another similar attack took place later in the afternoon and was also repulsed, each huge effort incurring horrible casualties. Driven back all along the British line, the French tried one further option. In an attempt to outflank the line to the north of the Medellín, they approached with cavalry down the wide valley. Here was the opportunity for the British cavalry to save the day. This they did, but a charge of cavalry against cavalry is a desperate business. The 23rd Light Dragoons charged headlong into an invisible sunken road and were severely mauled. The remaining regiments charged gallantly and the French outflanking movement withered, but at great cost.

The battle began to flag; all were exhausted, hungry and thirsty, but the light troops on both sides maintained a 'brisk fire', which continued on the left of the Medellín till late at night. By 11pm all was still, and there was a dim cheerless moon. Small parties went out to collect the wounded, whose pitiful cries of agony and distress upset the young soldiers. Both armies rested on the same areas as they had occupied the previous night. The Fusiliers had advanced about 200 yards in the day.

Long before daylight the British were alerted by the sound of drums beating in the enemy's lines. But when morning dawned, no enemy were to be seen. The French had retreated across the Alberche, taking away seventy or eighty carts of their wounded.

That morning after the battle the Light Brigade, consisting of the 43rd, 52nd and 95th Regiments, joined the army on that shocking battlefield, having made a phenomenal forced march in extreme heat over 24 hours.[38] They were received with loud cheers despite arriving too late for the fighting. These splendid soldiers under Robert Craufurd, after that gruelling endurance march, immediately took their place in the 3rd Division, which Craufurd took over in place of Major General John Mackenzie, who had been killed. Exhausted as they may have been after their epic march, the Light Brigade at once provided a professional screen on the Alberche, and helped with the battlefield fatigues.

Clearing the battlefield was the first task. Cooper thought there were 9,000–10,000 English[39] and French wounded to be taken into Talavera. The burial of the dead was a problem as the ground was mostly rocky and dry and there were no entrenching tools. Many dead were thrown into the dry beds of winter torrents, or in some cases cremated. A few mass graves were dug with difficulty. During the day the grass, which had been smouldering since the action, burst into flames and the crackling fire spread quickly among the unfortunate wounded. It had been a victory, perhaps, but famished soldiers trying to rescue or bury their comrades saw no glory in this sort of war.

On Thursday, 29 July, while still clearing the battlefield, Henry's Light Company was issued with 4 ounces of bread per man. At last some of the Commissariat waggons had got through safely from the depot at Plasencia, unmolested by fleeing Spaniards. Cooper thought this gave six or eight decent mouthfuls: not a lot for soldiers who had had no rations for over 48 hours. They had begun to suffer stomach cramps from hunger and dehydration.

Early that Sunday morning twenty-five Spanish soldiers, dressed in white and attended by 'popish priests', were marched to the front of the Royal Fusiliers and shot. Cooper continues:

> One young lad of 19 or 20 years of age, dropped before the party fired. But it was of no use, for after a volley at ten paces distance had been given by about 50 men, the whole party ran forward, and firing through heads, necks, breasts &c, completed their horrid work. The executioners having tools with them, the bodies were hidden in shallow graves in a few minutes.

These were the soldiers selected to be shot from one of the regiments which had panicked on that first evening. Cuesta had announced that he would shoot one in every ten men of the regiments. Wellesley pleaded to spare them. This was his grisly compromise.

The town of Talavera was choked with wounded men in every church and convent. The local people were horrified at the shocking sights. The British remained in the area until 3 August, by which time the uncleared battlefield had become putrid, foul-smelling and horrendous. The Spanish peasantry had been employed clearing the French dead. Before leaving Talavera the British collected the dead bodies in heaps and laid them on piles of faggots, 'which, being set on fire, were burned'.[40]

Cuesta's army and the French had been living off the land. No food was available, so the Spaniards could not honour their agreement to provide Wellesley with rations. Wellesley's idea of following up the defeated King Joseph to Madrid was, likewise, no longer a possibility. He supplemented his initial Talavera Dispatch of 29 July 1809 with a letter on 1 August, commenting: 'The extreme fatigue of the troops, the want of provisions and the number of wounded to be taken care of have prevented me from moving my position.' Discussing the battle of Talavera many years later, Wellesley said that Cuesta was no military genius, but that had he fought where he had agreed, it would have been as great a battle as Waterloo, and would have cleared Spain of the French for that time.[41]

The bigger picture now became urgent. Wellesley received intelligence that the French to his west were in danger of outnumbering him and cutting him off. His army had been reduced by almost a quarter. His supply situation was critical, lacking food, ammunition and reinforcements. He therefore reverted to his main aim: to defend Portugal. It was one thing to help the Spanish uprising and try to eject the French Grande Armée. This, however, was not his prime task. He could not justify his army becoming non-operational for want of resupply. He must withdraw westwards.

This left the problem of the wounded at Talavera. Wellesley had no option but to co-ordinate with Cuesta. They met at Talavera and Cuesta undertook to remain there and look after the British hospital and wounded while Wellesley would march against Soult who, it seemed from information received on 2 August, was threatening his rear at Plasencia, having brushed aside the Spanish blocking force at Puerto de Baños.

Wellesley had to accept this unpromising compromise, despite his worries about Cuesta. His dispatches are full of expressions of anxiety about the wounded. Still deeply anxious about his men, Wellesley ordered the westerly retreat to begin. Scarcely five hours after the British had marched out, Cuesta began to retreat too, abandoning the hospital. Talavera was occupied by the

French, who had kept a detachment waiting on the eastern side of the Alberche.

The majority of British wounded were well cared for by the French surgeons. There are many accounts of the kindness and efficiency of the French. The wounded were made prisoners of war; the survivors eventually reached northern France over a lengthy period, depending on their wounds, and were paroled at Verdun.

Wellesley's foray into Spain in support of the Spaniards had been a difficult experience. He now understood joint operations with Spanish allies. He had fought a severe general action, and even the inexperienced British troops had demonstrated their superiority over the French and their fortitude under sustained fire. Now, with his starving army in danger of being surrounded, they marched west towards the Portuguese border.

In England Talavera was treated as a major victory. Church bells were rung throughout the land, and Wellesley was later created Viscount Wellington, of Wellington in Somerset and Talavera.

Chapter 10

The Retirement to Badajoz, Portugal and Capture (August 1809–September 1810)

On Thursday, 3 August, Wellesley's exhausted and hungry army left Talavera and headed towards Oropesa, which the Fusiliers passed at midday. Meanwhile, Cuesta had received a captured dispatch which alarmingly revealed that the French troops reported to be at Plasencia were the two large corps of Ney and Mortier under Soult. Cuesta appreciated the danger and immediately sent the dispatch to Wellesley. Messages intercepted from Soult's command were becoming useful; first the interception of Franceschi[1] before Talavera, now this. Lord Fitzroy Somerset, Wellesley's ADC, was at this stage on his way to London with the Talavera dispatch.

Soult's presence at Plasencia had two consequences, as Wellesley had anticipated. Patients at the British hospital must have been taken prisoner; regrettable, but unavoidable. Critically, the Plasencia commissariat depot must also have been lost. This would deprive him of the essential rations he urgently needed for the retirement and, exasperatingly, would boost the French.

Henry and his men must have wondered what would become of their wounded friends left behind at Talavera. There were three officers, all wounded on the second day in the engagements in the olive groves; all were taken prisoner. The adjutant, Lieutenant William Page, had been slightly wounded, and could not yet be moved. Two captains, Richard Kirwan and Robert Muter, were severely wounded. The Royal Fusiliers had a surgeon and two assistant surgeons, so Sir William Myers agreed that the junior assistant surgeon, Montagu Martin Mahoney, who had volunteered to do so, should remain with the wounded. He stayed with them when they were taken back to France.

Kirwan, despite his wound being described as serious, was the first of the Fusiliers to reach Verdun, after three months, at the end of October. The adjutant arrived two weeks later, pleased to find a friend from his regiment already there. Assistant Surgeon Mahoney stayed with William Muter, whose wound seems to have been more serious. He cared for his patient till they reached Verdun together eleven months after Talavera. Mahoney was then repatriated to England under a dispensation for doctors, and rejoined the Royal Fusiliers, this time the 1st Battalion, in September 1810. This enabled him to be involved in all the major engagements of the war, surviving Albuera, Salamanca, Vitoria and the Pyrenees, up to and including Toulouse in 1814. Then he went to New Orleans in 1815, and arrived in France too late for Waterloo. He served twenty-seven years with the regiment, and in 1848 received a hard-earned Military General Service Medal with thirteen clasps.

From Oropesa the long line of troops trudged slowly south, in a huge cloud of dust, towards Puente del Arzobispo. Wellesley sent General Robert Craufurd ahead with his fast-marching brigade to Almaraz to prevent the French crossing the river and further disrupting his route.

The food situation was calamitous. Half-rations, if that, had barely seen them through Talavera. Now there was no regular distribution of food. The countryside became progressively bleaker. The Light Company had neither bread nor biscuit for six days. Famished as the soldiers were, the guns had to be pulled by drag ropes as many of the horses died. The few slaughter-oxen did not survive for long. The troops resorted to hunting wild pigs and stealing honey.

Henry's battalion stumbled into Puente del Arzobispo on 4 August, crossing the long bridge with its two high defensive towers. Cooper says the bridge was destroyed; perhaps he heard the explosion. It was another failed demolition, as had happened so often during the retreat to Corunna. The medieval bridge[2] was damaged, but remained passable.

Old Cuesta, now hungrily following up behind Wellesley, agreed to defend the bridge. Contrary to uncharitable accounts, he really did try, deploying a strong force of good repute. Their orders were to hold the bridge and the nearby ford at Azután until further notice. The force consisted of Bassecourt's (Spanish) infantry division and six regiments of the Duke of Albuquerque's cavalry. That made 5,000 infantry bayonets and almost 3,000 cavalry sabres, as well as a battery of twelve guns dug in to sweep the approaches to the bridge. On 6 August the Spaniards barricaded the bridge and manned its towers with infantry. This formidable Spanish presence was visible to the French.

Soult hesitated for the whole of Monday, 7 August. He did not know about the ford. In one of those stupid mistakes made by inexperienced soldiers, the Spanish cavalry compromised the shallows projecting from the southern bank by watering their horses far into the river. That night the French inspected the home bank carefully, and discovered a good ford not far upstream of the bridge.

Cuesta's efforts to hold the bridge were unsuccessful. On Tuesday, 8 August, the French made a series of vigorous charges at the bridge which were temporarily repulsed. At the same time they used the new-found ford upstream and began outflanking. Seeing themselves being bypassed, the defenders scattered, and the bridge and the guns were taken. These included French guns captured at Talavera, which Wellesley had given to Cuesta.

Nevertheless, by now the British had gained two days' march ahead of the French, thanks to Soult's hesitation at Puente del Arzobispo. So the Spanish presence at the bridge did at least enable the British to increase their lead by a further 24 hours.

The details of the retreat to Portugal are unimportant in Henry's life story, other than to recognize the fact that it was a gruelling journey of exceptional difficulty for want of rations, shoes and stamina. They camped at Deleitosa on the steep banks of the Rio del Monte. Dysentery broke out. The soldiers, without tents or blankets, dug scrapes in the ground, and put their legs through the sleeves of their greatcoats so as not to slide down the hill at night. From Deleitosa they moved on to Trujillo. Then as now, untidy storks' nests perched on the ancient towers in the town. The ungainly storks, with perfect timing, flapped into the clear air, protecting their young from the dive-bombing falcons. On 25 August the soldiers reached Mérida, founded by discharged Roman soldiers of the Army of Augustus, whose Roman aqueduct and amphitheatre survive today. No sightseeing for the classicist officers; just keep marching. This retirement, like every Peninsular withdrawal, became a serious test of discipline,[3] but unlike at Corunna, where atrocious weather, plenteous wine and the lack of a set-piece battle frustrated the shivering army, this time, after sanguinary Talavera, and in hot, rather than freezing, weather, the discipline held.

By 3 September, after almost a month's march covering 170 gruelling miles, the ravenous army reached Badajoz. Wellesley called a halt. Headquarters remained at Badajoz while the army deployed to divisional areas on the Spanish side of the Portuguese border. Henry's company was accommodated in a field near the woods at the hermitage of Nuestra Señora de Botoa[4] about 12 miles north of Badajoz. There they remained till 6 October. Rations and rest made all the difference, and Cooper tells us that soap, tobacco and other 'necessaries' were available to those who had money.

* * *

Wellesley corresponded copiously from Badajoz, organizing his strategy and ensuring that the authorities in London and the Central Junta in Seville were kept informed as necessary. His primary aim to defend Portugal was affirmed by London. There was much illness in the army, and many men were evacuated to hospitals at Elvas and Estremoz on the Portuguese side of the border. Gradually the army began to recover its health, physical strength and fitness. Drafts of reinforcements slowly restored the numerical strength. Morale began to improve, but prolonged inactivity is never good for soldiers; idle hands make mischief, and they did.

On Wednesday, 13 September Wellesley wrote to Mr Villiers at Lisbon, that 'everything appears so quiet that I may venture in a few days to Lisbon, where I want to look about me a little, and decide finally upon our plan of operations, in case Portugal should be invaded in the autumn or winter'. This letter reveals that Wellesley knew that alone he could not hold a combined French force on the Spanish–Portuguese border. Talavera had taught him to discount the Spanish Army in such calculations. Although the French were currently engaged in subduing resistance in Spain, Wellington knew Portugal was likely to be their next objective.

Written military appreciations of the situation, so beloved of Staff Colleges, were not produced in Wellesley's day. Nonetheless, his thought processes were very similar. Having analysed the options open to him, Wellesley dismissed any idea of invading Spain: there was no prospect of success, and every likelihood of risking his army, which could be easily outnumbered. He must therefore concentrate his army where he could hold and defeat the French whilst defending Portugal. The vital component was Lisbon.

In August 1808, after the Battle of Vimeiro north of Lisbon, Wellesley had taken a careful look at the country, and had noted the defensive potential of a wide position near Torres Vedras. While waiting for the French repatriation after Cintra, out of curiosity he had gone to look more thoroughly at the positions which the French might have used to defend Lisbon, had they not negotiated. It proved a useful visit.

Now, fourteen months later, his priority was clear. The British Army, even if raised to 40,000 men, could not cover both Seville and Lisbon. Lisbon must be held against what he saw as inevitable: a third French invasion of Portugal that would outnumber his combined Anglo-Portuguese Army. He must organize and secretly prepare a comprehensive defence of the Lisbon Peninsula by which could defeat that invasion.

In a letter to his brother he wrote: 'I do not take up my title[5] till I receive the Gazette, or some notification of it which is authority.' He wrote seven more long letters that day, 17 September, all signed 'Wellington' for the first time. He attended to administration at Badajoz[6] till Saturday, 7 October before leaving for Lisbon.

In a letter about the pay of British officers in the Portuguese service, Wellington remarked on the importance of establishing the means for paying these officers: 'Time is going apace: in three months we may have to fight for Portugal; and Great Britain will be much disappointed if, notwithstanding the pains taken, and the expense incurred, the Portuguese army should do nothing. I think much depends upon this increase of pay.'

For reasons we do not know, Henry Percy began to think about an exchange of regiment. No correspondence survives, but it must have been about this time that Henry began to negotiate a transfer to the 14th Light Dragoons. An examination of the nominal roll of the officers in his battalion who sailed for Portugal from Cove in 1808 shows this to have been a good survival aid, although Henry could not have known what lay ahead. Of his twenty-seven fellow Fusiliers only seven survived; the rest were either killed, wounded or had died of disease by the end of 1815.

In a lengthy correspondence, relevant by precedent to Henry Percy, Wellington struggled to prevent the Spaniards detaining French officers approaching under flag of truce to arrange exchanges of prisoners. This high-handed action prejudiced the delicate use of flags of truce, so crucial to sensible communication between the French and the allied commanders. He was much exercised by the case of Captain Victor de Thévenon.[7] Wellington wrote to the Spanish General Bassecourt at General Headquarters, that the detention of this French officer was against the laws of war. He should not have been sent to Seville, 'especially since he was sent there shortly after my request that he be released had been received from the hands of a British officer on my instructions'.

He requested that Captain de Thévenon should be sent to him at once with his ADC Captain Alexander Gordon, if Captain de Thévenon were still at the Spanish headquarters. 'I wish it to be explained to Captain Gordon where this officer is (if he is not at GHQ), and why he has been detained, so that we may ease Marshal Mortier's worry about this.'

Wellington also wrote directly to Mortier assuring him of his displeasure at the Spaniards' illegal detention of Captain de Thévenon, explaining that he was taking every possible step to arrange his immediate return. Wellington also wrote personally to Captain de Thévenon, apologizing and explaining that he had imagined he had been returned immediately to his own lines. The relationship with the intractable Spaniards deteriorated.[8] The case dragged on, involving several other prisoners whose chances of exchange were preju-diced. Wellington was obliged to drop the idea of a 'cartel' of exchange, which had been agreed between the French and British, at least on a temporary basis, owing to the conduct of the Spanish Army.

All negotiations for the exchange of wounded prisoners left behind at Talavera were cancelled when they were moved to France, even though, as Wellington put it, 'it is well known that they will not be set at liberty during the war'. The Talavera prisoners' fate had for a second time been badly influ-enced by the Spaniards.

Gordon, his mission to the Spaniards and French completed, joined Wellington at Lisbon and, conveniently for us, wrote to his brother, Lord Aberdeen, on 19 October,[9] giving a good account of his dealings with the French and Spaniards over the de Thévenon affair:

A French officer came some time ago with a letter for Lord Wellington to the advanced posts of the Spaniards which he wished to deliver in person, this could not be, but they allowed him to swim across the river and he was brought to their Head Quarters at Deleitosa, and there he has been detained contrary to all laws of War, against repeated remonstrances of Lord Wellington. My mission was to claim him in Lord W's name and to conduct him to the French Army. I however found he was detained by the Government at Seville, and not by the General, and consequently awaited their answer to Lord W's letter. They however refused to return him at present.

Gordon, an officer of initiative and remarkable maturity at the age of 23, then went to the French Army to explain the detention, and to deliver money for the sick, and inevitably to gain any information he could. He was conducted blindfolded to (Puente del) Arzobispo, where he remained with a French general for the day, and was treated with the greatest kindness and attention. They would not allow him to go to Mortier as he was at Talavera. Having spent a very pleasant day, he was conducted back to the Spanish lines, 'parting in the most friendly manner with the General and his officers'. He then made best speed to join Wellington at Lisbon, covering a remarkable 70 leagues[10] in 50 hours.[11]

Wellington visited Lisbon between 10 and 28 October. His energy was extraordinary. Over that short period he revolutionized the Portuguese Army, and set up the defeat of the French Army of Portugal. He took on three major tasks.

First, he put in place a fundamental reorganization of the Portuguese Army. This was intended to increase the manpower, strength and fighting efficiency of both the regular and part-time forces. Up to now there had been little experience of the Portuguese regular forces in contact with the French. Wellington intended that the Portuguese Army should be completely operationally effective, and form a major supplement to the British Army, even integrated into British formations. A complete revision of the order of battle was required, with the key command slots given by British officers. Basic training of Portuguese soldiers was to be based on the British standard training manuals. Similarly the commissariat arrangements for the Portuguese Army were completely restructured. This had to be achieved with agreement of the Portuguese Government, which he achieved. Wellington insisted that it should start forthwith.

The second task was to plan a means to defeat the French when they arrived near Lisbon, by the controversial method of food denial. Wellington set about a complete rejuvenation of the Ordenanza, the locally raised militia, organized in regiments, whose role was the vigorous harassment of enemy lines of communication and vicious guerrilla warfare. It had been historically understood that on the call-out of the Ordenanza the countryside should be cleared of all foodstuffs, means of transport, boats and other essentials. An invader would need his own protected and effective supply system. Wellington knew that the French could not possibly supply an army of the size needed to invade Portugal, especially given the very poor roads and their lack of a commissariat. He decided, when it became necessary, to evacuate the Portuguese population to the Lisbon area, to deny the French any locally procured food, and, while holding them firm at the Lines of Torres Vedras, to starve them. This required delicate political negotiation with the Portuguese, and detailed planning.

Wellington's third daunting task was to initiate the building of a series of stupendous field works, later known as the Lines of Torres Vedras, from which to defend the Lisbon peninsula. They were to be constructed in complete secrecy by a huge force of locally enlisted Portuguese labourers, closely supervised by 150 British senior non-commissioned officers, chosen for their integrity, sobriety and efficiency. The detailed plans for the Lines of Torres Vedras were coordinated between Wellington and his senior engineer, Colonel Fletcher. On 20 October Wellington gave Fletcher written instructions to draw up a scheme for the construction of two successive lines of trenches and redoubts, covering the whole stretch from the Atlantic to a point on the Tagus about 20 miles north of Lisbon. The works were to be on a vast scale: the fortified camp above Torres Vedras, for example, was to hold 5,000 men. The works at other locations would need 5,000 workmen to dig them, and work was to begin at once. The damming of rivers and creation of marshes was suggested. Fletcher, a dynamic genius, had only seventeen Royal Engineer officers for the project, and some 300,000 members of the local Ordenanza were employed.[12]

During Wellington's absence in Portugal various preliminary moves were being made in the deployment of the army from Badajoz and the border area to the new Mondego Line just inside Portugal. On Sunday, 8 October Henry Percy's Light Company marched to Olivenza,[13] some 15 miles south of Elvas. Cooper states that they were accommodated in the bomb-proof shelter of the castle. It was destroyed when the Spaniards stormed the castle later in the war.

Having set the huge Portuguese project in motion, Wellington, accompanied by Alexander Gordon, set off for Badajoz, arriving on Tuesday, 31 October. Irritatingly, the case of Captain de Thévenon had still not been resolved. Furthermore, the Spanish Government had just reorganized the Junta to be at Seville, and Wellington's brother, Lord Wellesley, was to return to England. His successor as Ambassador was unknown. Wellington, despite his time away in Lisbon, decided to deal with the prisoner question at once. Gordon, after only 24 hours at Badajoz, was sent to visit the French again, with letters for Mortier and Soult.

Wellington explained that he was doing all in his power to secure Captain de Thévenon's return, and was pressurizing the Spaniards. In the meantime, he told Mortier that he was sending Lieutenant Véron de Farincourt[14] in exchange for Lieutenant Cameron,[15] who had been returned by General Kellermann.[16]

In December 1809 the Portland cabinet gave way to Percival's new administration, and Wellington faced a different political situation at home. While his energy was going into the defence of the Lisbon peninsula, the government at home wavered, and insisted on preparations being made for evacuation in case the defensive operation was not successful. Perhaps they misjudged his capabilities, but they were right to be anxious. Talavera, hailed as a victory, had been a bloody engagement with no noticeable gain. The Walcheren expedition had ended disastrously. There was disquiet and 'croaking' in the army in the peninsula, and the public was questioning the Iberian involvement. Wellington had a plan, but security was vital. He could not tell his generals, nor his army. Surprise was essential; almost unbelievably he achieved it.

Thousands of Portuguese workmen secretly toiled away at the Lines of Torres Vedras. Training, re-equipment and the integration of new drafts lifted the British regiments.

Meanwhile, the French, too, were busy reorganizing and reinforcing. Napoleon's wish to subjugate Spain once and for all, and to eliminate British interference, was, he decided, to be achieved by a conclusive conquest of Portugal. With the Spanish ulcer eliminated, he could expand eastwards.

Wellington remained based at Badajoz until the end of 1809. Then he headed off for a confirmatory tour of the preparations for his withdrawal to Torres Vedras. By now he knew that the French Army in Spain had been reinforced, as expected after Austria's departure from the Coalition. French numbers reached 325,000 by mid-January, an increase of 100,000. As the precise order of battle became clearer, so did French intentions.

In order to complete his preparations at Torres Vedras, and to keep the Portuguese Government supportive of his drastic need for a mass evacuation and scorched-earth policy, it was important to prepare a delaying withdrawal towards Torres Vedras. Inactivity in the army, intentionally unaware of the plan, caused dissatisfaction and grumbling letters to the newspapers. The British newspapers were read to Napoleon each day at breakfast. It was one way for him to be better informed than his senior officers.

Wellington's confirmatory recce, in two halves, needed stamina. By the time he reached the new Headquarters location at Viseu on 12 January, after the first half, he had ridden over 300 miles. He combed the ground minutely for its defensive and delaying characteristics. He calculated the French

ptain Henry Percy, painted in April 1808 by Frederick Buck of Cork. Percy had spent a month
h the 2/7th Royal Fusiliers at Clonmel before leaving from England for Sweden as ADC to Sir
n Moore. Percy had no ADC uniform in Ireland, having ceased as ADC on return from Egypt.
route to rejoin Sir John he passed through London, so must have collected his ADC uniform
m home at 8 Portman Square. The image in this miniature has been questioned by experts, for
uniform is incorrect for any of Percy's regiments or appointments. It is Mr Buck's attempt at an
)C uniform. The reverse of the miniature is named 'Captain Percy' in Mr Buck's unmistakable
ting, similar to several of his other military miniatures. Furthermore, the recently discovered
atour Fontanet pair of miniatures painted in 1811 when Percy was a prisoner of war at Moulins
w facial similarities which bear out the identification. When greatly enlarged the eyes are even
e! So it is believed that this image does, beyond reasonable doubt, represent Henry Percy.
other Percy was serving in Ireland at the time, after all. (*With permission of, and gratitude to, the*
er, Ken Marsh, and to Philip Haythornthwaite who, as an expert, had doubts but nonetheless brought it
ttention)

(*Above left*) Algernon Percy, 1st Earl of Beverley (21 Jan 1749/50–21 Oct 1830), second son of Hugh Percy, 1st Duke of Northumberland. Henry Percy's father. He was detained in Switzerland and at Moulins in France from 1803 to 1814, and continued to live in France till his death. (*Collection of the Northumberland Estates*)

(*Above right*) Susan Isabella, Countess of Beverley, Henry's mother. Temporarily detained in Switzerland in 1803, she was repatriated with her daughters and youngest son Charles before 1808. She lived at 8 Portman Square. Died January 1812, while her husband and Henry were still on parole in France. (*Collection of the Northumberland Estates*)

(*Right*) Hon. Algernon Percy was visiting Italy with his parents and was detained in Switzerland on the return journey in 1803. He was individually sent to Verdun, but wrote to Napoleon in person and sought leave to go to rejoin his father, the Earl of Beverley, and family as his father was suffering from gout. Permission was granted after a police investigation. He moved with his father to Moulins, France, in the autumn of 1805. Algernon remained detained till 1814. (Henry Edridge, London, 1805) (*Collection of the Northumberland Estates*)

(*Above left*) Josceline Percy, twin elder brother of Henry Percy. A successful naval officer, whose courtesy to General Junot when his passenger in HMS *Nymphe* was later repaid to Henry when he was a prisoner of war. (*Courtesy of Levens Hall*)

(*Left*) Capt. Hon. Francis Percy (1790–1812), Henry's brother, served in the 7th Royal Fusiliers and the Royal Welsh Fusiliers at Walcheren and later in Spain, where he died near Ciudad Rodrigo while his father and brothers were on parole in France. (Henry Edridge, 1805) (*Collection of the Northumberland Estates*)

(*Above right*) Hon. William Henry Percy (1788–1855), Henry's younger naval brother, who commanded HMS *Mermaid* and carried the Duke of Arenberg to England as a prisoner of war in 1811. (Josiah Slater, London, 1810) (*Collection of the Northumberland Estates*)

Cintra Palace, after which the Convention was named in 1808. From George, Lord Lovaine's sketch book. He toured in Portugal and Spain while a military volunteer, more tourist than soldier. (*Collection of the Northumberland Estates*)

Lord Lovaine's sketch book shows he visited Oporto on 18 August 1808. The French had occupied the city in March 1808, and Wellesley retook it from them on 12 May. Henry Percy had been in the relieving force, and the follow-up. This is Fort St Johns. (*Collection of the Northumberland Estates*)

(*above left*) George Lord Lovaine (1788–1867), later 5th Duke of Northumberland. Henry Percy's eldest brother (of eight sons and five daughters). He visited Portugal as a volunteer with General Sir Charles Stewart in 1808, meeting Wellesley, General Junot and other contacts whom he lobbied successfully to exchange his father and brothers. (Henry Edridge, 1806) (*Collection of the Northumberland Estates*)

(*above right*) Major General Andoche Junot, Duke of Abrantes (1771–1813), who met Henry Percy and his brothers Josceline and George, Lord Lovaine at Lisbon in 1808. Junot was looked after

kindly by Josceline in HMS *Nymphe* when he was transported to La Rochelle after the Convention of Cintra. He later repaid the kindness by caring for Henry when he was made prisoner of war. (*Courtesy Musée de l'Armée, Paris, painted by Vincent Nicolas (1801–1865)*)

(*Left*) Major General Count Charles Lefèbvre-Desnouettes, protégé of Napoleon, was captured at Benavente, Spain, on 28 December 1809. He dined with Sir John Moore and met Henry Percy. Moore politely lent the disarmed general his sword before dinner. Evacuated to England from Corunna before the main body left, he was escorted by Moore's ADC Captain Henry Wyndham (later famous for his part in closing the gates at Hougoumont). Wyndham recovered the sword from Lefèbvre at Portchester Castle intending to return it to Moore. Moore, however, was killed at Corunna, and the sword is now in the Royal Green Jackets Museum, Winchester. (*Courtesy Musée de l'Armée, Paris*)

Castro Gonzalo bridge over the river Esla near Benavente. A reserved demolition, its destruction forced the French cavalry to ford and swim the river. In this action Major General Count Charles Lefèbvre-Desnouettes was captured. (*Author's collection*)

Capture of General Lefèbvre-Desnouettes at Benavente, painted by Robert Alexander Hillingford. On return to England after Corunna in January 1809, Levi Grisdale of the 10th Light Dragoons, wh was credited with the capture of the French general, was promoted corporal and visited the Prince Regent to be thanked for his valuable service. The regiment recognized its hero and the officers 'adjudged' this medal to him. A claimant from the King's German Legion, Johan Bergmann of Osnabruck, was awarded a pension for capturing General Lefèbvre-Desnouettes after a court of inquiry at Osterholtz in 1830. (*Courtesy Trustees of The King's Royal Hussars*)

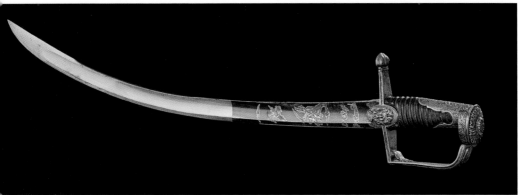

ord of the 1st Regiment of Hussars captured by Levi Grisdale from General Lefèbvre-Desnouettes
Benavente, December 1808, and presented by the 10th Light Dragoons to their Colonel, the Prince
gent. Originally in Carlton House. It is a Light Cavalry sword, about 1800, France (AL290.90).
Royal Armouries/Royal Collection)

edal 'adjudged' to Corporal Levi Grisdale, who greatly distinguished himself on 1 January 1809,
the officers of the 10th Light Dragoons. His action with Lefèbvre-Desnouettes at Benavente was
fact on 29 December 1808. (*Courtesy Trustees of The King's Royal Hussars*)

My attention has been called by a friend to an article which appeared in "N. & Q." of June 19, 1852, signed HALLIOLENSIS, where your correspondent says: "I believe the clergyman who read the service is now living in Hereford, and that he will state that the interment took place in the morning of the day after the battle."

I am the clergyman alluded to, who officiated on that memorable occasion. I was chaplain to the brigade of Guards attached to the army under the command of the late Sir John Moore; and it fell to my lot to attend him in his last moments. During the battle he was conveyed from the field by a sergeant of the 42nd, and some soldiers of that regiment and of the Guards, and I followed them into the quarters of the general, on the quay at Corunna, where he was laid on a mattrass on the floor; and I remained with him till his death, when I was kneeling by his side. After which, it was the subject of deliberation whether his corpse should be conveyed to England, or be buried on the spot; which was not determined before I left the general's quarters. I resolved, therefore, not to embark with the troops, but remained on shore till the morning, when, on going to his quarters, I found that his body had been removed during the night to the quarters of Col. Graham, in the citadel, by the officers of his staff, from whence it was borne by them, assisted by myself, to the grave which had been prepared for it, on one of the bastions of the citadel. It now being daylight, the enemy discovered that the troops had been withdrawn and embarked during the night. A fire was opened by them shortly after upon the ships which were still in the harbour. The funeral service was therefore performed without delay, as we were exposed to the fire of the enemy's guns; and after having shed a tear over the remains of the departed general, whose body was wrapt

"With his martial cloak around him,"—
there having been no means to provide a coffin,—the earth closed upon him, and

"We left him alone with his glory!"

A full and authenticated account of this interesting event will be found in The Narrative of the Campaign of the British Army in Spain commanded by His Excellency Sir John Moore, K.B., &c., authenticated by Official Papers and Original Letters. By John Moore, Esq.

I trust that I have satisfactorily answered the inquiries of your correspondent, and shall be happy to reply to any further inquiries which he may wish to make relating to that interesting event.

H. J. SYMONS,
Hereford.   Vicar of St. Martin's, Hereford.

The following are the names of the officers who were present, and assisted to bear the body of Sir John Moore to the grave:—Lord Lynedoch (then Colonel Graham); Lord Seaton (then Major Colborne); Col. Anderson; Major, now Gen. Sir G. Napier; Captains, now Colonels Percy and Stanhope; and Rev. H. J. Symons, A.M., Chaplain to the Guards, by whom the funeral service was performed.

H. J. Symons LLD
Chaplain to the Forces

From this Prayer Book I read the Burial Service over the body of Lieut General Sir John Moore KB who received a mortal wound while engaged with the French Army in the front of Corunna in Spain on the morning of 16th of January 1809

Prayer book used by the Reverend Henry Symons at the burial of Sir John Moore at Corunna, 17 January 1809. Pasted inside is an article in which Symons names those present. (*National Army Museum*)

The Reverend Henry Symons LLD, the chaplain who conducted Sir John Moore's burial at Corunna, by Georges de Galard, 1814. He is depicted carrying his pamphlet 'The Soldier's Friend, Advice to the British Army'. Mr Symons served in the latter stages of the war, receiving the Military General Service Medal with the clasps for Corunna (which was initially refused, but granted on appeal), Nivelle, Orthes and Toulouse, but he was not at Waterloo. He eventually became Rector of St Martin's Church, Hereford. (*Courtesy of Hereford Museum & Art Gallery, Herefordshire Heritage Services*)

The French ship *Ville de Paris*, flagship of the French admiral Count de Grasse, was captured at the Battle of the Saints in April 1782. She foundered while under tow to England as a prize. The British built their own HMS *Ville De Paris* in 1795. With 110 guns, she was the largest British warship at the time of her construction (*Victory* had 104 guns). Her captain at Corunna in 1809 was John Carden, cousin of Henry Carden who was a fellow prisoner with Henry Percy. Percy and Alexander Gordon, together with the wounded General Sir David Baird, returned to England in HMS *Ville de Paris* through a severe Bay of Biscay storm after Corunna. (*Courtesy the Webb-Carter family*)

brantes, assembly area for the advance to Talavera, summer 1809. View from the castle which dominates the area and the important bridge over the Tagus. (*Author's collection*)

(*Above left*) The fortress of Elvas faces Badajoz a few miles across the Spanish border. This statue of Seven Years War British grenadier bears witness to the long-shared history of this fortress which was much used in the Peninsular War. One of the oldest British military cemeteries in the world, with graves from Albuera and other Peninsular engagements, is maintained by the Friends of the British Cemetery at Elvas. The hospital at Elvas accommodated many of Henry Percy's Light Company in the winter of 1809, including Fusilier John Cooper. (*Author's collection*)

(*Above right*) Serjeant John Spencer Cooper, who made excellent 'Rough Notes of Seven Campaigns' was a private soldier in Henry Percy's Light Company of 2nd Battalion, 7th Foot (The Royal Fusiliers), during Henry's time in command in Portugal and Spain, including at Oporto and the battle of Talavera. If the exactness of his dates is occasionally adrift, his graphic eyewitness observation brings vivid immediacy. His Military General Service Medal, issued in 1848, had nine clasps. (*Courtesy of Philip Haythornthwaite*)

oulins in the Auvergne, where the Earl of Beverley and his son Algernon were paroled from 1808.
ey were joined there by Henry as a prisoner of war in 1811. They all remained here till 1814. Then
enry became ADC to Wellington in Paris, Algernon went to the Foreign Office and Beverley lived
France, with occasional visits to London, for the rest of his life. (*Author's collection*)

s Perrots, Coulandon. The Durands were *vignerons* who lived in an annexe of this big house. Here
enry's son, later Major General Sir Henry Marion Durand, was born on 15 November 1812.
uthor's collection)

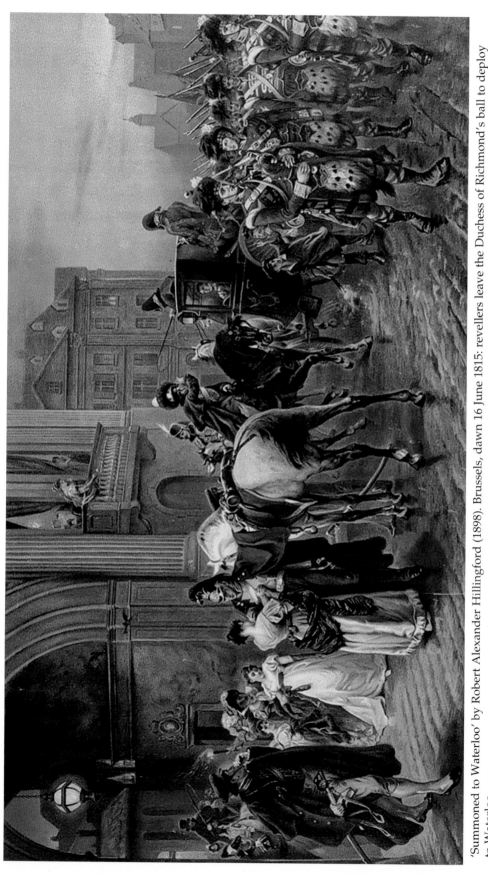

'Summoned to Waterloo' by Robert Alexander Hillingford (1898). Brussels, dawn 16 June 1815: revellers leave the Duchess of Richmond's ball to deploy to Waterloo.

The carriage in which Napoleon was fleeing after Waterloo was found at Genappe. The cloak was too heavy to 'liberate' so the finder removed the clasp of Imperial Bees. The clasp was in the possession of Henry Percy, although it is open to question whether he actually visited Genappe that evening. (*Courtesy of Levens Hall*)

The sword used by Henry Percy at Waterloo, which he forced into the chest of a mounted French officer; shocked at the prospect of killing him, Henry withdrew it, and the French officer did not fall from his horse. (*Collection of the Northumberland Estates*)

late 1815 Henry Percy visited the battlefield of Waterloo with Wellington. He painted this sketch La Belle Alliance, where he was with Wellington when they met Blücher after the battle. This esents a less romantic image of La Belle Alliance than is usually imagined. (*Collection of the rthumberland Estates*)

On 21 June 2015, the 200th anniversary of the event, the arrival of Henry Percy with the Waterloo Dispatch at Mrs Boehm's house in St James's Square was re-enacted. Here the post-chaise can be seen outside the door, while actors representing Major Henry Percy and Commander James White of HMS *Peruvian* hold replicas of the French standards which were delivered to the Prince Regent 200 years before. It is not confirmed whether Commander White actually went to London with Henry Percy, but the 'received wisdom', for which no evidence has been discovered, was that he did. Percy's former employer, Alexander Davison, may have watched the arrival of the dispatch from his house just round the corner. (*Photo Philip McCarthy, courtesy of the East India Club and Alex Bray*)

The Prince Regent's apology. Replica French eagle inscribed 'In commemoration of the STANDARDS brought by Major Percy to the Prince Regent at Mrs BOEHM'S on the 21 June 1815, taken from the French by the DUKE OF WELLINGTON AT THE BATTLE OF WATERLOO.' (*Private collection*)

...eguet pocket watch given by ...e Duke of Wellington to ...nry Percy for taking the ...aterloo Dispatch to London. ...ellington bought a second ...eguet watch, originally ...tended for King Joseph ...apoleon, engraved with the ...apoleonic arms of Spain, ...hich he always used ...ereafter. The firm of Breguet ...ntributed substantially to the ...furbishment of Hougoumont ... part of the Waterloo200 ...mmemorations in 2015. ...ourtesy of Levens Hall)

Henry Percy, painted at Moulins by Delatour Fontanet. This miniature, recently acquired by the Northumberland Estates, was given to Marion Durand by Henry. She gave it to her son Henry Marion, through whose descendants it became available in 2016. (*Collection of the Northumberland Estates*)

A newly discovered miniature depicting Major General Sir Henry Marion Durand, KCSI CB (1812–1870). Son of Henry Percy and Marion Durand of Moulins. He was brought up by foster parents, Mr and Mrs Deans, in London. Discreetly sponsored by Lord FitzRoy Somerset (later Lord Raglan), he served gallantly and successfully in the Indian Army. He died falling from an elephant as Lieutenant Governor of the Punjab at Tank in the North West Frontier. (*Collection of the Northumberland Estates*)

options for their main approach, and looked carefully at the area round the Busaco feature, identifying the danger of the ridge being outflanked. From this he decided on counter-measures to include in his plan.

Back at Viseu, he took up the case once more of the exchange of prisoners and his difficulties with the Spaniards. His dispatch of 27 January 1810 to the Earl of Liverpool (now Secretary of State for War and the Colonies) tells the story in his impatient style. Wellington was so 'politely exasperated' that he decided to send Lieutenant Véron de Farincourt to England so that he could be safely repatriated without interference from the Spaniards.

To the Earl of Liverpool   Viseu, 27th January, 1810.
MY LORD,
I sent home, by the vessel which will take this, Lieut. Véron de Farincourt, of the 2e regiment de l'infanterie legère of the French Army, with a cartel of exchange for Lieut. Cameron of the 79th regiment who was taken prisoner by the French on 27th July, and was sent to Portugal by General Kellermann from Valladolid.

Upon the location of sending this officer to England, and of requesting that he may be sent to France as soon as may be practicable, I think it proper to explain the reasons which have induced me to send him by this mode of conveyance.

I am concerned to have to inform your Lordship that since the British officers and soldiers were made prisoners in the hospital at Talavera, the Spanish government have thrown every obstacle in their power in the way of their being exchanged, and of every communication between the enemy's Generals and me which had for its object either their exchange or their relief by money or otherwise.

As the French prisoners taken in the battle of Talavera, and during the operations in Spain, were given in charge to the Spanish general at the time they were taken, I had no prisoners in my power to exchange for the officers and soldiers taken in the hospital.

Marshal Soult, however, proposed an exchange of prisoners provided General Franceschi, who had been taken in Old Castile in June, should be included in the cartel. This proposition having been referred to the Spanish government, they gave no answer to it for three months and at length refused to agree to it.

They then, in the month of September, detained Captain Thévenin [*sic.*], an aide de camp of Marshal Mortier, who had been sent in to the Spanish posts with a letter for me which was open: first, under pretence that it was necessary that he should wait for an answer; And afterwards, when I remonstrated against his detention, and declared that the letter required no answer, they detained him under the pretence that he had passed the Tagus at Almaraz, where they did not choose to receive flags of truce, although he was received at this same place with his flag by the officer commanding the Spanish outposts. After repeated remonstrances, they at length, in November, allowed Captain Thévenin to return to the French army, having detained him in close confinement for nearly two months.

In the month of September, General Kellermann sent Lieut. Cameron of the 79th regiment into Portugal from Valladolid, with a cartel of exchange for Lieut de Turenne, his aide de camp, who had just been made prisoner in Old Castille. I immediately requested the Spanish Government, through the Ambassador, to place Lieut de Turenne at my disposal, which, after some delay, they refused; and I then prevailed upon the Portuguese Government to allow Lieut Véron de Farincourt, who had been taken at Chaves and was a prisoner at Lisbon, to be exchanged for Lieut Cameron.

In order to avoid the difficulties which I had experienced in communicating with the enemy's generals regarding the prisoners, by the frontier of Estremadura, I determined to send Lieut de Farincourt at once into Old Castille, and he was attended by a Portuguese officer, Captain Gill, 24th regiment, who was to conduct him to the French outposts.

On their arrival at Ciudad Rodrigo, however, both were stopped, and Lieut de Farincourt was put in confinement, and Captain Gill was insulted and ill-treated. Brigadier General Cox, who commanded at Almeida, remonstrated upon this conduct, but in vain; at length when I was informed of it, on the 6th of December, I wrote to Mr Frere to request that he would make remonstrances on the subject; to which letter I received a reply on the 9th, a copy of which I enclose, stating that the orders had been sent to Ciudad Rodrigo to permit Lieut. de Farincourt to proceed to the French outposts.

I found, however, by a letter from Brigadier General Cox to Marshal Beresford, dated 18th December, of which I enclose a copy, not only that these orders had not been sent, but that the Duque del Parque stated that he has received others of a contrary tenor, and that Lieut de Farincourt and Captain Gill were to be sent back into Portugal.

The correspondence then ensued between Mr Frere and me, of which I enclose the copies, from which it is evident not only that the Duque del Parque had not received the orders under which he assured Brigadier General Cox that he acted, but that Don. A. Cornel had deceived his colleague Don F. de Saavedra. The result of this conduct, however, is an impossibility of having any communication with the enemy's Generals which has for its object either the relief or the exchange of the British officers and soldiers who were made prisoners, only because they were wounded in fighting the battles of Spain.

I have the honour to be, &c

Wellington

The Earl of Liverpool.

Having sent that off, Wellington began the second half of his tour, checking on progress on the second line of Torres Vedras. At Lisbon he concentrated on his relationship with the government, so as to be certain that the reasons for his mass evacuation and scorched-earth tactics were supported. If this were not enough of a diplomatic task, all the time he kept up a constant correspondence, sending a flow of cogent instructions from eight different villages during this tour. The preparations being well advanced, he returned to Viseu on 18 February.

Realizing that there were three main invasion approaches for the French, Wellington now had an outline plan. His 'troops to tasks' element of the plan was commendably simple. The most dangerous and most likely approach was the northern route, via Ciudad Rodrigo, Almeida and La Concepción. It divided further west in Portugal. To this route he allotted the 1st, 3rd and 4th Divisions, with the Light Division as rear guard. The other two possible invasion routes, to the south, were less likely to be chosen by the French, but must certainly be defended. Of these, the first went through Castello Branco, but this did not need a whole division. The second, the Badajoz to Elvas route, required the same. So he allotted the two southern routes to Hill's division, with a few attachments.

While Wellington's Headquarters was still at Viseu, the French began preliminary offensives under Napoleon's (remote) direction before the arrival of the Army of Portugal and its commander Marshal André Masséna.

Operations started, in bad weather, on 21 March when General Solignac of Junot's VIII Corps laid siege to Astorga with 10,000 men. The city, with its beautiful old cathedral, had experienced both sides of the war in early 1809, when Sir John Moore had passed hungrily through, pursued by Soult. Now it had 2,000 brave Spanish defenders with supplies for twenty days, but little artillery ammunition. To the French, Astorga was a key link in communications from Bayonne to Portugal. After thirty-two days under siege, Astorga finally fell on Sunday, 22 April. The defence had been a courageous, scientific and daring performance by the Spanish general José Santocildes. The defenders' ammunition, like the troops, was almost completely exhausted.

Ney's instructions were to move his VI Corps forward to the Portuguese frontier west of Ciudad Rodrigo and occupy the English to prevent them interfering with the city when it was besieged. On 26 April Ciudad Rodrigo was surrounded. That Saturday Wellington moved his headquarters in

Portugal 30 miles nearer the border, to Celorico. While he was there, Marshal André Masséna[17] arrived at Valladolid and set up the headquarters of the Army of Portugal. He had three corps:

- II Corps, Reynier's, arrived from the south. The idea for Reynier to besiege Badajoz was frustrated by the number of Spanish troops in the area.
- VI Corps under Ney was now besieging Ciudad Rodrigo and dominating the border area.
- VIII Corps under Junot (Josceline Percy's friend), former Commander-in-Chief of Portugal. It had just captured Astorga.

Masséna, not fully recovered from his latest wound, had been reluctant to go to Spain and Portugal, but was persuaded by Napoleon. He was accompanied by no fewer than fourteen ADCs, and the 'wife' of one of them as his mistress.[18] To the intense irritation of his corps commanders, Henriette Leberton, as she was known, was dressed as a cornet of dragoons wearing the Legion of Honour. The command arrangements were jealous and fractious. Masséna had an experienced Chief of Staff, 44-year-old General François Fririon, who been a brilliant brigade commander with Masséna at Essling and Wagram the previous year. The senior ADC was Jean Jacques Pelet,[19] a clever and influential engineer.

Wellington observed minutely the manoeuvrings of the Army of Portugal from Celorico while Ciudad Rodrigo was being gallantly defended by the Spaniards.[20] As the situation became more critical, pressure mounted on Wellington for a relief operation, but he resolutely refused to be drawn forward into an evident trap on the wrong side of the border.

While all this high-level strategy was going on, Percy had been busy. His Fusiliers had moved from the Badajoz area to Guarda, just over the Portuguese border. He stayed with the Light Company, although his diarist friend Cooper was sick, like many others, with a malignant fever in various hospitals, ending up in Elvas further west. We know from Cooper that Henry was still with his Light Company in a village not far from Guarda[21] when the sick returned. Cooper had memory troubles at this stage of his recollections. He says that while Ciudad Rodrigo was still under siege, Henry went out daily to reconnoitre. Being often observed by the enemy, they laid an ambush and took him prisoner. Not so; he was captured later. Cooper adds that just before this Henry had caused a Portuguese peasant to be flogged for striking his servant with a hoe. Captain Percy, he says, was a favourite with Wellington, and much, and deservedly, loved by his company.

Percy transferred by exchange[22] to the 14th Light Dragoons on 21 June 1810, well before the fall of Ciudad Rodrigo. He had known the 14th at Oporto, at Talavera and also on the long marches through Portugal and Spain. The cavalry formed a screen in the area of Guarda. When Henry joined them the acting commanding officer[23] was an Irishman, the experienced 'delightful, singular and eccentric' Lieutenant Colonel Neil Talbot,[24] who had been serving since 1794. Henry joined the regiment as a captain. His daily pay at 14 shillings and 4 pence appears on the 14th Light Dragoons' payroll of 21 June.

On 25 June Wellington moved well forward to the Vauban-style fortress of Almeida (a mile or two on the Portuguese side of the border) for five days, while Ciudad Rodrigo was still under siege. Seeing that Almeida was defensively well prepared under General Cox, Wellington moved west to Alverca village. From here he could conduct the affairs of his army while keeping the French moves under surveillance by his exploring[25] officers and a trickle of local information.

Probably unaware of Wellington's forward position, and of his intelligence capability, Junot made a daring reconnaissance with Brigadier General Sainte Croix, a recently promoted former ADC of Masséna's, to Fort La Concepción on the Spanish side of the border on 4 July.

Realizing that the French would soon move forward, Wellington warned Brigadier General Robert Craufurd of the Light Division not to be trapped east of the river Coa near Almeida by a superior force, as retirement by the single bridge would be perilous.

One of the most heroic and controversial engagements followed on 24 July, when Craufurd, for his own reasons, ignored his commander's advice and found himself in precisely the predicament foreseen by Wellington. The 14th Light Dragoons, including Henry, played a significant part in covering the very hotly contested infantry withdrawal, being praised afterwards by Craufurd. Henry, alas, wrote no account of the action. The Combat of the Coa demonstrated the superiority and tenacity of the Light Division, but at heavy cost. Wellington, displeased at being ignored, nonetheless supported Craufurd, despite his loss of over 300 casualties in a hair-raising 'scrape'. This left Almeida isolated, but Wellington was confident that its defences were sound. He remained at Alverca till 27 July, the anniversary of the Battle of Talavera.

All this time the undernourished defenders of Ciudad Rodrigo grimly held out under siege, till the town was stormed on 10 July; to avoid further destruction, the heroic General Herrasti[26] very properly capitulated. There was muttered criticism of Wellington's refusal to relieve the siege. In today's parlance, Wellington had obeyed the first principle of war: the selection and maintenance of the aim.[27]

On the day that Ciudad Rodrigo fell, Henry's eldest brother George, Lord Lovaine, tried again to secure the release of Beverley from France. Lovaine suggested to the Foreign Secretary that General Lefèbvre-Desnouettes,[28] a prisoner in England, should be exchanged. A sympathetic reply explained that the Government, on principle, would not enter negotiation, for to do so would recognize the legality of Beverley's illegal detention. Disappointing.

The fall of Ciudad Rodrigo enabled the French to advance. Wellington, writing from Alverca on 27 July, before he moved to Celorico for a fortnight, told the Secretary of State after the isolation of Almeida that 'I do not believe the enemy intend to attack Almeida. I have not heard of any preparations for that purpose and I suspect they are collecting a large force to make a dash at me.'[29] He also explained that the enemy had forced the evacuation of the Fort of La Concepción, and that it had been deliberately destroyed, a consequence of the Combat of the Coa.

Almeida had been isolated, but not besieged. A new friendly approach by the French to the locals was drying up intelligence to Wellington. He considered the French efforts at Almeida feeble, and their intentions 'so little distinct and the intelligence which we receive has lately been very bad, that I have thought it advisable to draw in the whole of the left of the army to the valley of the Mondego, holding Guarda still with a division of infantry. In this position I am equally prepared for any operation that it might be in my power to undertake for the relief of Almeida, if it should be attacked.'

Enemy movement was going on and it was daily becoming more likely that the French were on the verge of invading Portugal in strength. Wellington's plan was ready.

After spending two weeks at Celorico, Wellington returned to Alverca on 22 August. The French had now invested Almeida, opening ground on 15 August. They dug long approach trenches for a week without opening fire (their siege guns had not arrived). The garrison under General William Cox, consisting of the Portuguese 23rd and 24th Regiments of the Line and Ordenanza, made a spirited show of harassing small arms fire, to the great 'vexation' of the French. A former Portuguese Army lieutenant general, the renegade Marquis d'Alorna,[30] was now serving with the French. Previously the governor of Almeida, he had improved the fortifications and knew every detail. He was well known and popular with the local Portuguese militia soldiers.

Masséna and Junot moved in to the still habitable Commandant's house in the ruined, almost indefensible, Fort of La Concepción.[31] On 26 August the French began an intense bombardment at Almeida. This was answered by sustained heavy round-shot fire. The fighting pointed to an eventual bloody storm.

The next evening catastrophe struck. A shell must have ignited a powder train from a leaking powder barrel, which instantly detonated the main magazine containing some 150,000 pounds of gunpowder. There was a deafening, dazzling, violent explosion. Firing paused as huge lumps of masonry crashed terrifyingly from a great height onto the trenches and into the town. So massive was the explosion that it completely demolished the castle, which vanished to atoms. The cathedral disappeared and the roof of every house in the town was laid bare. Cox ordered the defenders to man the walls. Only thirty-nine barrels of powder survived intact for defence. The defenders' heavy casualties were hardly proportionate to the size of the explosion[32] but nevertheless they were shocking: almost 600 infantry, 200 gunners and about 500 local residents of the town.

After the explosion the French sent General Maximilien Foy (whom we last saw at Oporto) to negotiate terms with General Cox. But Cox would not accept the terms and refused to surrender. His Portuguese troops were severely shocked and dispirited. Perhaps they felt the French were going to be the winners after all.

Cox allowed some of his Portuguese officers to continue the negotiations in the French camp. While they were away being pressured by Masséna in person, Alorna and other renegade Portuguese officers circled the glacis, warmly greeting the Portuguese defenders. The Portuguese officers agreed with Masséna that the militia could return to their homes, but that regular soldiers would be made prisoners. Cox did not accept this; the French thought he was playing for time to enable Wellington to attack them. Further negotiations with Pelet, Masséna's senior ADC, broke down and the bombardment resumed. Defence was hopeless, and on the morning of Tuesday, 28 August, Cox surrendered. To his dismay, most of the Portuguese soldiers opted to change sides and join the French Army. The French, wisely, prevented them going as one group to a single regiment, regarding their reliability as questionable. The French admired Cox's brave defence. Baron Marbot[33] said that the Portuguese soldiers were terrified, and led by their officers refused to continue the defence. Cox, being unsupported, was compelled to capitulate.

Wellington had hoped that Almeida would resist for almost three months. Fortuitously, an unexpected factor intervened. Masséna's instinct was to push on westwards while Wellington was off balance. But, in a foretaste of future difficulties, the shortage of rations made it impossible to move without two weeks' supplies, so he waited till 15 September, thereby losing the advantage.

Wellington's aim remained unchanged: to delay the French advance, bring them to battle on his terms and then starve them before the Lines of Torres Vedras. This meant establishing which route the French would take. He thought they would probably advance to Coimbra. The Light Division, as so often, found the rear guard to delay them. Covering the rear guard, as before, was a cavalry screen of Slade's and Anson's cavalry brigades. While these manoeuvrings were going on, a general court martial was convened to try a young officer at Mello under the presidency of Major General Slade of the cavalry brigade. Henry Percy was nominated as one of the fourteen members. Wellington's dispatches were edited for public consumption, so the name of the accused and the charges are not specified. It is known, however, that the court was 'adjourned in consequence of operations' after hearing two days' worth of evidence. By Wellington's authority the officers returned at once to their regiments.

A key route indicator would be if the French captured the bridge over the Mondego at Fornos (de Algodres). This was the start of the difficult Viseu route. It must be watched. Equally, it was a possibility that Masséna might divert south to Oporto.

The 14th Light Dragoons and the 1st Royal Dragoons deployed squadrons to report activity between Guarda and Fornos, including the area of Celorico. Henry, back with his squadron from the court martial only 24 hours before, was now commanding a picquet forming part of the screen near Celorico on that sultry Sunday evening, 16 September. Given that the French seized the bridge at Fornos that night, the picquet from Henry's squadron must have been slightly west of Celorico. No operational report of Henry's capture has been found, but the English press helpfully reported 'Lord Henry Percy [*sic.*] of the 14th Dragoons (brother to Lord Lovaine) has lately been taken prisoner in Portugal: he had the command of the picquets, and his horse becoming restive at the approach of a French party, he was in consequence surrounded.'[34]

Next day the cavalry of Ney's VI Corps crossed the bridge at Fornos and no enemy went south. Two corps were identified going north. Masséna's decision was now clear, and Wellington was delighted that Ney's corps had been satisfactorily drawn to the most difficult possible route. He watched and reacted to the daily reports as he choreographed his army deftly towards Busaco, keeping his divisional commanders in constant touch.

Alexander Gordon discovered that his friend Henry Percy had been captured. Whether he had been wounded or killed was uncertain, but reports said that an officer, a serjeant, two rank and file and four horses had been wounded.[35] Wellington, busy with the move towards Busaco, wrote early the next morning, Monday, 17 September, to Masséna to ask about Henry, and to send him money and other necessaries. Alexander Gordon rode off under flag of truce to the French headquarters, some distance in the rear, since Masséna did not command from the front.

Masséna was having a torrid time, struggling with the awful roads. Food was critically short. So was ammunition. He was uncertain where the British were. He did not know of the existence of the Busaco ridge and his maps were terrible, his Lisbon-dwelling Portuguese guides hopeless in this wild unfamiliar country. Communication was extraordinarily difficult, and Masséna's uncooperative corps commanders tended to operate at their discretion. He almost lost control in the appalling country. Wellington wrote 'there are many bad roads in Portugal, but the enemy has taken decidedly the worst in the kingdom. I imagine Marshal Masséna has been misinformed, and has experienced more difficulty in making his movement than he expected.'[36]

Wellington adjusted his positions to allow for the peculiarities of the French approach. Masséna delayed for an extra day supposedly trying to reorganize his army, to the fury of his corps commanders, because it was said that Madame Leberton was recovering from the rigours of the journey. Pelet, regrettably, remained loyally discreet.

Wellington's Busaco deployment was exemplary, and achieved an emphatic victory over the French who failed to dislodge him from the ridge. The course of the battle is unimportant to Henry Percy's story, but it is necessary to understand that Busaco stunned the French. It achieved precisely the delay that Wellington wanted, and it shocked and damaged the already shaky French morale. When his line was about to be turned, Wellington withdrew, deftly controlled as planned, ahead of the French, leaving the country devoid of supplies, for a ravenous enemy to traverse. One difficulty was the evacuation of Coimbra. The population had been reluctant to withdraw, but this was achieved just in time. Now Wellington withdrew into, and occupied, his big strategic surprise: the Lines of Torres Vedras.

Chapter 11

Prisoner of War
(1810–1811)

They say the best chance to escape is in the first 24 hours. Not for Henry; wounded, disarmed and taken to headquarters under escort. Were he allowed to ride, his horse's bridle would have been roped to the escort.

Let us look in a little more detail at the events leading up to Henry's capture. By 15 September Wellington knew for certain that there was a general advance, so the critical route indicator must come soon. He constantly sent detailed instructions for the cavalry screen to Sir Stapleton Cotton,[1] verging on micro-management:

Gouvea, 15th Sept., 1810, ½ past 3 P.M.
Leave the hussars in front of Celorico. At all events you must get the regiments to the rear of Celorico in the morning at daylight.[2]
...
Probably you could put more squadrons into Celorico, and the others in the rear in the neighbourhood of that town, without making any great noise at night.[3]

Gouvea, 15th Sept., 1810, 20 minutes before 5 P.M.
I have received your note of 2 P.M. I have heard from Captain Cocks[4] from Misarelha that the enemy are pushing down Guarda hill; You had better retire everything on this side[5] of Celorico, or into that town for the night. It is very desirable that you should put the horses up somewhere for the night, and it would be best at once to move them to the rear. You may depend upon it that the movement is general. Let me hear from you as soon as the enemy appear to have taken their ground for the night.

Gouvea, 15th Sept., Midnight.
I was in hopes that I would have heard from you as soon as all was quiet for the evening; I am now apprehensive that the directions I shall give you may not suit the situation in which you may be. I have just received your letter of half-past 8.

I think you had better put the two heavy regiments in march to the rear at 4 in the morning. Let them be followed by the 14th, the 16th follow the 14th, and the hussars wait to follow the enemy's movements. Let the baggage go off, and pass through Sampayo and Pinanços.

The officers of the General Court Martial[6] [who included Henry Percy] will join their regiments.

There is some straw at Villa Cortez, which should be destroyed[7] by the rear regiment.

You had better draw the hussars through the town before daylight . . . Apprize Cocks of your movement.

Concerned not to exhaust the cavalry, Wellington wrote one final note that night, to Charles Stewart. His first letter, written before 8 o'clock the next morning, Sunday, 16 September, expressed his fear that 'we shall knock up the regiments if we do not let them get to their ground. [They] should be allowed to retire to their Cantonments. We have a good deal of work before us, and we must not knock up the troops.'

Beresford, a key figure in the Busaco campaign, was now updated. Wellington explained that he was retiring his headquarters to Cea (now Seia), and hoped Beresford's headquarters would move to St Ramao. 'Could you come over here?' Knowing the direction of the main French thrust, he ordered Beresford to evacuate the sick (from the British hospital in Coimbra in a convent in which one of Henry's Fusilier friends, Charles Auchmuty, had died a few days before), and prepare to destroy the ammunition and other stores.[8]

At Cea, Wellington turned his attention to Henry Percy. When Sir Arthur, as he then was, attended the Cintra Inquiry in early 1809 in London, Lovaine had sought help to influence an exchange of Beverley and Mr Percy.[9] Lovaine had also met Wellesley at Lisbon the previous August. Wellesley obligingly wrote to General Brenier,[10] but to no avail.

Alexander Gordon, Henry's friend from Corunna, was now Wellington's ADC and a trusted negotiator with the French. It is very likely that Gordon mentioned Percy's predicament to Wellington and encouraged him to write to Masséna (in French) on that hectic Monday:

To the Commander in Chief of the French Army [Marshal Masséna, Prince d'Essling]

Headquarters the English Army
17 Sept., 1810

Monsieur le Maréchal,
Captain Percy, in whom I am much interested, was wounded and taken, or killed yesterday near Celorico, and I would be much obliged if you would permit somebody to give news of him to my aide de camp, Major

Gordon; and if he is not killed, if you would allow him to receive this supply of money and necessaries which I send for him.

I have the honour to send you some letters which I received two days ago from the Governor of Elvas. I believe it is arranged between our Governments that non-combatant officers should not be prisoners of war, and if you understand it the same way, I will ask the Portuguese Government to allow M. Galland to be returned; but in any case I will have him given such money as he may need.

I have the honour to be, etc.

Wellington.

To His Excellency the Commander in Chief

Gordon went to Masséna under flag of truce from Cea. On such a task, he would usually travel with an orderly dragoon as escort. He must have headed for Managualde between Viseu and Fornos. Ney was already there, but Masséna was still en route from Almeida. It required careful judgement for ADCs to cross the lines safely, especially when both armies were on the move. Gordon achieved this and delivered Wellington's message. No answer survives, and Masséna's ADC does not mention his visit.

Gordon returned to headquarters, now at Cortiço.[11] On 21 September Wellington's staff retired to headquarters at Busaco Convent[12] on the ridge. By this time the British defensive deployment was starting. All three enemy corps were approaching from the valley of the Mondego, so Wellington knew to put his plan into effect. That Friday Gordon started a letter to his brother, describing over the next three days the progress of the enemy, and the positioning of Wellington's counter-measures. 'If Masséna does not mind what he is about he will yet get himself in a scrape.'[13] Gordon echoes much of Wellington's Busaco dispatch, which to his annoyance was taken to England by Captain Ulysses Burgh.

By now almost half of Wellington's army was Portuguese. Busaco was their first set-piece battle. Gordon reflects the popular view when he writes: 'The Portuguese Regts also have behaved uncommonly well. We are in high spirits at the Portuguese behaving so well.'[14]

The details of the Battle of Busaco need not concern us. It was a body blow for Masséna. He failed to turn Wellington's left flank, and his numerous costly frontal attacks on the ridge never had a chance. Valiant massed columns struggled up the steep slopes, harassed by skirmishers. As they neared the summit they were engaged by terrifying close-range artillery. Before they had time to recover, a long line of disciplined infantry charged down the hill, bayoneting the staggered columns.

French casualties were horrific, and included among others the truculent Brigadier General Simon, who was wounded[15] and captured (with his cantinière[16] and her donkey near the summit). Maximilien Foy was wounded yet again. Gordon discovered more about the casualties later.

* * *

A week after Busaco, Wellington was at Alcobaça, watching the French advance carefully towards Torres Vedras. Gordon again visited the French, returning on Friday, 5 October. The pretext was administration and Percy, another purpose intelligence. Henry's regiment had not been paid since 24 June, when Henry had received £2 17s 4d (£181.70[17] at 2016 values) for the four days since he transferred. (£1 in 1811 was worth £64.28 in purchasing power of January 2016.)

The regiment was next paid on 24 September, eight days after Henry's capture. The payroll shows he was owed £65 18s 8d (£4,178 at 2016 values) for ninety-two days' service. There is no signature against his name, but the paymaster added 'Prisoner of War. His pay remitted him by flag of truce.'[18]

Gordon stayed some time with the enemy and dined with Generals Sainte-Croix,[19] Soult[20] and Taupin.[21] Sainte-Croix and Taupin were both brigadiers in Junot's Corps, and we now know that Henry was being cared for by Junot.[22] It is not certain whether Junot was co-located with Masséna at this stage. Junot himself had been wounded at Busaco, as Gordon reported later. Gordon certainly did not see Henry, but he established for certain that he had not been killed.

Gordon reported that the enemy generals acknowledged they were 'completely beat' on 27 September. Optimism about the success of the campaign had vanished, and they told Gordon that their losses amounted to 3,000 men. He also reported that his friend Brigadier General Graindorge[23] had died of his wounds. Gordon was impressed by the impact the defeat at Busaco had on French morale.

The day after Gordon's return, the French continued their cautious move towards Lisbon, blissfully unaware of Wellington's trap at Torres Vedras, and still hoping to force a British evacuation. Wellington's cavalry screen covered the Light Division rear guard as usual. Lieutenant Henry Carden, from Tipperary, had recently joined the 1st Royal Dragoons. The Royals continued 'in connection with the 14th Light Dragoons':

> During the continued retrograde movement to the celebrated lines of Torres Vedras, the regiment held its post in rear; and on the 8th October near Pombal, the enemy pressing upon the line of march, a picket (of the Royals), led by Lieutenant Carden, charged gallantly, and drove them back with loss, but following up his advantage too far, the lieutenant and 1 man, both wounded, were taken prisoners. The picket, notwithstanding, captured and brought off a French cavalry officer.[24]

Henry Carden,[25] captured 4 miles north of Leiria in the direction of Pombal, was apprehensive. His reputation had suffered when he mistakenly allowed French flags of truce to enter the British line near Celorico without authority. He had been corrected, but longed to distinguish himself to erase this perceived smudge. When his squadron charged the French infantry, Carden keenly galloped ahead. His horse was shot down and he was wounded and taken prisoner. Like Henry Percy, Carden does not appear in British official casualty returns.[26]

In November 1809 Lovaine decided to contact his Lisbon acquaintance, General Junot, probably unaware that Junot was by then in Germany. Could Junot help over repatriating Beverley? No reply survives. The next year, in September 1810, just before Busaco, Junot, now in Portugal, discovered that the young prisoner was Moore's former ADC, Josceline and Lovaine's younger brother. He had met them all at Lisbon. Junot courteously repaid Josceline's kindness, and Henry was allowed to remain at Headquarters. When Junot was wounded at Busaco, Henry was transferred to Masséna's headquarters, although we don't know the date of this move.

Henry must have seen Junot before Busaco, and presumably met his ADCs. One of them was Lieutenant Mascarenhas, known to the French as Picot; a tall Portuguese officer from Junot's time at Lisbon, he belonged to a French cavalry regiment. Indeed, Henry may even have met him at Lisbon in 1808, and he might have been aboard HMS *Nymphe* as well.

After Busaco, Mascarenhas volunteered to carry Masséna's Busaco dispatch to Napoleon's Chief of Staff in Paris, disguised as a peasant in order to slip quietly through the mountains to Almeida. This was a perilous high-risk journey, even for a Portuguese speaker. Picot was recognized at Coimbra by a former school friend serving with Beresford. Claiming to be a peasant, Mascarenhas[27] was arrested, and Masséna's dispatch read with much interest. Both Masséna and Wellington considered the execution of Mascarenhas unreasonable, and Masséna's ADC wondered who was guilty of treason in this struggle in which the English and French wanted to subjugate Portugal.[28]

An acrimonious correspondence followed between Wellington's headquarters and Masséna's staff. In essence the message was simple: 'play by the rules and we will respect them. Officers captured in plain clothes will be treated as spies.' This ill-timed cooling of relations did not help the negotiations about a possible exchange for Henry. Nevertheless, although it has not been possible to find a record anywhere, Wellington's dispatches reveal, tantalizingly, that there must have been further negotiations.

The hints about an abortive exchange are found in a much later letter of Wellington's. Dated 8 November 1811, it was sent from Freneda to General Hill at Merida and concerned prisoner exchanges after the battle of Arroyo dos Molinos: 'take care that our Officers are at your posts when the French

Officers are sent in, otherwise they will play you the tricks they did on me last winter about Percy and Carden.'[29]

An explanation as to why the exchange efforts failed comes from Masséna's ADC, Pelet. His journal at Vincennes says:

> We exchanged a few prisoners. There were some difficulties on the subject of Lord Percy [*sic.*], whom the English were requesting. It was impossible to send him back because he had lived with us for such a long time and knew not only the strength and composition of the army, but also the secret details of our headquarters where he lived unconstrained. They also refused unconditionally to receive Portuguese officers in exchange.[30]

Wellington withdrew deliberately to the Lines of Torres Vedras over a period of several days, conducting a careful delaying action. The British were amazed at the vast defensive positions Wellington had secretly prepared, with dressed stone fortifications and redoubts, fully gunned and manned by Portuguese troops in the front line.

Masséna followed, and bumped into the Lines on 10 October. He was dumbfounded. Still smarting from his surprise Busaco reverse, now he was surprised again and halted abruptly.

Junot's corps, to the east, attacked the Great Redoubt of Sobral in bad weather on Thursday, 11 October. Then, on 12 October, they stumbled across one of the small Royal Naval signalling parties,[31] capturing Midshipman William Hains,[32] near Villa Franca at the Tagus end of the Lines.

There was a pause in the fighting at Sobral on Saturday, and then on Sunday, 14 October Junot tried again. The Battle of Sobral involved no fewer than three British divisions. Junot simply could not compete with Wellington's rapid reinforcements, made possible by the Navy's efficient land signalling system. That was enough for VIII Corps.

Several celebrated incidents occurred while the French tried to decide what to do. Masséna himself was spotted visiting the Lines. He was luckier than General Sainte-Croix, who had been killed by a naval round shot from the Tagus. This long-range cannon shot slammed into the wall of a building just beside Masséna. He politely raised his hat in salute and moved away.

A stalemate followed; Masséna had planned to capture Lisbon and drive the British from Portugal. He had anticipated a glorious victory, with food and spoils a-plenty in the Lisbon area. Now he was disappointed, hungry before the Lines, with no prospect of advance, no prospect of supplies, and no wish to retire to Spain in disgrace, having, after all that effort, achieved nothing but defeats. His situation was perplexing.

*   *   *

The Anglo-Portuguese Army waited comfortably throughout the bad winter weather until late February. Cantonments were arranged, and tactical reaction forces were positioned. The well-fed, well-rested and reinforced army was now in excellent condition. While hungry Masséna waited, comfortable Wellington sent a marauding force to disrupt French communications from the rear.

Although it took longer than he anticipated, Wellington's food denial strategy worked. There was no proper accommodation for the French; the winter was miserable, windy, wet and very cold. Eventually it became too much; starvation, low morale and desertion forced a withdrawal. The French began to thin out from the rear on 14 November. Wellington heard at once from French deserters. He sat tight.

Over the next four days Masséna withdrew into a loose defensive triangle of his three corps, and awaited Wellington's reaction, hoping to hammer a hasty pursuit. Knowing an attack would achieve nothing, Wellington denied Masséna the satisfaction, and relied on starvation to move the French: 'I have determined to persevere in the system which has hitherto saved all. And which will, I hope, end in the defeat of the enemy.'[33]

* * *

Henry Percy remained with the Headquarters of the Army of Portugal during November and December. During these early days, while he was recovering from his slight wound, negotiations of some sort went on to achieve an exchange for him and Henry Carden. Judging by the incomplete correspondence, there was a request from the French for the exchange of French officers which was agreed, subject to Percy and Carden being exchanged in their place. On 8 November the Adjutant General, Brigadier General Charles Stewart,[34] wrote to General Fririon, Masséna's Chief of Staff:

I have the honour to acknowledge receipt of your letter of 6th November which I have placed before His Excellency the Viscount Wellington KB, Commander-in-Chief of the Combined Armies, and I am to send you the following response.

In considering the proposal made by His Excellency Marshal the Prince of Essling, the Commander-in-Chief cannot forget that the same proposal was made with the stipulation of exchange agreed on your part for the exchange of the two English officers, Captain Percy of the 14th Dragoons and Lieutenant Carden of the 1st Dragoons in whom His Excellency has a lively interest, and that this exchange has not been concluded. The excuse which was given to the forward posts was that these two gentlemen had been sent to Spain.

In consequence, the Commander–in–Chief has decided that he will not agree to any other exchange of prisoners in which these two officers and Mr Hains are not included.

I am also to remind you, Monsieur General, that if Mr Percy and Mr Carden had been sent to Spain this ought to have taken place under the terms as proposed by His Excellency, the Prince of Essling, for the exchange, and at the time and place when it was decided to put it into effect.

I request, Monsieur General, that you place this response before His Excellency the Prince of Essling, and I have the honour to renew to you my assurances of highest consideration.[35]

As Masséna pulled back, his corps commanders assumed their positions in the loose defensive triangle. Henry Percy probably returned to Masséna's head-quarters at Torre Noval, judging by Pelet's later comments and the fact that Junot had been wounded. The next definite news of Henry is a letter, now at Vincennes, written by General Fririon to the Minister of War on 19 January 1811. It is notable how the revolutionary *égalité* of French military corre-spondence had been replaced by the Imperial flowery formality:

From the Army of Portugal
To His Excellency the Duke of Feltre [General Clarke],
   Minister of War
Monseigneur,
I have the honour to notify Your Excellency that Marshal the Prince of Essling will tomorrow, 20 January, send the undermentioned to Spain and thence to France:
- Taken the 16 7bre [16 September] near Celorico: N N Henri Percy, Captain 14th English Dragoons – prisoner of war.
- Taken the 6 8bre [6 October] near Leiria: Henri Carden, Lieutenant 1st Regiment of Dragoons.
- Taken the 12 8bre [12 October] near Villa Franca: William Heins [Hains], Ensigne de Vaisseau [Midshipman].
I hereby request General Cacault, the General Officer Commanding at Ciudad Rodrigo, to forward to Your Excellency a copy of the itinerary which these officers will follow en route for Bayonne.

I have the honour to be, with respect
To Your Excellency,
Monseigneur
Your most humble and very obedient servant
   Fririon
   Major General, Chief of the General Staff
   Torre Noval, 19 January 1811

Henry, with Carden and William Hains, began the marathon march on 20 January. Gordon, writing to his brother from Headquarters at Cartaxo on 2 February, said:

> The other day they sent a detachment of 2,000 men to escort a Courier by Castello Branco. With it went my poor Friend Percy to France. I received a very civil note from Reynier about him, and afterwards had an interview with his ADCamp. Junot's wound was *bien grave* but not dangerous, which I am glad of, as he is a good fellow and a bad General.[36]

News of Henry's capture had reached England and the *Worcestershire Journal* of 29 October 1810 reported his capture, as we have seen. The report continues with an explanation for the size of the escort for the courier and the prisoners, a tribute to the Spanish 'patriots':

> A considerable treasure, destined for the pay of the French armies, was intercepted on the great road leading from Bayonne to Madrid by the patriots who were inferior to the French force; but making their attack under cover of the night, they were, after a vigorous resistance on the part of the enemy, victorious. The booty obtained was estimated at 200,000 crowns.
>
> It is stated in letters from Holland that no less than sixteen couriers were imprisoned at Bayonne for refusal to proceed to the armies in Spain and Portugal with dispatches. Hardly one messenger out of six who takes the route of the Western Pyrenees is known to arrive at his destination.

The convoy and three prisoners set off that Saturday morning from Torres Novas on the first leg of 174 miles, through Castelo Branco and Guarda, which they passed on 30 January 1811. It was familiar to Percy. Arriving at Ciudad Rodrigo on Sunday, 4 February, they crossed the Roman bridge over the Agueda river and entered the fortress through its beautiful defended western gateway past the classical guardroom with oil lanterns on its door posts. Percy remembered the town: Sir John Moore had been welcomed here with ceremony by the Spanish Governor. Not this time; nor was there to be a comfortable night in the castle,[37] where General Cacault now presided. The Duchess of Abrantes, Junot's wife, was staying there at this time, but her journal does not help us.

From Ciudad Rodrigo, which a year later would be back in Wellington's hands, the convoy lumbered on towards Bayonne. The route was straightforward. The French had established garrisons in Spain, intending to pacify the surrounding country, but often unsuccessfully, hence the escort.

From Rodrigo the prisoners headed for Salamanca, 56 miles distant, a route again familiar to Percy from 1808. No comfortable Palacio de San Boal this time, nor time to find old friends. The convoy pressed on towards Valladolid, arriving about 18 February (326 miles marched; 600 to go to Moulins). Couriers could not delay, so prisoners, escorts and the courier (who was probably mounted), marched in short stages each day to prevent time being lost in rest days during long journeys.

The road to Bayonne passed through the open country of the high Castilian *Meseta*, passing decrepit, if beautiful, medieval Spanish towns. Between them lay miles of exposed open road, freezing, often snowy and windswept in February. Accommodation in the villages was draughty and primitive, and while individual officers were sometimes lodged in the mayor's house of a town, in peasant villages this was impossible. It was even more difficult when the party consisted chiefly of a huge escort.

The military escort was not supplied with rations in the way the British Army usually was. Forage depots needed guards – a drain on scarce manpower. Parties moving through Spain had to forage to some degree for themselves. Payment in cash was often needed when Spanish peasants refused French credit notes.

The route led via Valladolid, Burgos, Vitoria and San Sebastian. Then it followed the coast past St Jean de Luz, with the Bay of Biscay clearly visible, often with British naval shipping in sight. In early 1811 the road was crowded with carriages and marching troops. The tired prisoners arrived at the Citadel at Bayonne, a huge Vauban fortress, on about 14 March, after covering almost 600 miles. This was the same day that Masséna began his unavoidable withdrawal from Portugal into Spain.

Bayonne is a hilly city. Birthplace of the bayonet, the arsenal was the main depot for the French armies in Spain and Portugal, supplying weapons, ammunition and staging facilities for all troops moving to and from Iberia. There were hospitals for the wounded, camps for prisoners and gaols for the hundreds of French deserters returning in chains to France. British prisoners, civilian and military, were 'processed' at Bayonne, and forwarded to their destinations under escort. Most British officer prisoners were sent under Gendarmerie escort to Verdun, 682 miles further on. Several other towns, always well away from the coast, also accommodated paroled officers in smaller numbers.

The commandant at Bayonne, General Sols, was a polite officer of the old school. He had discretion, within certain rules, to decide where prisoners should be sent. Henry, aware that his father and brother were at Moulins, presumably asked to be sent there. Unless the Minister of War, Feltre, had sent instructions in advance of Henry's arrival, it would have been General Sols who chose Moulins.

Moulins lies 404 miles northeast of Bayonne, another long march. From this point, a small Gendarmerie escort sufficed; it changed daily, the men returning to their local barrack the following day. The route was almost certainly via Perigueux, Limoges and Mont Luçon to Moulins. Percy must have left Bayonne on about 17 March, so we may assume he arrived at Moulins about Monday, 16 April. The more direct (pilgrimage) route via Cahors,[38] with its magnificent Valentré Bridge over the river Lot, was no longer used by British prisoners of war. The records of the Gendarmes de L'Empire at Cahors show French military deserters and Spanish prisoners transiting through the town, but no British names are recorded after 1808.

Henry Carden, en route for Verdun, probably went by the direct route, not via Moulins. We know little more of his time as a prisoner save that he was listed in the *Caledonian Mercury*[39] of 20 August 1812 among those 'who are all well on the 2nd June' at Verdun. Midshipman Hains does not appear among the Midshipmen at Verdun, but midshipmen's names were seldom listed. So we lose sight of him at Bayonne.

Henry finally reached Moulins in mid-April, and was reunited with his father and Algernon.

Chapter 12

Life on Parole at Moulins

Moulins at last, after nearly a thousand miles; how wonderful not to be marching tomorrow. Henry Percy was escorted to the Gendarmerie Commissioner, and moved into his father's house at Moulins in late April 1811. He signed the parole form with General Le Poygne, commanding the Police at Moulins,[1] as instructed by the Duke of Feltre. The form was returned to the Bureau of Prisoners of War[2] at Le Bourget, and Henry was thereafter allowed freedom within the parole limits of Moulins, extended on request by Le Poygne. His family's reputation meant that he was only required to report to the police commissioner daily for the first short period, then '*surveillance*' was relaxed.

The Revolution had affected the Allier district less severely than elsewhere, and a number of landed estates survived relatively unscathed. Moulins itself lies on the wide river Allier, crossed by an enormously long bridge from the southwest. There are two notable churches, each with twin towers; one is now the cathedral. The streets of the old town are cobbled, twisting and very narrow, with timber-framed houses whose steeply-pitched roofs almost meet over the middle of the street. Large private houses, set back in their own gardens, are found in the newer part of the town, built in the late sixteenth century. Upstream of the bridge stand the extensive former cavalry barracks, known as the Quartier Villars.[3]

There had been a small English community at Moulins before the Revolution. Two elderly spinster ladies were still living in the town, having run a small sewing business. Occasional parties of British prisoners, often merchant seamen, passed through heading south for Besançon or other prisoner-holding towns. Beverley ensured that he gave them a good dinner, half a crown, tobacco and shoes. Glimpses of life as a *détenu* can be found in his letters to his son, Lovaine.

Henry had not seen his 61-year-old father for over seven years. Beverley had been at Moulins since his unexpected arrival in October[4] 1805[5] (just as news of Trafalgar was reaching France), having previously been detained for over two years in Geneva.[6] General Morand Dupuch, the Commandant of the Department of Leman (Geneva), had been friendly and issued a pass for Beverley (which is still at Alnwick) to move freely outside the town. Then, suddenly, presumably on instructions from Paris, he sent Beverley a written order to move to Moulins with Algernon at 24-hours' notice. The Moulins archives still have the order, together with the Mayor of Geneva's introduction, which was sent to the Mayor of Moulins. Beverley and his family were given a glowing reference, saying they were cooperative, well-behaved and the model of good behaviour. Consequently the police at Moulins relaxed the stringent daily reporting requirement after a few weeks. Beverley's move to Moulins with Algernon was accompanied by other British *détenus* from Geneva, William Wickham (probably not the well-known intelligence agent of that name, as he would never have been paroled), the two brothers Cazenove and Doctor James Clarke. Disappointingly, there is no record of where they lodged at Moulins, and Beverley makes no mention of them in his correspondence.

Beverley and Algernon settled in at Moulins in late 1805, being joined there by Henry in April 1811. Attempts at repatriation and exchange continued till the end of 1813. Lady Beverley and her three daughters, together with young Charles, aged 10½, had been allowed to go home from Geneva, when most wives and daughters of *détenus* were sent home,[7] before the Moulins move in the autumn of 1805.

In January 1808 Algernon had sought police permission to visit friends at Clermont. This was granted by Fouché because the Percys had always behaved honourably. Nonetheless, the duplicitous and scheming Fouché, a former monk and vicious murderous revolutionary who now headed the secret police, was suspicious. Police correspondence shows that the Pûy de Dome police were warned to ensure that strict surveillance was in place.

In March 1809, when Henry was in Ireland, Algernon applied for a licence to carry a shotgun so as to enjoy the pleasures of '*la chasse*' with the principal families of the area, from whom he always received a warm welcome. The local police commissioner referred his application to Paris, saying that the *Préfet* of Moulins supported it on account of the family's exemplary behaviour. In seeking the permission, it was noted by the police in Paris that the Duke of Northumberland allowed French prisoners to enjoy the pleasure of *la chasse* in his *parc*. After some hesitation, the licence was granted, encouraged by the Duke of Feltre. This was a carefully prearranged plan. Lovaine had written a few weeks before to the Duke of Feltre, asking, yet again, for an exchange for Beverley, and explaining how kind the Percy family had been to French prisoners, allowing them to shoot in the Duke of Northumberland's 'park'. The chances of an exchange were negligible, but with careful timing the application for a gun licence was approved. How satisfactory to find mention in one of Beverley's later letters at Alnwick that 'the boys are enjoying shooting'.

The year 1809 had been an anxious one for Beverley. His wife and daughters were safely ·at home, which was good, but Henry was on active service with Sir John Moore in Spain. The younger boy, Francis John, went on the disastrous Walcheren expedition between July and December as a lieutenant with the 2/23rd Royal Welsh Fusiliers, having recently transferred from the 7th Royal Fusiliers. The expeditionary force was smitten by a virulent and persistent fever, leaving Francis unfit thereafter for regimental service. A post was found for him at Fort St George in Guernsey as ADC to Lieutenant General Sir John Doyle. The whole battalion had been sent to Guernsey to recover after Walcheren. In due course he was sent to Spain, again as ADC, between June and July 1811, this time with Sir John's son, Colonel John Doyle, who commanded a Portuguese brigade. Francis was a good-looking, tall young man, but he was never strong after Walcheren. What role he held in Spain after the two months he served as ADC is not known; perhaps he was sick.

As 1810 progressed, England celebrated King George III's Golden Jubilee. At Cheltenham, General Lefèbvre-Desnouettes was living comfortably on parole. He and Brigadier Maurin, another paroled general, were popular in Cheltenham's social set, as evidenced by the *London Courier & Evening Gazette* in November, while Henry was with his company in the bomb-proof shelter at Olivenza:

> The day of the Jubilee was one universal holiday at Cheltenham and its neighbourhood. The shops are shut, divine service was performed, the poor were regaled from a subscription set on foot by Colonel Riddel, and fireworks and crackers made the streets ring in the evening. There was a great dinner at the town hall, at which about a hundred and fifty sat down, and gentlemen of the county uniting, the venerable Mr Delabere, father of the neighbourhood was in the chair.
>
> The next night the gentleman gave to the ladies, at the Bath hotel, a ball which was one of the most brilliant ever witnessed in this place. The company consisted of about 80 gentlemen and 100 ladies, all of whom were dressed in white satin or white silk, or the finest muslins with the most costly ornaments. Each put forth the whole of her taste and ingenuity, no expense being spared, and the blaze of beauty thus splendidly displayed in a room lighted even to excess could scarcely be borne by mortal Eye. The Countess of Belmoure, Lady Charlotte Goold, and Lady Elizabeth Mathew, were the patronesses, each being dressed to the utmost that expense and good taste could accomplish, and each having on their very best looks as well as best dresses. These ladies received the company, and were very assiduous in their attentions. The dancing began soon after 10 o'clock, and continued with spirit till one, when the supper rooms were opened, and everyone felt gratitude to the stewards, Messrs. Moore, Goold, and Stevenson, for the elegant and liberal

provisions they had made. The lady patronesses presided at three tables in the principal room, and after the fair visitors had retired, many loyal and appropriate toasts were drunk in good wine. The dancing was resumed and continued till daylight.

The Miss Winyates, and Miss Martin of Cawley, were much distinguished for their beauty, dress and dancing, as were the Misses Sheridan, the Miss Nixons, the Miss Joneses, the Miss Buckleys, the Miss Birds, and though last, but not least, Mrs Cathcart, Mrs Buller, and Mrs Busche; but to enumerate all the Ladies who justly excited admiration, not less than two-thirds of them should be named, as it has rarely happened that so great a proportion of beauty and attraction have been found in one assembly.

The French generals Lefèbvre and Morin[8] [*sic.*] were among the dancers with joy at King George's Jubilee. The ladies wore ribands with 'Long live the King' and 'God save the King' upon them, and medals were worn by both the ladies and gentlemen. Bright countenances and high spirits prevailed universally, so gay a party not having been before known in Cheltenham, notwithstanding the absence of the family of Colonel MacLeod[9] of Colbecks (usually the soul of the amusements in Cheltenham), in consequence of the recent death of the Colonel's only son, a most amiable and promising youth.

Official attempts were made to set up a formal exchange programme between the French and British Governments. It was intended to cover both prisoners of war and those detained by Napoleon. In April 1810 Colonel Colin Mackenzie was sent to Morlaix to negotiate. While in Paris he witnessed Napoleon's marriage festivities. The British Government, reluctantly waiving the principle of legality of arrest, suggested that the Earl of Beverley should be exchanged for a French general. A scale of equivalent ranks between French prisoners and senior detained British civilians was proposed. There was, however, a complication over the numbers of prisoners, for the French held far fewer British service prisoners. Negotiations foundered on the French insistence on Spanish and Hanoverian prisoners being exchanged or repatriated at unacceptable ratios. There were also difficulties over Portuguese prisoners (from the French service), whom the British handed over to Portuguese jurisdiction. On 6 November, while Henry was still a prisoner in Portugal, waiting at the French headquarters, Mackenzie returned with no agreement.

Despite this disappointment, individual contact was maintained with the French Government on the subject. Indeed, the *Morning Post* of 4 March 1811 understood (incorrectly) 'that the British Government agreed to take the Earl of Beverley, who has been detained in France since the commencement of the war, in exchange for Gen. Lefèbvre. This arrangement awaits ratification by the French Government. General Count Lefèbvre is now at Cheltenham. His Countess has recently joined him from France.'

Life was not always easy at Moulins, as for example when a certain Colonel William Whaley, who indulged in quarrelling, duelling and betting, arrived in 1808. He was notorious for 'immorality and extravagant conduct, and capable of the most desperate enterprises'. The British Government had refused him a passport for France in 1803, but still managed to get there. After six months' imprisonment in the Temple at Paris, where he fomented a mutiny among the prisoners, he had been sent to Verdun and thence to Moulins. He does not seem to have survived long at Moulins and was returned to Verdun. There, in 1811, out of spite for a perceived insult, he denounced General Lord Blayney, the benevolent senior British officer, as having secretly procured plans of French fortresses. The charge was investigated and declared unfounded.[10]

At Moulins there was so much to talk about, and so little to do. Henry wore plain clothes and mixed locally. The Earl, doubtless delighted to have Henry's company, lived well with his two sons. During this time Henry sat for a French miniature painter, Delatour Fontanet, at Moulins. He painted two miniatures of Henry. They show a handsome blue-eyed young man. The miniatures, which were in the possession of Henry's youngest grandson, Colonel Algernon Durand, have recently been acquired by the Northumberland Estates.

The Percys lived in a town house formerly rented by a friend, an erstwhile *Préfet* of Nîmes, Monsieur Dubois. Posted as *Directeur des Droits Réunis* at Moulins, Dubois had been a good conversationalist and liked the British. His son, Adolph, was a prisoner of war on parole at Bridgnorth[11] in Shropshire. In 1810 Beverley asked Lovaine to try to 'introduce some friends to this very intelligent young man whom I have met[12]'. M. Dubois senior had by now been dead for four years; he was a great loss to Beverley, but his house (used by Beverley since late 1806) was an improvement. Beverley found life expensive at Moulins, and often wrote to Lovaine on financial matters. Nonetheless, he had horses and a cabriolet,[13] and mixed freely in Moulins society.

The year 1811 must have been difficult, too, for Henry. Settling in to a quiet life with no purpose and little excitement with his father cannot have been easy, especially knowing that his friends were heavily engaged in the intensifying war. His opportunity to distinguish himself had gone, and promotion was impossible, but he was lucky to have missed the awful losses inflicted on his old regiment at Albuera and Salamanca. At Moulins Henry went riding, probably hunting and occasionally shooting. He met his father's local friends, although there were few like-minded young men in wartime Moulins, such were the demands of the *Grande Armée*.

The Beverley household employed servants from the local area, who under the surveillance regime were doubtless vetted by the Gendarmerie and required to report.

* * *

Henry's younger brother, William Henry, whom he had seen briefly in Lisbon and possibly at home after Corunna, was now commanding his first warship, HMS *Mermaid*, a frigate *en flute*, with half her normal guns, employed as a transport for 1,000 troops at a time between England and the Peninsula. In this role he was permitted by Admiral Berkeley to transport the Duke of Arenberg to England, as comfortably as possible, as a prisoner. A prince of the Imperial family, married to the Empress Josephine's niece, Arenberg, a rather hopeless cavalry colonel, had been captured at Arroyo dos Molinos. Interestingly, Wellington, who described him as 'a great card', was implored by the Marchioness of Santa Cruz to exchange the Duke of Arenberg for her husband, a Spanish general imprisoned in Italy. Wellington decided Arenberg was too valuable a prize, and suggested that the Government should exchange him for Lord Beverley[14] but nothing came of it.

Beverley still featured in the world of prisoner exchanges, and there was newspaper speculation over an exchange with General Lefèbvre-Desnouettes. On 7 March 1811, a few days before Henry left Bayonne heading to Moulins, the *Exeter Flying Post* reported:

> We understand the British Government has agreed to take the earl of Beverley, who has been detained in France since the commencement of the war in exchange for General Lefèbvre, Count of the French Empire, who was made prisoner in a rencontre between advanced parties of British and French cavalry near Sahagún, immediately previous to Sir J. Moore's retreat. The arrangement of this exchange awaits the ratification of the French Government. General Count Lefèbvre is now at Cheltenham where he has been, and continues to be, treated with the most liberal hospitality and attention. His Countess[15] has recently joined him from France.

The French Government would not ratify the plan.

The winter of 1811 was very cold at Moulins. A famous bright comet with a long tail was visible in the sky to the north for several months.[16] Superstitious French people said its coming explained the wonderful vintage wine that autumn. The people living near Moulins, especially in the commune of Coulandon 2 miles to the west of the river, were *vignerons*, and there were miles of vineyards. The large properties consisted of the owner's house, with estate workers' families accommodated in wings on either side of the main building, at right angles.

The next year, 1812, was different in many ways. Wellington was advancing in Spain, and in freezing weather Ciudad Rodrigo was successfully stormed on 19 January. Henry must have felt very much left out of it. Shortly afterwards word was received that his mother, Isabella Susannah, Countess of Beverley had died in London on the Thursday after the storming of Ciudad Rodrigo, on 24 January. She was 61. How sad that her two Moulins sons and their father had not seen her for so long. Awful, too, that young Francis was somewhere unknown in Spain. The naval sons, Josceline and William Henry, were both at sea, but at least Hugh, rector of Ivychurch, near Tunbridge, and Chancellor of Salisbury Cathedral, was available to support his brother George and the girls. George Lovaine must have had to take charge when Lady Beverley was buried in the Northumberland vault at Westminster Abbey.

The war raged on in Spain, and Henry must have sorely regretted his absence. Badajoz was stormed in April while Beverley was writing home saying that '4,000 men are expected here today, and an equal number the day after tomorrow, going to the Grande Armée. Hundreds of conscripts pass daily.' Wellington knew about the drain of French manpower from Spain for the Russian campaign, which enabled him to go on the offensive. Salamanca, with its cavalry glory, and the British occupation of Madrid all passed Henry by.

While this was happening on the continent, the Lefèbvre-Desnouettes family were enjoying their socially fulfilling life, living comfortably at No. 1 The High Street, Cheltenham, in company with Brigadier General Maurin. The general seemed to think that since he had been given to understand he would be exchanged for the Earl of Beverley, and it had not happened, he was absolved of his parole undertaking. After all, the Prince Regent himself had led him to believe the exchange would occur. Lefèbvre-Desnouettes chose to ignore the necessity of the French Government's agreement, which was not forthcoming. He decided that his duty lay in France: he must escape. To do so, he needed money and he raised it, quietly, by sacrificing a gold ring decorated with vine leaves,[17] given to him by Napoleon on his marriage to Stéphanie.

On 1 May 1812 Lefèbvre-Desnouettes made his getaway. With Stéphanie unostentatiously dressed in boy's clothing and travelling as his son, and his young ADC, Armand Le Duc, in the character of a valet, he made for London, supposedly disguised as a Russian count. After a night in a hotel in busy Leicester Square, where Sir Joshua Reynolds lived and the escapees could pass unnoticed in the crowd, they made their way quietly to Dover. Here, by previous arrangement, they met their boatman, Richard Tapper,[18] with whom they successfully evaded detection and crossed to France.[19] Lefèbvre-Desnouettes reported to Napoleon at St Cloud. Napoleon was having dinner at the time. His reception was cold at first. It is reported[20] by Napoleon's valet that, having first admonished Lefèbvre-Desnouettes for the loss of his chasseurs at Benavente, he listened to his account of his time at Cheltenham and his escape. Napoleon was delighted, and reinstated him in the army. Perhaps Lefèbvre-Desnouettes' timing was less than ideal, since he was just in time for the ill-fated Russian campaign.

The British were unimpressed. The *Public Ledger & Daily Advertiser* of Friday, 8 May 1812 thundered:

> ... He was much distressed at the idea that he would be blamed by Bonaparte for suffering himself to be taken in so foolish a way, and Bonaparte did accordingly blame him in the bulletin relating to the occurrence, although with some commendations of his courage.
>
> Besides being allowed to come to Cheltenham, and remain there on his parole, at the request of Colonel MacLeod, Lefèbvre was allowed to come to London for medical advice. And on that occasion he received polite attention from several persons of distinction. The physicians whom he consulted refused to take any fees from him. General Lefèbvre had a watch when he was taken, which he valued very highly; and such was the attention shown to him, that this watch, after three years bestowed in research and inquiry among the Dragoons engaged in the skirmish, and afterwards in guarding the prisoner, was at length, by the exertions of the Earl of Moira and the Prince Regent, recovered last summer and sent down to him at Cheltenham from the Prince by the hands of Major Camac, Private Secretary to Sir H. Wellesley.

According to the account held by the King's Royal Hussars (successor regiment to the 10th Light Dragoons) the Prince Regent appointed Grisdale a serjeant. As he was returning with the captured general to rejoin his comrades, they met a private of a regiment of Light Dragoons who took the general's watch from him. General Lefèbvre-Desnouettes had been equerry to the King of Westphalia who presented him with this watch, to which was attached his earldom of the New Creation of France.

> General Lefèbvre, it is said, was married to the daughter of an eminent banker at Paris, M. Perregaux.[21] This lady has been now above 12 months in England, being admitted to come over and reside with the General at Cheltenham, where she experienced the same polite attention so long shewn to her husband. It had for some time been proposed to exchange Lefèbvre for the Earl of Beverly; but no definitive arrangement was come to.

May 1812 was dramatic. In London the Prime Minister, Spencer Percival, was assassinated in the Palace of Westminster. This extraordinary news took time to reach France. At Moulins there were two unexpected arrivals. One was the one-armed Lieutenant General Sir Edward Paget, who had been so badly wounded at Oporto, had recovered and rejoined Wellington in Spain but was now a prisoner. The press quoted Wellington's dispatch:

> I am sorry to add, that we have had the misfortune to lose Lieut. Gen. Hon. Sir Edward Paget, who was taken prisoner on the 17th. He commanded the centre column, and the fall of rain having greatly injured the roads and swelled the rivulets, there was an interval between the 5th and 7th divisions of infantry. Sir Edward rode alone to the rear to discover the cause of this interval, and, as the road passed through a wood, either a detachment of the enemy's cavalry[22] had got upon the road, or he missed the road, and fell into their hands in the wood. I understand that Sir Edward was not wounded, but I cannot sufficiently regret the loss of his assistance at this moment.

General Paget was accompanied to Moulins by Colonel Raymond Pelly, a cavalry officer of the 16th Light Dragoons.

A week after General Paget's arrival at Moulins, the *Sussex Advertiser* published information from a French paper:

> The French General Lefèbvre, who lately broke his parole, is arrived in France,[23] from whence he has written an insolent letter to Mr Ryder (Secretary of the Home Department), in justification of his conduct. He travelled in a post-chaise as a German Count from Cheltenham through London to Dover where a smuggling vessel was in readiness to receive him. He was accompanied by Madame Lefèbvre, who in boy's clothes passed for his son, and his Aid de Camp [*sic.*] in the humble capacity of valet.

Beverley was delighted to have General Paget's company, and Henry was pleased to see his much-respected acquaintance of old. Beverley personally introduced the new arrivals to the *Préfet* and showed the general to his inn. Each evening the general spent two hours with Beverley, who appreciated his conversation enormously. Henry took the senior officers riding each morning for three hours. In a letter home Beverley asked Lovaine to tell Lady Uxbridge, Paget's mother, that the general was well, and was having no trouble with his eyes.

All they could do was live comfortably at Moulins. For Henry, the girl to whom he gave the paintings was some consolation for his absence from home and his regimental friends at war. He had a lovely 19-year-old local girlfriend, Jeanne Durand. He called her Marion and she lived in a wing of the big house at Les Perrots near Coulandon, a short distance out of Moulins. Her family were vineyard workers. How and where he met her we do not know.

Lovaine was tireless in his efforts to get the family home. An approach was even made to the Prince Regent in person, but it, too, stumbled on the principle of the illegality of Beverley's detention, which it was felt must not be negotiated.

Beverley took the opportunity to dabble in the French art market. Aristocratic properties had fallen victim to the revolution, leaving a thriving market of fine paintings, furniture and treasures. Beverley engaged a licensed civilian English agent to act for him at the Paris auction houses. Although he complained about the cost of living at Moulins, and asked Lovaine to send him monthly accounts of his business expenses in England under Power of Attorney, Beverley became acquisitive in France. He wrote to Lovaine on 7 December 1812:

> I have lately purchased two capital cabinet pictures, one of the crucifixion by Rembrandt,[24] and a Woreverman (?), the latter supposed to be one of the best pictures of that master. It cost me at Mr Clos's sale at Paris 4,980 francs, equal by the loss sustained by the exchange[25] to 270£. Mr Underwood[26] recommended and procured them. There was a beautiful (??) Claude, which I should have bid for, had it not been an oval picture. Mr Seymour bought it for 5,000 francs.

Just after midnight on Saturday morning, 15 November 1812, there was an important event at Les Perrots near Coulandon. Jeanne (Marion) Durand gave birth to her first child, Henry's son. The child was registered formally at the Mairie[27] at Coulandon, with two illiterate local *vignerons* from Les Perrots as *déclarant* and witness. The father is not named; it is recorded that Marion had a 'natural son'.

The attitude to such events seems to have been ambivalent. No very public notice was taken, and the infant remained at Coulandon for most of his early childhood, with occasional visits to Paris when Henry was there, until he went to England with Henry in 1818 and was fostered in London.

Late in the winter another sadness hit poor Beverley. Having lost his wife in January 1812, a letter arrived in November from Spain for Henry. It was sent by a Mr Ponsonby,[28] as Beverley describes him. It broke the news that Francis had died of exhaustion.[29] It is uncertain where he died, possibly at Cuellar, near Ciudad Rodrigo. The family was distraught, and old Beverley wrote sadly to Lovaine. They had heard the news in England, and Beverley does not mention it till a month after he had heard from Spain.

Henry was at Moulins as the war in the Peninsula headed for its dramatic victories of 1813. On 21 June Vitoria saw a French defeat and the flight of King Joseph to France. The French held out at San Sebastián, which eventually fell after a bloody storming. Pamplona surrendered, the Pyrenees were crossed and the British entered France. While engaged in his difficult

Pyrenees campaign, at Vera, just on the Spanish side of the border, Welling-ton answered yet another (rather fatuous) request from Lovaine. Would it be possible to ask Marshal Soult to exchange Henry? Wellington politely replied that he did not believe that it was within the responsibility of the Marshal (with whom he was engaged in a trial of strength in the mountains). The gallant General Foy was wounded again, his fourteenth wound, at Orthez, where a monument marks the spot to this day. His fifteenth wound came at Hougoumont, having met Wellington in the interval.

In the north the French were driven back all the way to Paris by the Prussians and Russians. Napoleon was forced to abdicate after the Battle of Montmartre, and under the Treaty of Paris was banished as King to the island of Elba.

Royalist in sympathy, the region of Bourbonnais, surrounding Moulins, had been home of the Dukes of Bourbon, so the people at Moulins had been unenthusiastic when Napoleon proclaimed himself Emperor. After all the misery caused by his expansionism, when he passed through Moulins en route for exile at Elba, he was hissed by the locals; he moved on, without spending the night there.

Like most prisoners, Henry went home in late April 1814. He left Marion in France with the child. Beverley, an admirer of the French, if not their politics, visited Paris, lunched with the distraught ex-Empress Josephine, and then went to England to deal with his affairs. He returned alone to Moulins, a free man. He loved France and lived there till his death sixteen years later.

Chapter 13

Paris and the Hundred Days (1815)

Most of the continent rejoiced that Napoleon had been expelled to Elba. Peace had been restored after all those terrible years of suffering and war. The tragedy of the bloody Battle of Toulouse (10 April 1814), before the news of Napoleon's abdication had reached either army, had been unnecessary slaughter. Now the army began to return to England from southern France, although a number of experienced regiments were already on their way to America for the continuation of the War of 1812. The infantry left for England by sea, the cavalry over land. Henry's regiment moved to the enormous French base cantonment area at Mont de Marsan near Bordeaux, where, nominated for America, they were reviewed. To their relief this was changed. The destination was now the new cavalry barracks at Hounslow.[1] Leaving Bordeaux on 10 June 1814, via agreed routes, with forage efficiently provided by the French, they reached Calais on 15 July, and Hounslow on the 18th.

Henry Percy had already arrived in London from Moulins. George's family was at Portman Square, although it is possible that Lovaine himself was in Paris, to which he had headed on 1 May. His journey had been delayed 24 hours by the discovery at Shooters Hill that the trunks containing his evening dress and plate, strapped outside the carriage, had been stolen.

On 30 April Wellington's dukedom was announced in the *London Gazette*, and he left Toulouse for Paris, taking only FitzRoy Somerset, his Military Secretary, from the family. While at Toulouse Wellington was surprised to be offered the ambassadorship in Paris, which he accepted with gratitude. The news of his appointment had not reached Paris and he was not yet formally the British ambassador to the corpulent King Louis XVIII, who had now returned from England to the French throne. Well before the signing of the Treaty of Paris on 30 May, which officially ended the war, French ships were leaving Plymouth and other ports with returning prisoners. British ships were docking with liberated prisoners from Verdun and elsewhere, in 'cartels' of up to 800 at a time.

There was justified anxiety in England that large number of fervent supporters of Napoleon returning to France might destabilize the fragile new

Bourbon regime. Indeed, in France it quickly became evident that while on the surface the restoration of peace was popular, respect for the Bourbon monarchy was superficial. British visitors to Paris soon noticed the virulently anti-British feeling of the returning prisoners of war who had been imprisoned on the hulks. No emperor; no glory; no work; no riches; and Wellington being favoured by the fat Bourbon king. It was perceived as a monstrous insult.

A day or two later a huge military review took place in Paris, and the *Morning Post* reported that:

> Yesterday, at the grand parade of the Allied troops, several foreigners suddenly recognised and named an illustrious stranger – a warrior who has for some years been the admiration of Europe for his great talents. But still more for the sublime principles of humanity which governed his conduct amidst the fury of war. The Hero of England, Lord Wellington, had arrived at Paris, and nothing was known of his arrival; he appeared in the midst of us, without any external decoration, dressed like a private individual. His Lordship stood between Lord Castlereagh and Mr. W. Pole [his brother].

That evening Sir Charles Stewart[2] gave a magnificent ball for more than 400 guests to celebrate the restoration. No longer was Wellington almost unnoticed and plainly dressed. *Bell's Messenger* enthused:

> The moment he entered the room the whole accompany a-crowded round him, struggling to get to the site of the man whom they universally acknowledged to be the first Captain of the age. I was standing close to Lord W. when Blücher was presented to him; they bowed and looked at one another for five minutes before they spoke one word; at last however, a conversation commenced which lasted for about ten minutes.
>
> The Emperor of Russia who was there, hardly had a circle around him, all having crowded round Lord Wellington. In short, for some time a complete stop was put to the dancing, such was their anxiety to see him. He was dressed in a British Field Marshal's uniform with the Orders of the Golden Fleece, Garter, Great Cross of Maria Teresa, Tower and Sword, Swedish Order of the Sword and another star which I could not quite distinguish.
>
> A splendid supper was served at one o'clock, after which the dancing recommenced with great spirit.

The newspaper lists eminent personages who were present, but the Earl of Beverley does not feature. Among the less visible was George, Lord Lovaine,[3] Henry's brother, who managed to wear evening dress despite the robbery in

London. He was invited as a friend, having been a volunteer in Portugal with Sir Charles, the generous host.

The Earl of Beverley and two of his sons[4] lunched at Malmaison with the distraught Empress Josephine who had been left behind, abandoned by Napoleon when he headed for Elba in April, after the capitulation of Paris. She had been appointed Duchess of Evreux. She told them that the English were the only people generous enough to speak respectfully of the fallen Napoleon. It seems that, unlike her husband in his heyday, she wisely did not read the *Morning Post*, which, on the same page as its expressions of delight at the Duke's presence in Paris, reported on Napoleon's journey to Elba the previous week:

> Bonaparte, after leaving Lyons, found the people every stage more and more discontented with him: at one place they attacked the carriage, tore off the eagles, and made him cry 'Vive le Roi! Vivent les Bourbons!' He then got frightened, stopped a day, and sent his carriages on with a servant, who was mistaken for him and cruelly beaten in consequence. He was put by his conductors into an Austrian uniform, but was recognized and pelted by the mob. At last, in order to escape, he was put into the dress of the postilion, and by means of the jack-boots and white cockade, got on board an English frigate at Fréjus,[5] when he said that for the first time for many years he felt himself perfectly safe. He has repeatedly solicited leave to go and live in England, but they say he will not be permitted to do so.

Among the crush of grandees who suddenly arrived in Paris at this time, General Lord Cathcart was accommodated by the widow Duchess of Abrantes. Junot himself had died (of unsound mind, it is suggested) on 29 July 1813 after recall from an erratic time as governor of the Illyrian provinces.[6]

After all the celebrations and activity in Paris Wellington returned to the army at Toulouse, where, having set the handover in train, he went urgently to Madrid. His purpose was to consolidate the Spanish regime, since the released King Ferdinand VII was taking a controversial absolutist line likely to reignite the civil war. Having done his best, Wellington returned, delayed by broken carriage wheels at Vitoria, to Paris and thence to London.

Henry, back in London, was still a serving officer, much behind in promotion, but unable to visit his regiment which was still in France. By the time they arrived at Hounslow in mid-October, he was in Paris, a major on the Duke's staff.

In June 1814 Henry opened a bank account at Hoare's Bank in London. His (closed) account is still at the bank in Fleet Street. He received a monthly allowance of £50[7] from his father, but his army salary[8] does not appear in the account. His outgoings show little of interest till September, when there is frequent mention of money being transferred to Perregaux bankers, Paris. Furthermore, his parson brother Hugh instructed the bank that Henry should be permitted to draw up to £40[9] on his account at Paris.

During the summer the season in London was lively, notwithstanding the Corn Laws and festering political difficulties with radicals; there was peace, in Europe anyway. On midsummer's day, 22 June, the first cricket match was played at Mr Lord's ground, followed on Thursday, 23 June, by a naval review at Spithead, with fifteen ships of the line and thirty-one frigates taking part. The review was attended by most of the crowned heads of Europe. The war, however, continued in America.

By the end of June all the French prisoners had been repatriated from Norman Cross[10] in Huntingdonshire, a purpose-built depot which had held the largest number of enemy prisoners in England.

Arrangements gradually took shape for Henry to join Wellington's 'family' in Paris. Henry probably met Alexander Gordon on leave in London, which may explain how he came to be appointed extra ADC to Wellington. At long last, Henry was promoted brevet major on 12 July. His surviving regimental contemporaries had mostly overtaken him while he was a prisoner. That Friday, 15 July, Algernon, 'on return from abroad' (no mention of being a *détenu*), attended the Queen's Drawing Room in the state apartments at St James's Palace, a colourful and lavish affair. Such events were conducted with much formality and hand-kissing. They were fully reported in the press.

Next it was Henry's turn, and on Friday, 29 July, Major Henry Percy attended the Prince Regent's Levée at Carlton House in full uniform of the 14th Light Dragoons, 'on his return from France and promotion to major'. Also present was his late brother Francis's brigadier, Colonel John Milley Doyle, who was knighted, as also was the deserving Dr James McGrigor, Wellington's chief medical officer.

Preparations went on during the season for Wellington to become ambassador in Paris. Henry had new ADC's uniforms built (as the saying went), but his tailor could not obtain the proper gilt buttons with the royal cipher for a scarlet uniform coatee which he later wore at Waterloo. It survives at Alnwick, with plain gilt buttons. He needed to be equipped as an ADC, but with no serious prospect of fighting, his expenses were not as high as some ADCs going on operations, who bought mules, camp gear and the like. Nonetheless, it was paid for by the officer, not by the Treasury. An ADC's cocked hat, for example, cost about 4 guineas (about £260 today). So perhaps, if it was serviceable, he used his old one from his days with Moore, with a new plume. A sword (the French had taken Henry's in Portugal) was about £8, and he had other responsibilities to provide for, such as horses and servants. We know, however, that Henry had two horses, one of which he sold in Paris during the Hundred Days to an old Talavera adversary, General Sebastiani; it was an unwise transaction.

The family for the Duke in Paris was small and hard-working. The Military Secretary was Lord FitzRoy Somerset,[11] who had been in his family throughout most of the Peninsular War, and carried the Talavera dispatch to London in 1809. He had been Military Secretary from May 1810. His experience, intelligence and reliability were remarkable for a man aged almost 26. More remarkable was his appointment as Minister Plenipotentiary to France, when Wellington left for the Congress of Vienna in January 1815, an appointment which he discharged with notable distinction.

Brevet Lieutenant Colonel Ulysses Burgh was a Gordon Highlander who had served in the Peninsula from January 1809, and was present at every one of Wellington's battles, miraculously being wounded only twice, slightly at Talavera and Toulouse. He received frequent awards and was mentioned in dispatches four times. To Gordon's irritation, Burgh had been chosen to take the Busaco dispatch to London. He was knighted, KCB, and later became Lord Downes.

Brevet Lieutenant Colonel John Fremantle was a Coldstreamer, who had also served in the Peninsula since January 1809. Like Ulysses Burgh, he had been ADC to General Cradock. He had served in Hanover in 1806 and in South America in 1807. At Talavera he fought with the Coldstream close to Henry Percy's position in the line. He took the Vitoria dispatch to England, together with the colour of the French 100th Regiment and Marshal Jourdan's baton, which inspired the Prince Regent to design a British field marshal's baton for Wellington. He also carried the Orthez dispatch, and was annoyed to be technically too junior to be promoted or awarded a gold medal or CB at the time.

Brevet Major Henry Percy joined this experienced team as Extra ADC. He was well qualified, being a fluent French speaker, with infantry and cavalry active service under his belt and ADC experience with Sir John Moore. Being an Extra ADC meant that the holder was not entitled to ADC pay.

Mr Lionel Hervey was a young civilian, the younger brother of Colonel Felton Hervey of the 14th Light Dragoons, who had lost his arm at Oporto, but had continued to serve with distinction.

On 17 August John Fremantle, en route to Paris, went first to Ramsgate and then set off from Dover for Calais with Lionel and Dr John Hume, former surgeon of the 79th, who had served with them till he joined Wellington's headquarters as Deputy Inspector of Hospitals in 1811. Arrangements had been made by Lionel for two equipages (carriages) to be available at Calais. Henry did not travel with them, although Fremantle may have been expecting him. By Sunday, 21 August Fremantle and Henry were both in

Paris, complete with baggage and horses, on which, through an administrative oversight, duty had to be paid.

The first major event took place on 25 August when Wellington, with a heavy cold, presented his credentials as British Ambassador to King Louis XVIII. Fremantle describes Henry's and his part in it:

> We were at court all day yesterday. We went in the King's carriages; Percy and I had one to ourselves drawn by eight horses with running footmen. We bowed condescendingly to all the people who pulled off their hats, excepting an old bitch who put out her tongue at us, and I did the same.[12]

To put life in Paris into context, on this day the British Army entered Washington. Major General Ross's account in his dispatch,[13] carried by Captain Smith, his Assistant Adjutant General, is shocking in its way:

> I reached the city at eight o'clock that night. Judging it of consequence to complete the destruction of the public buildings with the least possible delay, so that the army might retire without loss of time, the following buildings were set fire to, and consumed, – the Capitol, including the Senate House, and House of Representation, the arsenal, the dock-yard, the treasury, war office, President's palace, rope walk, and the great bridge across the Potowmack: in the dock-yard a frigate nearly ready to be launched, and a sloop of war were consumed ... The object of the expedition being accomplished I determined, before any greater force of the enemy could be assembled, to withdraw the troops, and accordingly commenced retiring on the night of the 25th.

This unpleasant war was achieving nothing for either side. Behind the scenes talks were going on to end the war with America, and the Treaty of Ghent, ending the war, was signed on Christmas Eve.

Life in Paris was hectic and expensive, but it did not stop Fremantle from attending Berthier's grand dinner for the Duke, and sitting next to Marshal Ney. During this period Wellington bought the splendid Borghese Palace from Napoleon's financially embarrassed sister Pauline, to be the British embassy, which it remains. A difficulty for Wellington was the French Government's refusal to tackle the unpopular abolition of the slave trade. There was a conflict of opinion between England and France, and despite strenuous efforts little was achieved. It was the one advantage of Napoleon's return; a dictator can achieve such things, and he abolished the slave trade on 29 March 1815.

In September the office was busy. FitzRoy had not arrived and Ulysses Burgh was in charge of the team. Fremantle was in charge of passports, while Percy and young Lionel were what they described as the scouts. By the end of

September the pressure was endless: requests and applications, passports and invitations needing attention, with no clerk established for the embassy. At the beginning of October, after the Duchess had arrived in Paris, Henry suddenly became dangerously ill. His ailment was unspecified, but sounds like malaria to judge from later correspondence which says he had severe recurring rheumatic headaches. Fremantle was concerned for the office and for Henry's welfare. By mid-October Henry had improved, but it was some time before he was fit for work. This is the first mention of the debilitating malady which afflicted Henry for the rest of his life.

The family managed to hunt near Paris with the royal hunt, which was described as the greatest burlesque, but the office remained oppressively busy. The staff claimed that Parisian social life in the evening was boring and expensive. The political climate was uncertain, and there was a sudden government reshuffle in early December after a rumoured conspiracy to kill the king on his way to the theatre. The new Minister for War was Marshal Soult, former adversary of both Moore and Wellington. The streets were thronged with troops after the scare over the king. Threats were beginning to be felt against Wellington, it being believed by the mob that his victories were responsible for placing Louis, ironically nicknamed 'Le Desiré', on the throne. Castlereagh wished to remove Wellington from very real danger in Paris. It had been planned that Wellington's two sons would go to Paris for the Christmas holidays. The government, fearing for Wellington's safety despite his reluctance to give in to threats, solved the difficulty by sending him after Christmas to Vienna as Great Britain's representative at the congress to redraw the map of Europe. His prestige was invaluable. Wellington did not speak German but took John Fremantle as ADC and interpreter.

Wellington's departure left an ambassadorial vacancy in Paris. Who should be appointed in his place? The surprise choice was Lord FitzRoy Somerset, who at the age of 26 was appointed Minister Plenipotentiary to the French Government, as arranged by Wellington with Castlereagh. In the event it proved an inspired decision for what was a very testing time. Things began badly when FitzRoy discovered that Wellington had taken away the keys of his precious 'office box' containing the Prince Regent's authority for him to hold office. It had to be broken open. On 7 February he presented his credentials to Louis XVIII.

There were plenty of delicate matters for the new minister to manage diplomatically, such as dealing with the protocol of the estranged Princess of Wales's visit to Paris, and the disposal of British deserters demobilized from the French Army. His chief duty was keeping the home government aware of developments affecting security. At the end of January Lord FitzRoy reported that the ceremony of reburial of the murdered Louis XVI and Queen Marie Antoinette in an elaborate state ceremony was ill-attended by the lower classes, and there was no 'very lively interest in the royal family'. There was no doubt that the Bourbon restoration was unpopular throughout northern France. There was, as he reported, anxiety about Napoleonic political manoeuvring. Such fears were well grounded, for on 7 March the news reached Vienna that Napoleon had escaped from Elba on 26 February.

Prince Metternich at Vienna immediately recognized that Napoleon would head for Paris, so negotiations began at once for an allied army to assemble in the Netherlands under Wellington's command. The reaction of France was of key importance. The telegraph system was 'down' in thick weather to start with. Lord FitzRoy kept in touch with Wellington in Vienna and of course with London. He told Wellington that he believed Napoleon would succeed in reaching Paris. The French telegraph system remained serviceable after the departure of Napoleon to Elba, while the British, with undue haste, econo-mized and dismantled key telegraph installations in 1814. This false economy later had a direct bearing on Henry Percy, preventing the news of Waterloo reaching London more quickly.

It was made clear from London that the Embassy in Paris was accredited to the King, and not to any usurper French Government. Wellington, con-cerned at the situation, independently sent Lieutenant Colonel Sir Henry Harding[14] to France to report on Napoleon's movements to Vienna, via His Majesty's Minister at Paris. Harding was able to report Ney's defection, which was initially disbelieved.

The Embassy, in common with other diplomatic missions, took the pre-caution of requesting their passports, since the king would probably flee rather than face up to Napoleon. Only six days after Lord FitzRoy had warned Wellington of Napoleon's likelihood of success, his prophecy was fulfilled. Napoleon entered Paris on 20 March. Requesting the post horses for departure, since the king had by now left, it was discovered that Napole-onic instructions had immediately caused bureaucratic obstruction.[15] Lady FitzRoy, heavily pregnant, was still in Paris; this was a cause of anxiety to Castlereagh, but not apparently to the busy Minister, who explained that she would not leave him.

After several frustrated attempts, new passports were produced, contro-versially, by the new regime. The diplomats were able to leave on 25 March. Originally the intention had been to go to Dieppe, but they reached Calais at midday on 28 March. Henry, like all the diplomatic corps, left Paris six days after Napoleon's arrival. He travelled with Lionel Hervey, and his notebook, now at Alnwick, tells us his itinerary:

- (Sunday) 26 March (1815) left Paris
- (Monday) 27 March left Beauvais

- (Tuesday) 28 March arrive Calais. (Lord and Lady FitzRoy arrived the same day).

A newspaper report states that the Earl of Beverley arrived in town [London] from Paris that Tuesday. He crossed from Calais. So it seems certain that Henry saw him either at Calais or even in Paris before he left. The significance is that Beverley would have been in London when Henry reached there with the dispatches after Waterloo. He certainly could not have returned to Moulins while Napoleon's army rampaged round before Waterloo.

- (Wednesday) 29 March. No comment
- (Thursday) 30 March. Arrived Ostende. King left Ostende in the morning. Arrived at Bruges, Hotel de la Commerce.
- (Friday) 31 March. Quitted Bruges, and arrived Gand (Ghent).
- (Saturday) 1 April. Sir Charles Stewart arrived, also Sir Henry Harding. Mails arrived (from England). Wrote to MD (Marion Durand).

On arrival at Ghent Lord FitzRoy found, probably to his great relief, that he was to be succeeded as Ambassador by Sir Charles Stewart, an experienced former ambassador, whom he knew well. He therefore resumed his appointment as Military Secretary to Wellington. Before doing so, as part of his final report FitzRoy was kind enough to tell Lord Castlereagh of the good work done by Percy.

Henry's notebook says he wrote to MD, who of course is Marion Durand, the mother of his two-year-old son, Henry Marion. We do not know whether she had been in Paris before Napoleon's arrival, but it is reasonable to assume that she would have made her way back to Moulins during the Hundred Days. She certainly went to Paris after Waterloo, with little Henry Marion.

Henry stayed at Ghent for a day or two, in anticipation of the Duke's plans becoming known, and making arrangements about a horse to replace the mare he had sold to Sebastiani.[16] Wellington arrived at Brussels on 6 April. The next day Henry got there, and notes that the Duke went to Ghent for a night with 'Mr Pole' (his elder brother,[17] originally Wellesley, later Wellesley-Pole). He and the Earl of Harrowby (Lord President of the Council) were at Brussels for discussions with Wellington about the allies and the coming campaign. Henry may not have seen much of Harrowby in Brussels, but he was to meet him again, and fall asleep in his dining room at 44 Grosvenor Square, on one epic night in June.

There was a certain amount of complicated administration to deal with in the early days at Brussels. When Wellington had gone to Vienna, some of his possessions had been left in Paris (now occupied by Napoleon). These now had to be recovered, a difficult matter which was successfully achieved through contacts in Paris. There were also questions about horses and baggage, and it seems that Lionel Hervey had made something of a fumble of the administration before the move from Paris. When Mr Pole returned with the Duke, the ADCs were busy because a courier[18] was sent to London.

By now the immediate staff was gathering in Brussels. Lord FitzRoy was back as Military Secretary. On 10 April Percy was formally appointed Extra ADC, which appeared in orders the following day. Ulysses Burgh, senior to Fremantle, had rejoined, and Percy was the junior of the trio. Fremantle calculated he would be paid an additional 9s 6d aide-de-camp pay, although he was told by FitzRoy that he had objected to it in favour of Percy, who in the Duke's first arrangement was not to have any pay. FitzRoy had suggested to the Duke that there should be three assistants, which gave an allowance to Percy. FitzRoy was perceived by Fremantle (who denied any jealousy) as being very attentive to Percy, which is hardly surprising since Henry was originally senior to FitzRoy, but had been a prisoner.

There was much work to do at Brussels. Wellington had a difficult task to combine his diverse army into a coherent force, using his old technique of mixing the formations in each corps so as to ensure that the experienced regiments would be near the young or less reliable allied units. He depended on his British and his King's German Legion infantry, around whose regiments he built his formations. He also had the delicate task of ensuring that understanding and liaison was fully implemented between the allies, many of whose soldiers had previously fought for the French.

Wellington visited Blücher at Tirlemont on 3 June, attended by Percy, and then travelled to Ghent to see King Louis and Sir Charles Stewart, now the ambassador. He reviewed the detachments of troops as they assembled, combining military business with an appearance of normality and a hectic social life. He held two balls in June, exciting acid comments on the character of some of the female guests. Brussels was a fashionable place to visit, the cost of living being less than in England. For this reason the Duke and Duchess of Richmond and their family were in Brussels, the Duke's generous spending as Lord Lieutenant of Ireland having left him financially strained. The Duchess of Richmond proposed a ball to commemorate Wellington's victory at Vitoria, to be held on 15 June. Then rumours started to circulate that Napoleon was approaching. The duchess wondered if the dance should go ahead. Wellington said yes, even though he knew that the rumour was partly true. Many on the guest list had served under Napoleon, and 'there was much intrigue'. The recently repatriated Duke of Arenberg (the 'great card'), with his two sons, was present.

All the Duke's ADCs attended, as did Lionel Hervey and his brother Felton, but FitzRoy Somerset stayed in his lodgings with Emily and the baby. The romantic story of the ball is well known. The Prince of Orange's ADC, Captain Henry Webster, delivered a dispatch to Wellington from General Constant

Rebeque at Braine-le-Comte, saying that the French were at Quatre Bras and that a division was heading there to try to hold the village. Quatre Bras was key to the vital road linking Wellington's army with Blücher at Ligny. Napoleon would try to divide the allies. His aim would be to engage one half, and assault the other, destroying one at a time. After looking at the map, and apocryphal remarks about humbugging had perhaps been said, orders were quietly given, and the uniformed figures disappeared quickly into the night to deploy southwards in the rain. As he left the ball, Henry's unknown partner gave him a keepsake, her crimson velvet lady's sachet. It remained in his evening uniform pocket till he reached London after Waterloo. Henry quickly bade her farewell, and hurried off to war.

Chapter 14

Waterloo, London, France (1815–1818)

To move the army from Brussels at short notice in the middle of a wet night was complicated. Divisional commanders were alerted at the ball, the brigades mustered their regiments, and marched off when ready, to an assembly area. Thence the army headed south as quickly as possible for Quatre Bras.

The Duke's family at Waterloo was larger than normal. We know of Lieutenant Colonels Gordon[1] and Fremantle, and Major Percy. The others in the team were:

- Lieutenant Colonel Charles Fox Canning, 3rd Foot Guards. He was ADC to Wellington from May 1809 before Talavera throughout the Peninsular War, being involved in all fifteen major engagements, including Toulouse. He had four gold medals for engagements in southern France. He only rejoined the family just before Waterloo, at his father's request. He was killed at Waterloo.
- Lieutenant Lord George Lennox, 9th Light Dragoons, second son of the Duke of Richmond. He served in the Peninsula from September 1812 to April 1814, seeing much operational action in the 9th, and then as ADC to Wellington from Freneda in April 1813 all the way to Toulouse, via Vitoria and the battles in the Pyrenees and southern France. He was a very experienced ADC.
- Captain Lord Arthur Hill, on half-pay. He had served from 1809 in the 10th and later the 24th Light Dragoons, but was in the Peninsula only from February to September 1813. He, too, had served at Vitoria.
- Lieutenant Hon. George Cathcart, 6th Dragoon Guards. Commissioned in the Life Guards in 1810, he had served in America and Flanders. He had been at Vienna at the Congress, and knew Wellington from there.[2]
- The Hereditary Prince of Nassau-Usingen. He was the son of the Duke of Nassau, who sent a contingent of troops to fight at Waterloo. Wellington considered him a brave young man in the battle.

So now to the deployment. Henry found his horse, and moved in the rain to Quatre Bras, where the French were, indeed, pressing heavily. It was a very anxious battle in which Ney, with his customary panache and gallantry, nearly overran the allies. The British really arrived too late, and they did not all arrive at once, and it was largely thanks to the staunchness of the Saxe-Weimar troops and the Dutch that Quatre Bras was not lost before the British arrived. Even then, the battle ebbed and flowed critically. During the continual close-quarter fighting, cavalry charges, and heavy artillery cannonades with smoke obscuring the view in the confused battle, Henry's horse was killed. He must have fallen, extricated himself and taken another horse from a cavalryman, as was the system, so that the Duke's orders could be delivered. He seems to have been unhurt, if shaken.

Had Quatre Bras not been eclipsed by Waterloo it would stand out as one of the most sanguinary and dramatic of Wellington's battles, on a par, perhaps, with Talavera, even though the duration was much shorter. The life of an ADC in a set-piece battle was not for lightweight fashionable aristocrats; it was a very high-risk, responsible role. At Quatre Bras, in addition to Henry's horse being killed, John Fremantle's was also killed and one-armed Felton Hervey's was wounded for the first of three times.[3]

By the end of 16 June Quatre Bras had been held. Owing to confusion on the French side, it was possible next morning to withdraw in order to take up a position at Mont St Jean, since Blücher's Prussians had been forced to retire after a ferocious battle at Ligny, and Wellington needed to conform. Early the next morning, 17 June, the senior ADC, Gordon, was sent with an escort of a complete squadron of 10th Hussars to communicate to the Prussian headquarters that Wellington was retiring to the Waterloo position. Napoleon's plan to engage one element and destroy the other had not worked, but he thought the Prussian withdrawal was a retreat to Prussia, and that he would therefore only have Wellington to defeat on Sunday, 18 June.

The intensity of the fighting and the slaughter at Waterloo have been compared with the mechanized killing on the first day of the Battle of the Somme 101 years later. At Waterloo, edged weapons made the wounds horrifying and the limited medical facilities lacked anaesthetic or knowledge of sepsis. The pain and suffering at each battle was indescribable. The immense personal sacrifice and bravery displayed at Waterloo – the extraordinary cohesion and gallantry shown by the soldiers to stand firm in a square being bombarded by round shot, then charged by cavalry – is difficult to understand.

The hard pounding of Waterloo almost ended in defeat; 'a near run thing', saved by the timely arrival of the Prussians and the stalwart defence of the key features of Hougoumont and La Haye Sainte and the extraordinary infantry on the slopes of Mont St Jean who turned the tide. The often-described details of this hideous battle, which dragged on till late evening, need not concern us. Lord Uxbridge, the cavalry commander, had been wounded while sitting beside Wellington, and lost his leg: 'By God, sir, so you have!' FitzRoy Somerset was hit while leaning over to show Wellington a scrap of paper;

so close. He lost his arm. Gordon was wounded in the leg and taken back to the Headquarters inn at Waterloo. Canning was killed. Wellington, to the amazement of his personal staff, survived physically unscathed, but mentally distraught, having been in the thick of the fighting all day.

Henry left no account of the battle, but we do know it was Henry who was sent by the Duke to deliver the message to Colborne to attack the Imperial Guard from the flank while the Foot Guards pushed them back from the front. In fact, as is well known, Colborne had already used his initiative and was moving to attack the flank, in the decisive move of the battle, when Henry arrived.[4]

In February 1865 a French lady called Clemence wrote to Henry's brother George, shortly after he succeeded as 5th Duke of Northumberland, and reminisced about Henry. She had asked him if he had killed many men at Waterloo. Henry replied:

> Me? I don't know; in the battle, we never know where the bullets go, but after the fight, I found myself face to face with a French officer. As I was stronger than he was in the wrist, I made his sabre jump, then I pushed the tip of mine into his chest, but when I felt it going in, a shiver passed through my elbow and into my heart. I withdrew my sabre and I hope that I didn't kill him. I watched him for a long time, he did not fall from his horse. I hope that I didn't kill him.[5]

With the battle over, and the French in headlong flight from the unforgiving Prussians, Wellington and Blücher met at La Belle Alliance, as portrayed by Daniel Maclise[6] in 1861, some 36 years after Henry's death. Each commander was accompanied by some of his staff, among whom Henry was Wellington's only ADC. The following November Wellington took Henry from Paris to visit Waterloo. At La Belle Alliance Henry painted a small amateur watercolour sketch. It lacks the romance and glory of Maclise's gigantic version, and the inn looks like a run-down country cottage of no significance.

According to Henry's daughter-in-law, Mrs Bagot, on the evening of the battle Henry was moving round the battlefield and saw a cloak on a mound of earth. Stopping to take a closer look, he realized it had been the Emperor's, with groups of Imperial bees forming the clasp. The cloak was too heavy to take, so Henry removed the clasp, which he gave to his brother Josceline,[7] in whose family it remains. However, the inscription in the case declares that the bees from Napoleon's cloak, in possession of Major Henry Percy, were found in Napoleon's carriage at Genappe.[8]

The battlefield was a nightmare of carnage and horror, with wounded and dead lying in piles so close together as to make movement difficult. Wellington, Henry and some of the staff went slowly back to the Headquarters inn at Waterloo. Dr Hume was there, doing what he could for Alexander Gordon, lying grievously wounded on Wellington's bed. Wellington's charger, Copenhagen, which he had ridden for the whole day, kicked out at him as he dismounted. Wellington's cook, James Thornton, had supper ready, and they waited for the little family to gather. It was distressing how few arrived. Everyone was dead-beat, some still wearing their dancing clothes, first drenched by rain, then spattered with mud and blood. Wellington was too tired to write, so after supper he agreed that a single report of the battle could be given to King Louis at Ghent, written by the Corsican opponent of Napoleon, Carlo Andrea Pozzo di Borgo, who was the Czar's representative in Belgium.[9] Worn out, Wellington soon lay down on a pallet to sleep without even washing. At a very early hour the next morning, 19 June, he was woken by Dr Hume, who quietly told him of Gordon's death and gave him news of other casualties. Wellington was much affected, and wept. He exclaimed to Hume, 'Well, thank God, I don't know what it is to lose a battle, but certainly nothing can be more painful than to gain one with the loss of so many of one's friends.'

Wellington could not sleep. Instead, physically drained and psychologically deeply affected by the horrors, he began to write his official report to the government, before dawn. During the early hours Wellington decided who would take the news to London. FitzRoy Somerset, badly wounded, was not there to help. Alexander Gordon had just died of wounds. John Fremantle, the senior survivor of the family, would be needed in Paris, and had done well at Vienna. Charles Canning was dead. George Lennox was too junior in rank. So it had to be Henry Percy, who had excelled in the battle and deserved the promotion which would result from delivering the dispatch.

After breakfast Wellington and Henry, still wearing his red evening uniform from the ball, rode to his quarters in Brussels. There, Wellington wrote the rest of his dispatch, which was copied by a clerk, possibly Serjeant McRae.[10] He also wrote briefly to his young friend Lady Frances Wedderburn-Webster. Still struggling with fatigue and emotion, he wrote to the Duke of Beaufort about FitzRoy's wounding. Next he wrote to Gordon's brother, Lord Aberdeen, expressing his 'extreme grief' at the death of his gallant brother, and asking what to do with his black horse, a present from Lord Ashburnham. Wellington's letters seldom communicate his feelings; these articulate intensely his acute sadness and care.

Henry carefully folded the dispatch into the purple velvet sachet and put it safely in his pocket. Then, taking several important letters, including one from Creevey, and the two captured eagles with 10ft poles (one broken) and gold-embroidered tricolour regimental colours, Henry set off by carriage for Ghent, 30 miles ahead, which he had visited before, to call on Louis XVIII on his way to London. He arrived three or four hours later, called briefly, if politely, on the delighted King, and continued to Ostend via Bruges. He may have collected a King's Messenger with dispatches from Sir Charles Stewart at Ghent. Henry probably had difficulty changing horses, say five times, during his journey. We know of Beverley's horses being requisitioned (in France) in April.

Unbeknown to Percy, a false French declaration had been circulated, supposedly from the royal palace at Laecken, north of Brussels, trumpeting Napoleon's glorious victory. Many disgruntled French-sympathizing Belgians were delighted.

In Ostend at about mid-day on Tuesday, 20 June Captain Benson Hill, a young British gunner officer recently arrived from America, was awaiting transport to Brussels. He was surprised by the Belgians' truculent mood, and discovered the Napoleonic proclamation. Shocked by this news, which implied that Brussels itself had fallen, he went to the Ostend Naval Headquarters to report to the admiral, Sir Pulteney Malcolm.[11]

Hill recorded:

We hardly had time to talk over the subject when a loud huzza was heard at some distance. Scarcely had we gained the window, ere a cabriolet drove up to the door, in which Major Percy was seated, displaying to the hundreds who had followed him the eagles of the 45th and 105th regiments, taken from the foe on the glorious plains of Waterloo. Admiral Malcolm's first inquiry was for the Duke. 'He is safe and well, and in full march on Paris,' shouted the gallant major. His countrymen, on learning that their noblest captain had escaped unhurt, rent the air with shouts, whilst the brave *Belges*, hearing that he was about to visit Paris, instead of taking his ships, sneaked off, uttering abundant *sacrés* and other emphatic epithets. Major Percy alighted, and in a few words related to the admiral the leading features of that fight, on which the destinies of Europe depended.[12]

HMS *Peruvian*, a 200-ton brig-sloop with eighteen guns, had arrived at Ostend that morning in 'fresh breezes'. The admiral authorized Percy to sail for Deal in her at once. Commander James Kearney White, the captain, took Henry on board with the unknown King's Messenger. They weighed anchor at 2pm on 20 June, with the breeze by now 'moderate'. The crossing to Kent is 75 miles. With a favourable wind, that could mean landing at midnight. From the coast to London was another 75 miles. So that might just mean London by midday. A fast vessel, even the speedy *Peruvian*, needed wind. They sailed slowly in light, then lighter winds, and Henry became increasingly anxious. And then the wind dropped completely, and every inch of sail was tried, 'out studding sails' says the log. They were becalmed, hoping and praying for wind, as they went below for a meal. The night passed restlessly, but almost silently, drifting. Just before 11am land – white cliffs – was sighted from the rigging. Even Commander White was getting worried now by the delay. He suggested taking the gig, with a crew of sailors to row to the shore. He picked four strong sailors. The log gives their midday position as 15 miles west of Ramsgate, and records: 'Out gig. Captain and the Hon. Major Percy left the ship with the dispatches.' According to legend, but, alas there is no evidence, Percy, an old-Etonian oarsman, and the captain himself each took an oar. The eagles and their standards lay in the stern. They rowed for all they were worth over the glassy sea, leaving *Peruvian* in the care of the first lieutenant.

At about 3pm they landed on Broadstairs[13] beach. There was an inn, and a 'post-chaise and four' (horses) was immediately engaged. Legend has it that Commander White accompanied Henry Percy to London, although documentary evidence of his involvement ceases when they cast off in the gig from *Peruvian*. The ship's log does not mention the gig's return, nor her captain. She went to Ramsgate and then to the Downs (anchorage), while an East India convoy came up the Channel.

The post-chaise with Henry (and possibly Commander White) hurriedly clattered off, through the cheering local crowd, at about 3.30pm, at best speed for London, the eagles and standards protruding from the windows as they were too long to fit inside. The first stop to change horses at Canterbury was a longer run than usual, almost 20 miles. They passed the cathedral, and made the change in one of the inns on the main road. The excitement must have been terrific. The crowds would have seen the standards, and followed the post chaise, cheering and waving.

Each time they stopped to change horses the reaction was the same. England had been awash with confusing, worrying, contradictory rumours for days. Now here was real news of victory, and these people were among the first to see evidence of it with their own eyes.

It had rained in London that afternoon, but it still felt sultry. The post-chaise covered the 15 easy miles to Sittingbourne and changed horses quickly at a well established coaching inn there (it might have been any of several). The only delay at each change came from the eager crowds wanting to hear the news. Twice more, at Rochester and Dartford, the horses were changed, taking only a few minutes each time. A receipt was needed as a tax was levied on post-horses. (As Henry was approaching London, Napoleon, exhausted too, was approaching Paris, still vainly imagining he might resist the allies.)

About 11pm the yellow post-chaise crossed the old Westminster Bridge; there, on the right, was the Duke of Richmond's house where old Scotland Yard now stands. To the left was Westminster Hall and the old palace of Westminster, a jumble of medieval buildings. By now the crowds were beginning to notice the standards protruding from the windows: they cheered.

The post-chaise entered Downing Street to find Earl Bathurst, the Secretary of State, to whom Henry must hand the dispatch. A crowd by this time followed the carriage. No answer. Luckily the Secretary to the Treasury, Charles Arbuthnot MP, had just returned from an evening in Parliament. Hearing the noise in the street, he went to investigate and saw the chaise and four, with eagles poking out of the windows, at the door of the Colonial Office. Arbuthnot knew that Lord Bathurst was dining with the rest of the cabinet at Lord Harrowby's in Grosvenor Square, 'upon which he stepped into the chaise and drove there with Percy'.[14] There is no mention by name of James White now or later, so it is possible that he never went to London, contrary to the legend. There is, however, one more possible, tantalizing, appearance of Commander White, in Grosvenor Square.

The moon was full, the night stuffy and the streets crowded. With much excitement and noise, the post-chaise reached Grosvenor Square. Harrowby's 14-year-old daughter, Mary Ryder, was woken by the cheering outside. In her night-dress she looked over the banisters, and saw an officer in a scarlet coatee (Henry), followed by two other men (Arbuthnot and White, perhaps), rush into the house asking for Lord Bathurst, crying out 'Victory! Victory! ... Bonaparte has been beaten!' She noticed how tired and dishevelled Major Percy looked. He went into the dining room, and a moment later she heard cheering. Then her father came out and stood outside the front door facing the crowd, drawn by the standards which were still in the post-chaise, and announced the news. So the first public announcement of the victory was made at 44 Grosvenor Square.[15]

Henry, worn out after his epic journey, waited in the dining room. He answered a few questions, and then sat down. He must have dozed, but woke to hear Lord Harrowby proposing a toast[16] with Lord Liverpool, the Prime Minister,[17] to the victory and the bearer of the good news.

Henry's next duty was to hand the dispatch and the eagles to the Prince Regent. Members of the cabinet followed as they set off for St James's, followed by an excited, noisy crowd. The procession headed to Piccadilly and down St James's Street, passing gentlemen's clubs where distorted defeatist news (arising from the retreat after Quatre Bras) was being discussed. The noise again drew people to the windows, and the post-chaise and eagles could be seen passing with the unmistakable signs of victory.

The carriages turned into Pall Mall and left into St James's Square, heading for Mrs Boehm's fine house in the corner, Number 16. Here, at the zenith of her social success, Dorothy and her husband Edmund Boehm were entertaining the Prince Regent and the cream of society to dinner and an extravagant midsummer ball. This was to be her greatest moment of social glory: midsummer's night. Mrs Edmund Boehm's guests included the Prince Regent and his brother, the Commander-in-Chief, the Duke of York, the Foreign

Secretary, Lord Castlereagh, and enough celebrities to dazzle the most ardent socialite hostess. The sash windows upstairs were wide open towards the square, facing Mr Davison's[18] house, number 11, a few doors along to the left.

Dinner was over and the ball was beginning on the first floor with the guests forming for the first quadrille. The orchestra was ready. The popular melody of the day, '*The Downfall of Paris*', adapted from the French revolutionary song 'Ça Ira', was undoubtedly on the music stands for that evening. But it was not played, for suddenly through the windows came sounds of shouting. Not another Corn Laws protest at that hour, surely? People forgot the dance and rushed to the windows. A post-chaise and four came into view below from the right, pursued by the mob, with French standards sticking out of its windows. It drew up and a figure in scarlet uniform emerged, taking the standards up the steps below. All went to the landing and saw the tired 'dusty' Henry Percy hurrying upstairs into the ballroom; stepping quickly up to the Regent, he dropped onto one knee, laid the flags at his feet and pronounced the words 'Victory, Victory, Sire,' as he handed over the dispatch from its purple sachet.

The Regent, having promoted Henry to lieutenant colonel, retired to a smaller room with Lord Liverpool, the Prime Minister, who read the dispatch aloud, including the long list of casualties. Nobody felt like dancing while this was happening. All waited anxiously. Poor Dorothy Boehm; what an interruption – could 'they' not have waited? When Liverpool had finished reading, the Prince appeared, much affected, he said, by the loss of so many friends. He said a few sad words to the Boehms, sent for his carriage, and left.

The party broke up in about 20 minutes, leaving Mr and Mrs Boehm and the servants disconsolately looking at the debris of an unfinished extravaganza. Outside, the guests mingled with the crowds for a little, and 'God Save the King' was sung at full chorus. The flags were displayed in front of the Boehms' house. Lord Bathurst, his office manned in anticipation, sent bulletins to the press and to the Lord Mayor. Then arrangements were made for the *London Gazette* to publish the dispatch in a *Gazette Extraordinary* as early as possible.

Henry, his duties at last complete, and appointments made for the next morning, went home to Portman Square, with appointments made for the next morning. His father was there, but not, of course, expecting him. The house was besieged by an anxious throng. Henry gave them the news briefly, and went inside, and soon to bed.[19]

Realizing that he had inadvertently wrecked Mrs Boehm's party, the Prince Regent had a gilded replica of a French eagle made as a present for her, suitably inscribed, stating that it was presented by the Prince Regent to commemorate the arrival of the news brought by Major Henry Percy of the

Victory by the Duke of Wellington at Waterloo. Mrs Boehm remained inconsolable, and often referred to those 'horrid French eagles'.

Next morning the press was full of the victory, expressing satisfaction with patriotic and euphoric superlatives. The Tower guns fired a *feu de joie*, and Henry Percy attended the Duke of York, Commander in Chief, at 9.30am in St James's Park at a great display by all the regiments in London. The Life Guards, the Foot Guards and the Oxford Blues formed a line from Carlton House to Birdcage Walk. A double salute from the guns at 10am preceded three hearty cheers, the cavalry flourishing their swords, and the infantry waving their caps with sprigs of oak. Grand manoeuvres followed, the bands playing stirring tunes all the while. The parade ended with another artillery and musket salute, after which the Duke of York, with Lieutenant Colonel Percy, properly dressed, standing beside him, read passages from the dispatch. The troops then returned to barracks.

Henry had two more duties to perform. First he had to visit 19-year-old Princess Charlotte of Wales, to tell her formally of the death in action of her mother's father, the Duke of Brunswick. This was delicate, since Princess Charlotte's mother was estranged from the Prince of Wales, and she had recently, at the age of 17, turned down an arranged marriage to the Prince of Orange, which her father tried to force upon her.

Next Henry had to call upon Lord Castlereagh at Loring Hall, Bexley, to collect dispatches to take to Wellington. He was as a consequence in London for the evening of the illuminations, when all public buildings were decorated even more lavishly and patriotically than after the victory at Vitoria.

On Sunday (only one hectic week after Waterloo) Henry, accompanied by his brother Charles, now aged 21, left for Brussels, arriving at Ostend early on Monday after a rough passage. There were no delays this time; they stopped for dinner at Brussels, before continuing towards Paris to find Wellington.

Henry Percy's health had not been good in Paris before Waterloo, but he had recovered sufficiently to demonstrate enormous physical stamina from the few days before Waterloo till his return from London to join Wellington. The story that a Waterloo musket ball was found in his shoe at Portman Square seems doubtful. We are almost certain he was wounded in Portugal when he was captured in 1810. But Wellington, for all the fatigue of the battle, would surely never have entrusted the vital victory news to a wounded and unhealthy officer. The musket ball ring may indeed have existed, but it has disappeared, and the source of the musket ball story remains unsolved. Suffice it to say that Henry was not healthy, being subject to bouts of severe headaches, which recurred at shortening intervals.

In August 1815 Russian orders of chivalry were distributed for recommended officers, and Henry, in addition to his Companion of the Bath which was awarded on 22 June for his part at Waterloo, now received a Russian Order of St Anne, which he was permitted to wear.

The Duke's personal staff had responsible and unusual tasks during the occupation of France. Colonel Felton Hervey, for instance, by now Assistant Military Secretary (in the absence of FitzRoy Somerset), represented Wellington in the negotiations for the formal capitulation of Paris. John Fremantle became involved in preventing the Louvre being emptied of exhibits, which the Prussians tried to remove as reparations. It was one thing to reclaim the items looted by Napoleon's armies, but unauthorized reparations in kind from the Louvre were not permitted, so British soldiers guarded it.

In the late summer or autumn of 1815 Marion Durand visited Paris with the 3-year-old Henry Marion. Wellington, as Ambassador, was based in the Hotel de Charost, which had been bought the previous year as the embassy. Henry took the little boy to see the Duke there. While running into the great man's room he tripped and fell, cutting his forehead to the bone against a projecting corner of the chimney piece. He was treated with much kindness and the visit remained fresh in his memory for the rest of his life.

For some of the time the staff were at Cambrai, at the British military headquarters. We learn that Henry took to his bed for several weeks in the winter of 1815/16. Health was a problem for the staff, Wellington being susceptible to severe colds, and Hervey and Percy, too, were often unwell. In May 1816 Henry went to visit his father at Moulins, and to see Marion and his son. Marion may by now have had her second son with Henry, James. We do not know when he was born, but when Henry left France and returned to England in 1818, Marion did not go with him, nor did she ever visit England as far as is known. Henry and Marion never married, and her fate is unknown. The boys, who used their mother's surname, Durand, were happily fostered in London by Mr John Deans, Beverley's faithful confidential servant, and his very kind wife, and their father maintained a keen interest in them. He also regularly remitted money to France for Marion.

Henry was unfit, but returned to his regiment at Hounslow in 1820. This was unsatisfactory, since his promotions had each been brevet promotions, dependent on his remaining on the staff. So he had to revert to his substantive rank, which is shown in the Army List as captain, local lieutenant colonel (meaning that his majority and lieutenant colonelcy were both brevet ranks). His health was still causing problems, and on riding for two days to Brighton in early August he was seized with a pain severe enough for him to be asked by Headquarters to send a surgeon's report. This has recently come to light.[20] It was written by Surgeon Denis O'Flaherty of the 14th Light Dragoons, who sent a detailed report at Henry's request. The symptoms described by O'Flaherty have been examined by Mr Michael Crumplin, an expert in Napoleonic era medicine and surgery, who is also a surgeon and a trustee of the Waterloo Association. Reading the symptoms, he believes the recurring illness could have been benign (i.e. not cancerous) tertian malaria, perhaps picked up in Egypt. Headaches are often manifestations of fever, as are a furred tongue and malaise. Discomfort in the left side and fullness in the left hypochondrium would indicate enlargement of the spleen.

As his father had foreseen, Henry retired from the army on the grounds of ill-health in 1821. He became an inactive Member of Parliament for the family constituency of Bere Alston in Devon from 1820 till his death, aged 39, on 15 April 1825.

Epilogue

Henry Percy's life leaves various unfinished sub-plots. So let us tidy the loose ends. We saw how Henry, while on parole, lived comfortably in France, and served again at Waterloo. Then came his moment in the spotlight, delivering the dispatch to the Prince Regent.

So what about Charles Lefèbvre-Desnouettes? He escaped from Cheltenham, wrote his 'insolent' letter to the Home Secretary, and joined Napoleon's campaign in Russia. He was slightly wounded on 29 January 1814, at Brienne, fighting against Blücher. During the First Restoration he continued serving and was treated indulgently. However, upon learning of Napoleon's landing in France in March 1815, Lefèbvre-Desnouettes went to La Fère to seize the arsenal for Napoleon. When this plan failed, he travelled to Compiègne and tried to subvert his regiment to Napoleon. This was a fatal mistake.

During the Hundred Days Napoleon renewed Lefèbvre-Desnouettes' appointment as commander of the *chasseurs à cheval* of the Imperial Guard. He led his division into action at the battles of Quatre-Bras and Waterloo, where he was wounded and fought with the 'rage of desperation'. After Waterloo, Lefèbvre-Desnouettes was a wanted man. He fled to America, leaving Stéphanie in France. Tried by a Council of War at Paris in May 1816, *in absentia*, he, like Ney, was found 'contumacious' and condemned to death.

In 1817 French military émigrés[1] acquired land in Alabama and set up the Vine and Olive Colony in Marengo county. Disputes over land-holding caused at least two moves. Ten senior officers and about 200 other émigrés set up a centre and named it Demopolis. Unfortunately Demopolis was incorrectly sited and had to be abandoned. Lefèbvre-Desnouettes' property there included a log cabin, in the centre of which stood a bronze bust of Napoleon, surrounded by swords and pistols; the walls were draped with imperial flags. He wrote that he had 'a commodious house and a good life'. He hoped he would be joined by Stéphanie and their daughter Charlotte, who was born after he left France. But Stéphanie was unable to make the crossing. A new settlement named Aigleville ('Eagle Town', what else?) replaced Demopolis. Life was boring, and the agriculture unsuccessful. Lefèbvre-Desnouettes' papers in the University of North Carolina illustrate the loneliness and frustrations faced by the Emperor's exiles. Lefèbvre-Desnouettes pleaded with Louis XVIII for a pardon to enable him to return to his family in France.

In 1821 permission was granted. Longing to meet his 6-year-old daughter for the first time, he set off, travelling under the assumed name of Gravez. The packet ship *Albion*, Captain Williams, sailed on 1 April from New York for Liverpool. Before daylight on 22 April, in a fearsome storm, *Albion* was hurled against the rocks near Old Head, Kinsale, Ireland. Local people tried to help, but the ship was dashed to pieces and forty-four people, including Charles Lefèbvre-Desnouettes, aged 48, were drowned. It is said his nephew, a M. Chabut of Paris, was also on board. Of the twenty-three passengers and six steerage passengers all but one perished. A Mr Everhart survived and wrote in September 'when the ship was thrown on her beam ends a prodigious destruction took place below; the doors of the state rooms, the tables bound with iron, the furniture, were all destroyed, and thrown into heaps. Gen. Lefèbvre Desnouettes [*sic.*] had one of his arms broken.'[2]

This left Stéphanie a widow in Paris. In 1852 she erected a monument to her husband at Sainte-Adresse, near Le Havre. It is known as the *pain de sucre* (sugar loaf) memorial. Stéphanie died in 1880, aged 93, and was buried in the monument. Charlotte, who sadly never met her father, inherited the legacy of 100,000 francs left by Napoleon in 1821 to her father. A lady of the court, she married in 1836, becoming Madame Sancy de Parabère, after whom a charming old-fashioned pink rose is named.

*   *   *

Levi Grisdale and Johann Bergmann are two other unfinished elements of the Lefèbvre-Desnouettes story. The mystery, however, seems to be solved by witness statements made by Private Bergmann himself. His statement is corroborated by several other German hussars who had taken part in the action, and by letters written by German officers who were present. Bergmann's testimony at Osterholtz in 1830[3] states that:

> ... at the third charge, or in reality the pursuit, he came upon the officer whom he made prisoner. He was one of the first in the pursuit, and as he came up with this officer, who rode close in the rear of the enemy, the officer made a thrust at him with a long straight sword. After, however, he had parried the thrust, the officer called out 'Pardon'. He did not trouble himself further about the man, but continued the pursuit; an English Hussar, however, who had come up to the officer at the same time with him, led the officer back.

Bergmann did not know the officer was Lefèbvre-Desnouettes until later, when he was told he should 'have held fast the man'. He added that he was young and 'did not trouble' himself about it. All he remembered was that the officer 'wore a dark green frock, a hat with a feather, and a long straight sword'.

The other German witnesses and letters confirm Bergmann's story, and state that the General had fired a pistol at Bergmann: 'which failing ..., he offered him his sword and made known his wish to be taken to General Stewart'. But Bergmann 'didn't know General Stewart personally, and while he was enquiring where the general was to be found, a Hussar of the tenth English joined him, and led away the prisoner'.

So this seems to be the truth of the matter: Lefèbvre-Desnouettes was surrounded by a German troop and captured by Private Johann Bergmann. Levi Grisdale, with the 10th Hussars, might have arrived at the scene at the same time as Bergmann or very slightly later. Lefèbvre-Desnouettes asked to be taken to General Stewart, so Bergmann, 'not knowing General Stewart personally', handed him over to Private Grisdale who 'led the prisoner away'.

Grisdale served to the end of the Peninsular War, and also at Waterloo. He was promoted sergeant major and remained with the 10th Hussars till he left the army in 1825, aged only 42, with twenty-two years' service and thirty-two engagements behind him. His discharge papers state that he was suffering from chronic rheumatism and was 'worn out by service'. His army pension was 1*s* 10*d* a day.

Why did the regiment consider Grisdale such a hero? Maybe because before Sahagún, Grisdale was picked as 'coverer' for the 14-year-old George Augustus FitzClarence, illegitimate son of the Duke of Clarence and nephew of the Prince of Wales, the regiment's Colonel-in-Chief. It was unusual for well-connected young men to proceed on active service so young.

Grisdale became the landlord of the Stag and Star public house in Barr Street, Bristol, but by 1832 he and his family had moved home to Penrith. Grisdale was something of a celebrity, and was interviewed by the *Carlisle Patriot* on 17 March 1849.[4] It reported that he had presented Lefèbvre-Desnouettes' sword to the Prince of Wales on his return from Spain. Some versions of the story say he was promoted in person by the Prince Regent, others that the sword was handed to the Prince Regent by the commanding officer.

It is thought that Grisdale named his pub the *General Lefèbvre*; he even hung a large picture of the General over the entrance.[5] He died on 17 November 1855 at Penrith, aged 72, and is buried at Christ Church, Penrith. His occupation was given as 'Chelsea pensioner'.

* * *

Henry Percy had two sons with Marion Durand. The first, Henry Marion Durand (hereafter described as Henry Durand to avoid confusion), is well documented. The second child, however, is something of a mystery, because his date and place of birth are unknown, and even his Christian name is unconfirmed. We know he existed. First, he is mentioned in Henry's will, although there is confusion about his Christian name, which has been widely taken to be Percy, when really this is part of his father's signature at the bottom of the document. Second, he is mentioned, without a Christian name, in the biography of Sir Henry Durand (his brother). And third, the present-day Durand family[6] know about him, and say he was called James.[7] He lived at some stage in London, and, like Henry Durand, was happily fostered by the kind Deans family at 48 Connaught Terrace, Edgware Road, London. We know from Henry Durand's biography that 'James' died young, but we do not know where or when.

Henry Durand, as we have seen, was born at Coulandon near Moulins on 6 November 1812. His father returned from Moulins to England in April 1814, leaving the little boy at Coulandon with his mother. Henry Percy arrived in Paris as a member of Wellington's staff at the end of August 1814. We do not know of him visiting Moulins that year, but he did in 1816.

When Napoleon escaped from Elba in March 1815, Beverley headed for London (losing his horses en route) with Algernon, and stayed there till after Waterloo, so Marion remained with her family with no local Percy contact once Paris had been evacuated. After Waterloo, Paris was occupied, Marion visited and the child saw Wellington. Then, in 1818, the occupation ended, the troops departed, and Henry left too.

We do not know when Mrs Deans took over the care of the two boys, but it could have been in late 1817 or 1818. Henry paid Mr Deans £50 in May 1817. Henry Durand was by now 6, and James perhaps 4. The Durand family today believe that Marion was regarded by the Percy family in England as an 'enemy alien', although there is likely to have been a more practical view: that a French country girl would not have fitted comfortably into the English society in which Henry lived. So far as is known, Marion remained in France; she and Henry certainly never married, but they almost certainly did correspond.

Mr Deans always hoped Henry Durand would enter the Church, but he wanted to be a soldier. A friend of Percy's offered him a nomination to Haileybury for the Indian Civil Service; he declined. Another friend offered an Indian Cadetship, upon which he set his heart. When Henry Durand was 8 he was sent to Leicester School, after which he moved to Mr Carmalt's special training establishment at Putney. Here he met many useful contacts for the future in India. Small in stature but big in spirit and clever, he had an interest in mathematics and astronomy.

On 15 April 1825 Henry Percy died in London, aged 39, and was interred in the crypt of St Marylebone church.[8] This left Henry Durand a lonely young man; he had already lost his only younger brother, he had not seen his mother for years (she probably only spoke French and his must have been rusty), and now his father had died very young, worn down perhaps by recurrences of the tertian malaria. Luckily the lad had the emotional anchor of the wonderful Deans family.

That year Henry Durand joined the East India Company's College at Addiscombe. His mother, he recorded on enlistment, was living in Paris. That is the last we know of poor Marion. Sadly, her remittances from Henry's bank to Laffitte bankers in Paris stopped when he died.

Henry Durand prospered. Before he was 15 he had overtaken all his contemporaries, but a cadetship was delayed on account of his youth. Such was his success, however, that the rule was waived for him. In June 1828 he left Addiscombe early, as a Cadet of Engineers, having won seven of the eight possible prizes, and the sword for good conduct. He was commissioned under age, a second lieutenant in the Bengal Engineers, on 12 June that year, spending a year at Chatham on the engineers' course. His superior reported to Lord FitzRoy Somerset, who had made inquiries about him:

> He was one of a party of seven who joined at the same time. He is one of the most distinguished young Engineers whom I have ever had under me, both in respect to diligence, ability, and conduct. He was in all my monthly reports of progress &c., returned exemplary as to conduct.
>
> If your Lordship can procure or give him any recommendation to the authorities in India, you will not only serve a young man of great merit, but do good to the service there.[9]

The journey to Calcutta was dramatic, with storms, piracy and even a shipwreck near Cape Town. Poor Henry Durand lost all his possessions, salvaging only his mother's Bible, which he treasured all his life.[10]

Less famous than his father, Henry Durand nevertheless achieved a great career in India and indeed outshone his father. In the early days he worked with the Public Works Department in the Himalayas. A secondment to the Canal Department followed and then came the First Afghan War. Henry Durand was afterwards known as the Hero of Ghazni. It was decided to enter Ghazni by blowing the Cabul gate. It fell to Durand to place the powder bags and fire the train. His little party advanced without cover, exposed to fire from the outworks, approaching the gate by a narrow, winding roadway, lined on each side by a loopholed wall. The 300 pounds of powder were carried in hessian bags by local sappers. A sergeant carried the hose, and Henry Durand led. As they came within 150 yards of the gate, the defenders opened fire on them. They dashed forward under fire and reached the gate without loss. The charges were quickly laid against the gate, and Durand, helped by the sergeant, laid the hose to a nearby sally-port, from which he fired the train. The gate was successfully blown in, the storming party succeeded, and Ghazni fell on 23 July 1839.

Henry Durand was engaged in places familiar to recent campaigners in Afghanistan. After several appointments throughout India, he fought in the terrifying battle at Chillianwalla in the Sutlej campaign of the Second Sikh War. 'Disaffection' in the Native Army of Bengal boiled over, leading to strenuous action to contain what became the Indian Mutiny.

In April 1843 Henry Durand had married Mary, daughter of Major-General Sir John McCaskill, KCB, one of the divisional commanders in the Afghan campaign of 1842. Mary bore him three fine sons, Edward, Henry and Algernon, whom he wisely left for safety in Switzerland in 1856. They all prospered greatly later in life. Sadly, though, in 1857, during the forced marches of the strenuous Central India campaign, under a burning sun, his brave and pregnant wife fell ill and died shortly after her arrival at Mhow.

Like his father, Henry Durand was made a Companion of the Bath (CB) in 1858 for his part in the Indian Mutiny. Awards of the CB for distinguished operational service were replaced by the introduction of the Distinguished Service Order (DSO) in 1886.

In 1859 Henry Durand married his second wife, Emily, née Wallnut, widow of the chaplain killed at Lucknow, the Reverend Henry Polehampton. They had two sons who were blind, and a daughter who died aged 2. Emily outlived Henry, and died in 1905.

More senior appointments earned a worthy knighthood in the Most Exalted Order of the Star of India (KCSI), and Sir Henry was appointed Lieutenant Governor of the Punjab in 1870. This was the second most senior post in India, previously exclusively civilian.

Uneasiness on the frontier prompted a visit to Tank in December 1870. Entering the gateway on an elephant, in full splendour, the howdah hit the arch, and the Lieutenant Governor was knocked to the ground, and badly injured. Some 24 hours later, on 1 January 1871, he died. He was buried at Dera Ismail Khan, in North West Frontier Province (now Pakistan), where his tomb lies in the compound of St Thomas's church.

The Durand and Percy families maintained contact for over a century, and correspondence in the Alnwick archives shows a close relationship, with advice on Indian investment a long-lasting topic of mutual interest. Indeed, Colonel Algy Durand lent his Delatour-Fontanet miniature of Henry to the 7th Duchess to be copied, and the 7th Duke allowed him to take his son to fish on the family beat on the North Tyne. It is clear that the illegitimacy was no bar to friendship, and the Durands were kindly treated.

The kind Mr Deans corresponded with Henry Durand in India after his father's death. That, too, faded as Deans aged. The 5th Duke of Northumberland, as George Lovaine became, kept in charming avuncular touch. Indeed, the 6th Duke of Northumberland, George Lovaine's son Algernon George (born 1810), was General Henry Durand's cousinly executor in 1871.

So shocking was Henry Durand's sudden death that the electric telegraph from India to London was closed for 48 hours for the exclusive use of traffic concerning his death.

Over the years the families drifted gently apart. The Durands have lived in Ireland for many years, and these days there is no contact. Alnwick Castle stands, splendid as ever, adapting to changing times, at the forefront of innovation, heritage, conservation and visitor attraction, to complement its historic roles. Its archives must still have undiscovered treasures, but that's for another day.

*   *   *

The relationship between Henry Percy and the Duke of Wellington became very friendly. Wellington gave Henry one of two Breguet watches which he bought in Paris, as a present for taking the Waterloo dispatch to London. The other, originally made for Napoleon's brother King Joseph Bonaparte of Spain, he kept and used himself.

When Henry was in France even long after Waterloo, Wellington was constantly on the move and used Henry to organize his communications. There are detailed instructions as late as 1818 from the Duke concerning dispatches sent over a period of two weeks from London, Calais, Menin (near Ypres), Liège and Valenciennes. Some involve the sending of dispatches, others refer to sending officers to collect incoming news. These dispatches concerned arrangements for the reduction of the armies of occupation.

In the correspondence between Percy and Wellington there is often a nice personal element; it is not all politics and military matters. Some nice examples from August 1818 show their closeness:

> Wellington to Henry: London, 17 August 1818: I was at Vauxhall on Wednesday, & made a visible attempt to cut the Duchess of Richmond *en revanche* for her cut of you. The attempt failed as she turned my flank and got across the Head of my column but she observed it, became *toute rouge*; & it answered all the purposes of success!!

And then on 11 August 1818 he wrote to Henry at Cambrai, the British Army Headquarters:

> I have promised Lord Stewart to give him two couple of good fox hounds viz two dogs and two Bitches, & that Wattler should have them. I shall be very much obliged to you if you will give orders to Crane accordingly; & tell Wattler that Lord Stewart begs he will go over and chuse the dogs, & send or take them up to him at Paris where he will be about the 15th or 16th.

Henry evidently got on well with the Duchess of Wellington, and in 1820 she wrote a long chatty letter to him, full of gossip about members of the Duke's military family:

> I really wish you were here Dear Percy, I am sure you would enjoy seeing the Duke at his real home, good and happy I trust he is, beloved by all who approach him, going regularly to Church giving the brightest example of unaffected piety, indeed Percy it would make even you good to see him. As yet we have no party here.

She closed with a gentle joke about his children:

> If you can read this you must be a cleverer man than I am, for I declare I can not. Somebody said the other day of a friend of mine 'He has <u>christened</u> his child Henry Fitz Henry!' Oh Percy! Percy! I thought [it] was a new one and my Heart sunk within me! But I find it is not, so I revived. God bless you Percy.
>   Most truly yours,
>   C[atherine] S[arah] D[orothea] Wellington

In 1820 the Duke wrote to Henry from Stratfield Saye:

> My Dear Percy, I think you told me that my horse was in your stable; and I should be very much obliged to you if you will let me know where I shall send for him. I shall be here till toward the end of next week; & shall be very happy to see you if [you] will come down.

Henry's untimely death and interment at St Marylebone almost closes his story. There remain curiosities, of course. He always wore a locket containing a lock of Sir John Moore's hair, and that has disappeared. There must be more evidence about his second son, James. Where he died is unknown. What really happened to Marion Durand after the glimpse of her living in Paris when young Henry Durand went to Addiscombe?

And then there is the follow-on from Henry Durand. After the disastrous accident at Tank on New Year's Day 1871, how did the family fare? Henry Percy would have been immensely proud had he lived to see his grandsons, all of whom were much more successful and highly decorated than him. The three sons of Henry Durand's first marriage were all very successful in India and, comfortingly, their achievements show how the Victorian stigma of illegitimacy could be overcome by strength of character and the passing of time.

The eldest son, Edward Law Durand (1845–1920), was a soldier in the 97th Bengal Infantry, reaching the rank of lieutenant colonel, after which he became involved with civil affairs, also earning a CB. He was a fine watercolour painter and became the Resident in Nepal, following which he was awarded a baronetcy.

The second son became the Rt Hon. Sir Mortimer Durand, GCMG, KCSI, KCIE (1850–1924), 'Boundary-Maker' and 'Peace-Maker', and architect of the Durand Line, which established, in Victorian terms, the frontiers of the Indian Empire with Afghanistan. He wrote a comprehensive biography of his father. This was the first indication of the existence of his uncle James, who died young. Henry Percy's will and probate corroborated the information, but did not add to it. It seems likely that none of the three sons of Henry Durand knew anything about their long-deceased uncle, and since he died before the introduction of death certificates in 1837, we, too, know no more details.

The third son was also a success: Colonel Algernon George Arnold Durand, CB, CIE, of the Central India Horse (1854–1924). Better known to his friends as Algy, he had a successful military career, and fought in the Afghan War of 1879–1880. His greatest achievement was his command of the brilliant little Hunza Nagar campaign of 1891, during which he was wounded, in the hitherto unexplored wild mountainous Karakoram region near the Chinese border. He then became district agent at Gilgit. He wrote wonderful graphic accounts of his experiences describing the towering wild Himalayan nature of the countryside and the people with whom he dealt. His much-read book, *The Making of a Frontier*, is an impressive tale of the happenings in that remote part of the Empire at that time, reflecting admirably the attitudes of the day. A short quotation will give a flavour:

> A man does not rule a frontier state for forty years for nothing. He saw that, so far as his dynasty and country were concerned, safety lay in alliance with us, danger in any closer intercourse with Afghanistan. For this reason he was delighted to have an unconquered Kafirstan on his flank as a buffer between him and the 'God-given Government'. He might occasionally, in retaliation for too numerous murders on the part of the Kafirs, raid their country with the object of getting some slaves, but he had no desire to see it conquered, and he was delighted that the Kafirs had made the road down towards Asmar, and up the Ashreth valley to Lowari Pass, their happy hunting-ground, and murdered stray Pathans. The more dangerous the road was, the more isolated and safe his state. We discussed many questions, to which I cannot refer, with daily increasing interest and amusement on my part. Some of his ideas with all his shrewdness were very quaint; one of his most persistent demands was that, given any agreement with Government, it should be engraved on a sheet of copper. Some ruffian had persuaded him that no treaty would be binding on us if only written on paper.

Colonel Durand coupled this tactical, political and administrative ability with great competence as a staff officer, and was twice employed by Viceroys, latterly as Military Secretary dealing with appointments in the entire Indian Army. On retirement this distinguished officer became a member of the Honourable Corps of Gentlemen at Arms in 1902. He owned the two miniatures of Henry which were painted at Moulins, which have recently been obtained by the Percy family on the open market.

*   *   *

There are other mysteries too, enough to keep the inquiring mind busy for years, but a few thoughts are below:

- The mysterious Lisbon meeting of all the brothers in 1808 needs corroboration, and it would be nice to find a diary entry from somebody mentioning it. Was William Henry Percy, the naval officer at Lisbon in 1808, to join the party? It seems improbable.
- What happened to the jewels reputed to have been given to Josceline Percy by Junot at La Rochelle in 1808, which was considered such a 'bad show'? Indeed, were they ever jewels? Mrs Bagot says that when paying to fit out HMS *Hotspur*, Josceline sold a fine dressing case given to him by Junot.
- Francis John Percy was at Walcheren. He was lucky to survive, since in addition to the immediate fever casualties, his battalion lost 265 officers and men in the shipwreck off the Dutch coast of their transport, the Dutch frigate *Valk*, on their way home. But why was he near Ciudad Rodrigo when he died, and was it really Walcheren fever? His brother Henry, after all, also died very young, also of an unproved malady, which was probably also acquired while campaigning.
- The Durand story is complete from Henry Durand onwards. But it is sad not to know what happened to his poor mother after Henry Percy's death.

Notes

Chapter 1: Early Days (1785–1808)

1. Beverley, detained in France, suggested that General Paoli, living in London, would be a good person to intercede with Napoleon. Lovaine did not know Paoli, but the retired family tutor, Monsieur Dutens, did. So he was asked to see Paoli. As Dutens expected, it came to nothing, because Paoli was at loggerheads with Napoleon, and in effect a refugee in England.
2. He retained the name Wesley till 1798 when his eldest brother Richard was created Marquess Wellesley, and Arthur adopted it as the family name.
3. The story of Davison, as relevant to this period, is extraordinary, and beautifully told in Martyn Downer's intriguing account of his 2005 discovery of a cache of Nelson's jewels and treasures and quantities of previously unknown correspondence. See Martyn Downer, *Nelson's Purse*.
4. Alexander Davison, Noel, Templer, Middleton, Johnson and Wedgwood, 34 Pall Mall.
5. Henry Percy is shown on the payroll at Clonmel from 24 March to 24 May. From 25 May to 24 June he is noted as 'on Sir John Moore's Staff'. This shows he remained on strength of his battalion, but was detached to Sir John Moore.

Chapter 2: Sweden (1808)

1. Colonel Willoughby Gordon, Military Secretary to the Duke of York.
2. The Duke of York, Commander-in-Chief of the Army.

Chapter 3: Portugal and Spain (1808)

1. Nicholas Trant was a highly successful leader of Portuguese troops, with notable successes at Coimbra and after Torres Vedras. Some of Trant's correspondence with Marshal Beresford, Commander of the Portuguese forces, can be found at the Woodson Research Center, Rice University, Houston, Texas. His reputation was somewhat rough, and Wellington wrote critically that he was 'a very good officer, but a drunken dog as ever lived'.
2. The clasp on the Military General Service Medal awarded in 1848 to those who were present at Roliça was inscribed Roleia.
3. In 1901 a party of officers and men of the Worcestershire Regiment returning from the Boer War in South Africa staged through Lisbon. They visited Roliça and refurbished Lieutenant Colonel Lake's grave. A button from his uniform found during this visit can be seen in the museum at Obidos. A street in Roliça is named after Colonel Nicholas Trant and lavish tile representations (*azulejos*) of the battle adorn the local park.
4. The clasp on the Military General Service Medal awarded in 1848 to those who were present at Vimeiro reads Vimiera.
5. First demonstrated in 1787 at Gibraltar, and used successfully at the Battle of Fort New Amsterdam in Suriname in 1804, the invention was developed at his own expense by Shrapnel. In 1814 the British Government recognized Shrapnel's contribution by awarding him £1,200 a year for life. He was appointed to the office of Colonel Commandant, Royal Artillery, on 6 March 1827 and rose to the rank of lieutenant general on 10 January 1837. The shrapnel shell was replaced by the high explosive round at the end of the First World War in 1918.

6. Wellesley said 'The action of Vimeiro is the only one I have ever been in, in which every-thing passed as was directed, and no mistake was made by any of the officers charged with its conduct.'

7. Distinguished at Marengo (1800) and Austerlitz (1805), he commanded a cavalry division under Junot in the 1807 invasion of Portugal. He remained active throughout the Peninsular War, and went on to serve at Quatre Bras, where he led the famous cavalry charge. He was wounded at Waterloo.

8. An interesting surviving link to the battle is the local delicacy known as the *Bolo dos Generais* – a fruit cake that, according to tradition, was baked for Wellesley by a local woman. In the village of Vimeiro, close to Wellesley's headquarters building, facing the church there is a small roundabout, in the centre of which the local council erected a fine statue of a British infantryman to commemorate the 200th anniversary of the battle. It is, for reasons of economy, made of fibreglass, but it looks exactly like marble.

9. HMS *Nymphe* was a fifth rate 36-gun ship, captured off Ushant on 10 August 1780 by Captain William Peere Williams. After a long period of service in which she took part in several notable actions and made many captures, *Nymphe* was wrecked off the coast of Scotland on 18 December 1810.

10. Junot's influential 'official mistress' while in Portugal was Juliana de Almeida e Oyen-hausen, also known as Julia Stroganova (1782–1864), a Portuguese noble lady-in-waiting and daughter of the 4th Marquise of Alorna. Junot, like many senior French officers, led a complicated life with the ladies; he was alleged to have a second mistress aboard HMS *Nymphe*. As Secretary to Napoleon, he was involved in the delicate difficulties of Napoleon's divorce from Josephine, being scarcely forgiven for his attempts at mediation. Madame Junot, Duchess of Abrantes was left at Ciudad Rodrigo during Junot's second visit to Portugal in 1809–1812. There she wrote a spirited journal, but no hint of such goings-on is to be found.

11. General Sir Harry Burrard lost all his three sons in the Peninsular War and, it is said, died of a broken heart. He surprised Moore by asking him to accept his 18-year-old eldest son, Paul Henry (Harry) Burrard of the 1st Foot Guards, as an ADC. Moore was embarrassed but could not reasonably refuse. Harry Burrard was severely wounded by the same shell which mortally wounded Moore at Corunna on 16 January 1809. Moore never knew. Harry Burrard was put aboard HMS *Audacious* (the ship in which Moore had travelled to Portugal), but died of his wounds on 21 January 1809. General Burrard's second son, Midshipman John Burrard was drowned in a boat sent ashore from HMS *San Fiorenzo*, also in 1809. His third son William, an ensign in the 1st Foot Guards, was mortally wounded storming San Sebastian in August 1813. His death notice appeared in the same issue of the *Gentleman's Magazine* as his father's death, which took place on 17 October.

12. Younger brother of Henry Paget, later Marquess of Anglesey, who was also feeling slighted by Castlereagh having, as a cavalryman, been given command of a small infantry division.

13. Probably transported to La Rochelle by Commander Josceline Percy in HMS *Nymphe*.

14. Wellington lay in state in the Great Hall at the Royal Hospital, Chelsea from 10 to 17 November 1852. Two candlesticks which stood at the corners of his coffin are in the State Apartments at the Royal Hospital.

15. The journal, a treasure at Alnwick Castle, was presumably given to him by Hon. Captain Alexander Gordon (Corunna campaign ADC to General Sir David Baird), since his name is embossed, in the archaic style, in gold lettering on its cover.

16. Elvas, a huge fortress on the Portuguese side of the Hispano–Portuguese border, has been a familiar stamping ground for British soldiers since the Duke of Marlborough's time. On the southeast gate there is a delightful statue of a British soldier wearing a Grenadier cap. There

is also a Peninsular War British cemetery at Elvas which is neatly maintained by the Friends of the British Cemetery and is well worth visiting.

17. In a footnote Henry remarks 'This Brigade passed with great difficulty the mountains of Portugal.'

Chapter 4: Salamanca, Sahagún and Benavente (1808)

1. General Joyaquín Blake y Joyes (1759–1857) was the son of an Irish father from Galway and a Galician mother. He took part in the unsuccessful Spanish siege of Gibraltar and also the Spanish reconquest of Minorca in 1783. An able commander with weak officers, he was usually outnumbered in his brushes with the French. He ultimately found himself besieged in Valencia, where his eventual surrender was the high point of the French advances in that part of Spain.

2. The Palacio de San Boal, a honey-coloured gem, was used as headquarters by successive commanders of Salamanca. Its later occupants were the French Army of Marshal Soult in 1812, and Wellington advancing towards Vitoria in 1813. It is now the Hispano–Japanese Cultural Centre. The exterior façade is decorated with rare tinted designs scratched into the wet plaster, known locally as *sgraffitos*.

3. Parades took place in the huge classical Plaza Mayor, where later Wellington reviewed the entire newly formed 7th Division in 1812. A medallion of his head, in company with other Salamantine *prominentes*, graces the square. Baffled by his dizzying ascent in the British peerage, the Spaniards wisely entitled him Lord Wellington.

4. Sir J.F. Maurice, KCB (ed.), *Diary of Sir John Moore*, vol. 2 (London: Edward Arnold, 1904), p. 352.

5. Nicholas Jean de Dieu Soult (1769–1851). One of Napoleon's most able generals, he started his military career as a private soldier in the royalist infantry. A protégé of Masséna, he became one of the few senior officers in Spain to retain his reputation throughout the war. He was appointed Marshal of the Empire in 1804, and after the Peace of Amiens collapsed he was made Commander of the Army of England, intended for invasion from Calais. Appointed Duke of Dalmatia by the Emperor, the British troops nicknamed him the 'Duke of Damnation'. In 1838 he represented King Louis-Philippe at the coronation of Queen Victoria, where he met his old adversary Wellington, who is said to have seized his arms and said 'I have you at last!' – a tribute to his difficulties in Spain.

6. They were the 15th (The King's) Light Dragoons (Hussars) from Charles Stewart's Brigade and the 10th (Prince of Wales's) Light Dragoons (Hussars) from John Slade's Brigade. 'Black Jack Slade' was a former commanding officer of the 10th Hussars. Each of these regiments had been Light Dragoons till 1807 when they became Hussars. The title was, for a time, a combination of Light Dragoons and Hussars, which thereafter caused endless confusion.

7. General Henry, Lord Paget, later Earl of Uxbridge and Marquess of Anglesey. The elder brother of General the Hon. Edward Paget, in 1809 he eloped with Wellesley's sister-in-law, whom he later married, and thus did not feature in the Peninsular War under Wellesley's command. The Duke of York insisted on him commanding the cavalry in the Waterloo campaign, against Wellington's wishes.

8. Colonel Tascher was a relative of the Empress Josephine. He was certainly the commanding officer at the time but it is not certain that he was present at Sahagún.

9. The Battle of Emsdorf (Hesse, Germany) took place on 14 July 1760 during the Seven Years War. The 15th Light Dragoons had won the unique battle honour of Emsdorf for breaking five battalions of enemy foot and taking over 1,000 prisoners.

10. The 15th Hussars were awarded 'Sahagún' as a unique battle honour, and the tradition of celebrating Sahagún Day was maintained, including the singing of a rollicking

contemporary song called *Sahagún*. It is still celebrated today by the Light Dragoons and B Battery, 1st Regiment Royal Horse Artillery.

11. The 15th Hussars claimed to have captured two lieutenant colonels, eleven officers and 154 private soldiers, as well as 125 horses and several mules. In addition, a quantity of baggage was abandoned by the French in their precipitate retreat to Santarbas.

12. P. Haythornthwaite, *Corunna 1809*, p. 45.

13. C. Hibbert, *Corunna*, p. 78. A King's German Legion witness.

14. Johan (or Joaquin) Bergmann does not appear on the role of recipients of the Military General Service Medal awarded to soldiers of the 3rd Hussars of the King's German Legion. A number of the soldiers of this fine regiment fought at Waterloo, and a Private Heinrich Bergmann is shown as having been at Sahagún, Benavente and Waterloo, and to have received the Guelphic medal. Two other Privates Bergmann served at Waterloo with the 3rd Hussars KGL, but Johan Bergmann was not there. Four officers of the regiment fought at Sahagún, Benavente and Waterloo, possibly more, some having died before 1848 when the Military General Service Medal was issued. Of the soldiers of this regiment at Benavente in 1808, no fewer than seventy-three fought at Waterloo in 1815.

15. Levi Grisdale seems to have moved up and down the ranks. The silver medal given to him by the officers of the 10th Hussars shows him as corporal (with his name spelled Grisedale). He did eventually achieve promotion and finished his service as a serjeant major. The medal is now in the possession of the successor regiment, The King's Royal Hussars. It is mistakenly dated 1 January 1809. The engagement was on 29 December 1808. A fine oil painting in the Royal Collection, by Dennis Dighton, shows the supposed capture of General Lefèbvre-Desnouettes at Benavente by Levi Grisdale.

16. The story of Lefèbvre-Desnouettes' watch is told at page 122.

17. The Prince Regent was Colonel-in-Chief of the 10th Hussars, in whom he took a paternal and generous interest. So we can assume that when Grisdale relieved Bergmann of Lefèbvre-Desnouettes, he still had his sword. The sword is now at the Royal Armouries at Leeds, on loan from the Royal Collection. The fine sabretache worn by Lefèbvre-Desnouettes at the time of his capture is in the National Army Museum. These ornamented pouches were normally worn fixed to the sword slings and scabbard, but in this action it is likely that the sabretache, which usually contained notepaper, had been unhitched from the scabbard to keep it dry while crossing the Esla. In any event, it is highly probable that it was one of the items which Levi Grisdale delivered with the general.

18. The celebrated diarist Rifleman Harris of the 95th Rifles, of Blandford, was part of Lefèbvre-Desnouettes' escort, on foot. The young general in a splendid uniform rode a fine horse. Harris made his views clear. He was on foot, but the general, a prisoner, was mounted. And, as the crowning indignity, the general was wearing a British officer's sword (Moore's, of course).

19. Napoleon wrote to his wife Josephine a slightly tetchy account of events: 'Lefèbvre has been captured. He took part in a skirmish with 300 of his chasseurs; these idiots crossed a river by swimming and threw themselves in the midst of the English cavalry; they killed several, but on their return Lefèbvre had his horse wounded; it was swimming, the current took him to the bank where the English were; he was taken. Console his wife.'

Chapter 5: The Retreat to Corunna (1808–1809)

1. His escort (Captain Henry Wyndham, see below) reached Corunna with Lefèbvre-Desnouettes before the main body of the army. Moore wanted the prisoner out of the way, especially since the retreat was becoming increasingly difficult. Henry Wyndham took General Lefèbvre-Desnouettes and a servant on board HMS *Cheerful* (cutter, 10 guns), Lieutenant D. Carpenter, Royal Navy. They sailed for Portsmouth so as to deliver

Lefèbvre-Desnouettes to Portchester Castle, the reception centre for all French prisoners of war. Circumstantial evidence suggests that they sailed before the Battle of Corunna.

2. Henry Wyndham (1790–1860) was ADC to Sir Arthur Wellesley at Roliça and Vimeiro. On Wellesley's return to England for the Cintra Inquiry, Wyndham was taken on as ADC to Sir John Moore. Wyndham must have recovered Moore's sword from Lefèbvre-Desnouettes on or before arrival in England, with the intention of returning it to Sir John. He was the natural son of the 3rd Earl of Egremont. He was present at eight general engagements in the Peninsular War. He was also at Waterloo in the 2nd Battalion, Coldstream Guards. He took part in the famous closing of the gates at Hougoumont and was said to have been so disturbed by the incident that he would never again close a door, preferring to sit in a room in a howling draught. After the battle, seeing the carriage of Jerome Bonaparte in the wake of the general retreat of the French at Waterloo, he made an attempt to capture Napoleon's brother, but Jerome leaped out through one door while Wyndham opened the other. He became a full general and Knight of the Order of the Bath. His memorial is in St Mary the Virgin Church, Petworth.

3. The soldier in question had been found guilty of looting the rum store (and of course sharing out his spoils, to the detriment of discipline). The shooting took place in front of the Ayuntamiento (Town Hall) in the Plaza Mayor of the village.

4. In this famous incident the French general Auguste-Marie-François Colbert was shot by an Irish Rifleman of the 95th, Thomas (Tom) Plunkett, using a Baker Rifle at a range of about 600 yards. As they say in Irish regiments, Plunkett was 'a very good man in the field'. This was a very impressive feat. Plunkett reloaded and with his next shot felled the trumpet major who had come to the general's aid. After the repulse of the French attack on the bridge at Cacabelos, and the skirmishing which followed, General Edward Paget discovered some soldiers of the Rear Guard plundering in Cacabelos. After an immediate drumhead court martial, he ordered some to be flogged and others to be hanged. As the last two were being prepared for the noose, the French began another surprise attack. Telling the offenders and spectators they would be pardoned if they fought well, he galloped off to deal with the enemy. They were soon repulsed, and the soldiers spared. Tom Plunkett was noted for 'being the life and soul of the party' and a good companion, possessing a quick and wry wit. 'Plunkett ... was a bold, active, athletic Irishman and a deadly shot – but the curse of his country was upon him.' The 'curse' in question here was habitual drunkenness, which saw Plunkett's promotions to corporal and sergeant lead each time to a flogging and a reduction back to the ranks.

5. This officer is sadly not identifiable from the casualty rolls of either the 95th Rifles or the 60th Royal American Regiment.

6. Los Nogales, now known as Nogais.

7. Santa Maria de Constantin, a village which seems to have changed its name. It is a parish of Neira de Jusa on the right bank of the river Neira.

8. These guns had been abandoned because the exhausted draught animals were unable to pull them.

9. Captain the Hon. James H.K. Stewart, 95th Rifles, was wounded on 12 January 1809 at the ridge at Barba. He had a long and distinguished career, winning gold medals at Salamanca and Vitoria, and eventually a CB.

10. J. Paget, *Wellington's Peninsular War*, p. 78.

11. It remains ruined to this day, having been replaced, not repaired, as is also the case at Talavera.

Chapter 6: The Battle of Corunna and the Death of Sir John Moore (January 1809)

1. British eccentricity? Probably not. Lord William Bentinck, while commanding his brigade, rode a mule at Corunna in preference to a charger. Second son of the Prime Minister, the Duke of Portland, Lord William Bentinck was wounded in the arm by a cannon ball, exactly as Moore would be later, but less seriously. He did not command in the Peninsula after Corunna. He died in 1839.

2. *Voltigeurs*, French skirmishers who went ahead of the columns of infantry. Each French battalion had a company of ninety *voltigeurs*, chosen for their shooting and fieldcraft skills. During the retreat to Corunna they sometimes travelled with the cavalry, riding two-up, so as to be fresh for skirmishing with the British rear guard.

3. Lieutenant Colonel James Wynch, shot through the body, was being conveyed off the field in a spring waggon which overtook Sir John Moore, who was being carried in a blanket by soldiers under a serjeant of the 42nd. Having been told who was in the blanket, the colonel desired to be lifted out. Sir John asked one of the Highlanders whether he thought waggon or blanket best. The man answered gently, 'The blanket, Sir. It will not shake you so much, and we shall keep step and carry you easy.' Sir John agreed, 'I think so too.' (Obituary, *Gentleman's Magazine*, February 1811, p. 88.)

4. Lieutenant General Sir David Baird was wounded but was, however, able to walk to the town. Probably his nephew, Captain Alexander Gordon, and some of his staff accompanied him. From his quarters in the town he was taken aboard HMS *Ville de Paris*. T.E. Hook, *Life of Baird*, vol. 2 (1832; reprinted Nabu Press, 2011), pp. 308–10.

5. James Stanhope was Moore's youngest ADC. His sister, Lady Hester Stanhope, wrote to Moore at Salamanca asking him to take 'my little brother James'. His elder brother Charles was commanding the 50th (Royal West Kent) Regiment. James had only arrived from England a few days earlier.

6. Charles Napier (later General Sir Charles Napier of 'Peccavi' fame), although listed as killed, was in fact missing, wounded. He had a leg and several ribs broken by grapeshot, a bayonet stab in the back, contusions from a musket butt, and severe concussion from a sabre cut on the head. His life was saved by a French drummer boy who stopped an Italian soldier administering the *coup de grace*. Marshal Soult's own surgeon attended Napier. Shortly after the evacuation, Lady Sarah Napier persuaded the First Lord of the Admiralty to send a sloop-of-war, HMS *Cadmus*, under flag of truce, to find the truth about Napier. Soult had by now been relieved by Ney, who made a magnanimous decision. 'If his mother is old and blind, let him go himself to tell her he is alive.' Napier arrived in Plymouth with twelve wounded soldiers and fifty-four women and children in April 1809, finding his family in mourning. Recovered, he rejoined his regiment the following year and was again severely wounded in the head, at Busaco in 1810. An ornament to his profession, as Wellington described him, Napier was distinguished in India as conqueror of Scinde. He suffered headaches all his life after Corunna and Busaco. His statue stands in Trafalgar Square, erected by the subscription of admiring private soldiers.

7. Reverend Henry John Symons (1781–1857), Chaplain to the Brigade of Guards. When the Military General Service Medal was authorized in 1847, his eligibility to receive the clasps Nivelle, Orthes and Toulouse was unchallenged. His claim for Corunna was granted on appeal after he had proved his presence. The Army List only showed his service at the three battles of 1813–1814. He remained an Army Chaplain till 1816. His final living was All Saints with St Martin, Hereford, where he died and was buried in 1857.

8. François David, a former French hussar of the *émigré* corps whom Moore adopted as his valet at Barbados in 1796. He was very French, very young and totally loyal to Moore. He replaced Moore's old servant, Boyd, who was smitten with Calvi fever and had to stay behind in Scotland when Moore sailed for the West Indies in 1795.

9. Paul Anderson, of Grace Dieu, Waterford, was a devoted friend and companion of Moore. They served together from St Lucia in 1796, when Anderson was his brigade major. Thereafter they were together in Ireland, Holland, Egypt, Sicily and Sweden.

10. Lieutenant Colonel J. Willoughby Gordon of the Royal African Corps was Military Secretary to Frederick, Duke of York, Commander-in-Chief of the Army. (This short-lived regiment consisted of pardoned military offenders who were excused a prison sentence in exchange for service in the West Indies and West Africa.)

11. From the accounts of others we know that Anderson glared enough to prevent Moore being told of young Burrard's mortal wound. Percy, of course, knew.

12. Lady Hester Stanhope, Pitt's niece, whose warm attachment to Moore is well known. A seal which she gave him was cut off Moore's fob by Colborne. He gave it to Mr Carrick Moore, who returned it to Colborne.

13. The members of Moore's 'family' present at his death were Paul Anderson, John Colborne (later Lord Seaton), Henry Percy, James Stanhope and François. The Reverend Henry Symons and the two surgeons were also there. Thomas Graham and General Edward Paget were in the house, but probably in another room.

14. Charles Wolfe (1791–1823), curate of Ballyclog, later rector of Donaghmore, Co. Tyrone. He wrote 'The Burial' in 1814, when he was aged 23. It was inspired by a passage in the *Edinburgh Annual Register* for 1809 describing the burial of Sir John Moore. The poem appeared anonymously in the *Newry Telegraph* of 19 April 1817, and was reprinted in many other periodicals. The Reverend Henry Symons wrote to correct several details.

15. Colonel Thomas Graham (later Lieutenant General Sir Thomas), Lord Lynedoch (1748–1843), was one of the most distinguished and oldest officers in the Napoleonic wars. He won four gold medals. In 1791 his wife's health had collapsed. He took her to France but she died there. The violation of her coffin by Revolutionary soldiers at Toulouse motivated his resolution to support the war. He spent £10,000 raising the 90th Perthshire Volunteers, but the second battalion badly strained his finances. His career took a rewarding turn in 1808. He acted as Moore's aide-de-camp in the Swedish fiasco and then accompanied him to the Peninsula, serving with distinction as a very senior ADC in the retreat to Corunna. He commanded a division at Walcheren and returned to Portugal in 1810. His dashing personal triumph at Barossa on 4 March 1811 earned him the Order of the Bath, and the thanks of Parliament.

16. Captain William Maynard Gomm. Aged 14, he had carried the colour of the 9th Foot as an ensign in Holland in 1794. For part of the retreat to Corunna he acted as brigade major to Major General Disney's Brigade. He was mentioned in Wellington's Vitoria dispatch. He was wounded at the Nive, 9 December 1813, and won a gold medal for his service there. One above Henry Wyndham in the Army List, he served on the staff at Waterloo before transferring to the Coldstream Regiment of Foot Guards in July 1814. He was appointed Knight of the Bath in January 1815.

17. Brevet Colonel (Brigadier General) Robert Anstruther of the 3rd Foot Guards was in the Peninsula from August 1808 till his death on 14 January 1809. He was mentioned in dispatches at Vimeiro, and awarded a Gold Medal, which he never received, for Vimeiro. He commanded one of the brigades of General Edward Paget's Rear Guard during the retreat to Corunna, with much distinction. His death has been attributed to exhaustion, dysentery and pneumonia. Whatever the cause of death, the rigours of the retreat certainly contributed to his demise. His uniform is in the Guards Museum.

18. The military habit of referring to a chaplain as a *padre* originates from the Peninsular War, though whether it was in use in January 1809, so early in the war, is not certain.

19. It is normally accepted that only four officers were present. However, the Reverend Symons, who conducted the brief service, recorded that Colonel Graham, Major Colborne,

Colonel Paul Anderson, Major George Napier and Captains Henry Percy and James Stanhope were present and helped to bear the body of Sir John Moore to the grave. He wrote as much in the front of the prayer book which he used, and which is now in the National Army Museum.

20. Later Lord Seaton (1778–1863). Inspiring leader of the 52nd, he was one of the great heroes of the Peninsular War. His action at Waterloo in moving his 52nd Regiment to attack the Imperial Guard's flank was a major contribution to the success of the incipient rout begun by Maitland's Guards.

21. Hon. J.W. Fortescue, *A History of the British Army*, vol. VI.

22. HMS *Ville de Paris* (Captain Carden) carried General Baird and twenty-three officers of the 50th, three of the 43rd, four of the 26th, three of the 18th, one of the 76th, two of the 52nd, two of the 36th, four Royal Engineers, and two Royal Artillery – a total of 45 officers 'exclusive of their servants'. Napoleon Series: *Corunna Evacuation*.

23. Captain John Surman Carden RN had twenty years' service. His father, a major, had been killed in the American Revolutionary War. He was related to Cornet Henry Carden of the 1st Royal Dragoons, who in 1810 was taken prisoner after Busaco and was escorted to Bayonne with Henry Percy in 1811.

24. The January 1809 weather was unusually severe and cold. Among the losses at sea were HMS *Primrose* (Brig-sloop, outbound for Spain) and the transports from Corunna *Dispatch* and *Smallbridge*, which foundered on the Manacle Rocks. In all, 104 men of the 7th Hussars were lost in *Dispatch*, while five officers and 209 King's German Legion soldiers perished in *Smallbridge*. Observations from naval vessels provide a complete picture. See David E. Pedgley, 'January 1809 Synoptic Meteorology of Floods and Storms over Britain' (Royal Meteorological Society Paper no. 16, 2015).

25. Baird had been described by one of his subordinates as a 'bloody bad-tempered old Scotchman'. It is clear from Alexander Gordon's letters that he disagreed fundamentally with Moore's strategy, and expressed his views to his nephew.

26. Gordon could not be promoted because he had not served seven years as a captain as stipulated in the regulations. The regulations trap occurred again after Vitoria and Orthes in 1813, causing ill-feeling with Major John Fremantle, the messenger.

27. To the Glory of the Most excellent Sir John Moore | General in Chief of the British Armies | And to his valiant soldiers | Spain thanks you. | Battle of Elviña, 16 January 1809.

28. http://wonderingminstrels.blogspot.co.uk/1999/06/burial-of-sir-john-moore-at-corunna

29. Foy, *History of the War in the Peninsula*, p. 74.

30. Coote Manningham was one of the founders of the 95th Rifles. He died in April 1809 at Maidstone of an illness contracted in the retreat to Corunna. He was succeeded as Colonel of the 95th by Sir David Dundas.

31. Henry Warde of the First Foot Guards. He was born in 1766. He received the thanks of Parliament for his service at Corunna. Later he served in India and Mauritius, becoming a General and GCB. He died at Alresford, Hampshire, on 1 October 1834.

Chapter 7: England, Ireland and Back to the Peninsula (January–April 1809)

1. The day after the Battle of Roliça.

2. Francis John Percy missed the Corunna campaign. He was commissioned lieutenant in Henry's regiment, the 7th Royal Fusiliers, in April 1808 (Army List, April 1808). He transferred on 18 May 1808 to a captain's vacancy in the 23rd Foot, the Royal Welsh Fusiliers. He was not allotted to a battalion till the Walcheren expedition between July and December 1809. At Walcheren in the 2/23rd, Francis served in Beresford's Brigade, which was badly affected by Walcheren fever. Francis, unfit after Walcheren, acted as ADC to Lieutenant General Sir John Doyle in 1810 at Fort St George, Guernsey. He stayed there

till June 1811, before moving as ADC to Sir John Doyle's nephew, Colonel John Milley Doyle, commanding a Portuguese brigade in the Peninsula. Francis was ADC for only two months. He died, as his cousin Sophy Bagot correctly says, in Spain, at Cuellar near Ciudad Rodrigo, on 23 August 1812, probably from Walcheren fever.

3. By the British from the French in 1808 before the Convention of Cintra. Josceline remained with *Nymphe* until he moved to HMS *Hotspur* in 1810 (an unusually appropriate choice of billet by a naval appointer with a sense of history).

4. William Percy's first command was HMS *Mermaid* in 1811. He was promoted lieutenant in 1807, but we have no reason to doubt he was in Lisbon. It was possible.

5. Henry was not in the 14th Light Dragoons during either of his two visits to Lisbon. But the first time, in August 1808, the only time the brothers could have met, Henry was in the 7th Royal Fusiliers, when he was ADC to Sir John Moore. He transferred on 21 June 1810 (Army Lists and Regimental Payroll, National Archives). Francis Percy never served under Moore's command

6. Lovaine was a volunteer in the Peninsula in August and September 1808, with Sir Charles Stewart (Castlereagh's half-brother), commanding a cavalry brigade in Moore's force. Lovaine met Henry and Josceline at Lisbon, as well as Junot and Wellesley. He probably met Sir John Moore.

7. There must have been a meeting of some of the brothers. We can forgive Mrs Bagot confusing some details. So, when was the Lisbon meeting?
   - Francis could only have been present in June 1811. Lovaine was not there that year. So it seems almost impossible that the August 1808 meeting included poor Francis.
   - Josceline was commanding HMS *Hotspur* in the Channel (November 1810 to 1815), but could have gone to Lisbon.
   - Henry was at Lisbon before the Corunna campaign from late August to 28 October 1808 and for three days again, on returning in April 1809, but never again.
   - We know Lovaine visited Lisbon in August 1808 as a volunteer.
   - William Percy by 1811 was commanding a frigate *en flute* (i.e. with reduced guns for use as a troopship).

   The meeting can only have happened in the late summer of 1808, when William was not commanding.

8. The present Clonmel barracks were built in 1780 but the town had been a garrison since 1650 when it was captured by Cromwell. Extended in 1805, the town became an important military centre. Renamed Victoria Barracks in 1837 in honour of the Coronation, in 1882 it became the Depot of the senior Irish infantry regiment, the 18th Royal Irish Regiment. It was renamed Kickham Barracks after 1922, and till 31 March 2012 it housed the 12th Infantry Battalion, Irish Army. Tipperary County Council acquired the site in 2012, when the historic military connection ended, although the old Royal Irish Depot war memorials for the 1879 Afghanistan campaign and the Boer War 1899–1902 remain, respected and preserved.

9. Cove, in Cork, was renamed Queenstown in 1844 after Queen Victoria's first visit to Ireland. It is now spelled Cobh.

Chapter 8: The Peninsula: Oporto (1809)

1. Ponte de 25 de Abril.

2. The 1st Coldstream Guards (strength 1,120) and the 1st Third Foot Guards (Scots Guards) (strength 1,361). These two strong battalions formed the 2nd Guards Brigade in England in 1803.

3. The boots and shoes issued to British soldiers were often of poor quality and had no distinction between left and right. French soldiers had left and right boots so French casualties were quickly relieved of their boots. Officers bought their own footwear, so it fitted.

4. James Wellington (no relation) served in the Peninsula from September 1808 to April 1814, and was killed at Plattsburg in America in August 1814 (Challis, Peninsula Roll Call and Army Lists).

5. Wellesley made special arrangements for this officer to be evacuated to England and properly looked after.

6. Swiss and Irish battalions in the French Army wore red uniforms, the latter in memory of the Jacobite Catholic King James.

7. Felton Hervey recovered and commanded his regiment in 1811. In September 1811 he was involved in a 'brisk series of actions, and a French officer, whilst striking at Felton Hervey, perceived he had only one arm. With a rapid change, [he] brought his sword down to the salute and passed on.' A character, Felton was a German speaker, and became involved in a celebrated incident when he rode up to an enemy vedette manned by a German. He conversed with the sentry and the visiting Officer of the Picquet before making his escape. His orderly's bridle was grabbed and he was taken prisoner.

8. Wellesley's nine-page Oporto dispatch (WO 1/238) was taken home by James Stanhope, Moore's former ADC. It was dated 12 May 1809 – a long and busy day.

9. A Portuguese *vintin* was worth just over one English penny.

10. Sir William James Myers, 2nd and last Baronet, was wounded at Albuera on 16 May 1811, and was 'since dead', according to the *London Gazette*. He was 27.

11. Hugh Percy became Bishop of Carlisle in 1827. He died in 1856. John Cooper wrote his reminiscences from his notes many years after the event. They are occasionally inaccurate about dates, but provide an excellent eyewitness reflection on attitudes in the ranks, an all-too-uncommon feature in the copious writing about the Peninsular War.

12. J.S. Cooper, *Rough Notes of Seven Campaigns*, p. 16.

13. General Foy was a much-wounded and brave soldier, always in the middle of the action. By the start of the Battle of Waterloo he had been wounded fourteen times; he suffered his fifteenth wound while attacking Hougoumont during the afternoon.

14. *Record of The Royal Regiment of Fusiliers, 1809*, p. 96.

15. In 1815 Henry Percy met General Sebastiani in Paris while Napoleon was in exile at Elba. He arranged to sell a horse to Sebastiani.

Chapter 9: The Talavera Campaign (1809)

1. John Randall Mackenzie commanded the 2/78th (Seaforth Highlanders) at the Battle of Maida. He was highly regarded by his Sutherland soldiers. He was killed at Talavera. (*Gentleman's Magazine*, August 1809, p. 780.)

2. C. Oman, *History of the Peninsular War*, vol. II, p. 358.

3. Gurwood (ed.), *Wellington Dispatches* (1838), vol. 4, p. 349.

4. Gurwood (ed.), *Wellington Dispatches* (1838), vol. 4, p. 323.

5. Rt Hon. John Villiers (1757–1838), later 3rd Earl of Clarendon. Envoy to Portugal, 1808–1810.

6. Colonel Richard Bourke of Limerick served in the 1st Foot Guards in the Netherlands in 1799 and was badly wounded in the jaw. He was Superintendent Junior Department of the Royal Military College. A brilliant confidential member of Wellesley's staff, it was his responsibility to arrange the junction of the armies, discover information on strength, morale and discipline in Cuesta's army, and assess the chances of securing assistance from Venegas' army in the south.

7. The Hon. Edward Cadogan died of wounds at Vitoria on the Heights of Puebla while commanding the 71st (Highland Light Infantry). He was thrice mentioned in dispatches, most glowingly by Wellington for his 'behaviour' at Fuentes de Oñoro.

8. J.S. Cooper, *Rough Notes of Seven Campaigns*, p. 18.

9. Alexander Campbell, late 13th Foot (Somerset Light Infantry), was promoted lieutenant general on 29 April 1802 (Army List, 1808). He was wounded in the thigh by grapeshot at Talavera while commanding the right wing of the army (Royal Military Calendar, vol. 2, p. 407).

10. Gurwood (ed.), *Wellington Dispatches* (1838), vol. 4, p. 413.

11. Castello Branco is where the Idanha a Nova militia, who were overrun at Alcántara, were mustered.

12. Old Spanish bells, it is said, contain less tin than English bells, making a less mellifluous ring to the English ear.

13. General Jean Baptiste Marie Franceschi-Delonne. There is a letter in the National Archives requesting that the news of Franceschi's captivity be sent to his wife in Paris. This was done. He was imprisoned by the Spaniards at Granada and later at Cartagena and kept in close confinement within four walls. He was treated with unjustifiable rigour. This also happened to the hero of Saragossa, General Palafox. Franceschi died of fever on 23 October 1810, after two years' captivity. (Oman, *History of the Peninsular War*, vol. 2, p. 402.)

14. General Latour-Maubourg's 1st Dragoon Division. Strength 3,179.

15. General Zayas. Napier, as ever, is biased and critical of the Spaniards.

16. It has been suggested that Cuesta had heard that the Junta offered Venegas the chief command of the Spanish armies if he relieved Madrid. This was anathema to Cuesta. The precise reason for Cuesta's decision is much debated. Perhaps his army could not attack at such short notice. Surprisingly, Victor unwisely remained static long enough to be attacked by an allied force, but equally unexplained, Cuesta would not react until too late.

17. This seems to confirm that Cuesta wanted to relieve Madrid before Venegas, but was annoyed that Wellesley would not help.

18. Sherbrooke's 1st Division and Mackenzie's 3rd Division were east of the Alberche on 26 July.

19. Anson's Brigade consisted of the 1st Light Dragoons KGL and the 23rd Light Dragoons. (Oman, *History of the Peninsular War*, vol. 2, p. 650.)

20. Mackenzie's Brigade only had the 1/45th (Sherwood Foresters) with any experience. This battalion had been at Buenos Aires fighting the Spaniards in 1806. It had been at both Roliça and Vimeiro, so was a steady experienced battalion. In Donkin's Brigade was the headquarters of the 5/60th, and at least one company of highly experienced skirmishers. The 2/87th (Irish Fusiliers) were inexperienced. The experienced 1/88th (Connaught Rangers) had also been in South America.

21. While Wellesley was talking to Lieutenant Colonel William Guard when, according to Fortescue's account, two musket balls hit Guard's sword and another went through his shako. Colonel Guard was wounded and left behind in hospital, becoming a prisoner of war. He was one of the senior officers on parole at Verdun, where he arrived on 3 November 1809.

22. Señor Don Gregorio Martín Tostón to the author when visiting with the Duke of Wellington, 1990.

23. It has not (yet!) been possible to discover who the French officer was, so the Casa de Salinas telescope remains to be found.

24. Alexander Campbell's Brigade consisted of 2/7th, the 2/53rd Shropshire Light Infantry and a company of the 5/60th Royal American.

25. Tilson's Brigade consisted of the 3rd Buffs, the 2/48th Northamptonshire, the 2/66th and one company of the 5/60th Royal American.

26. Stewart's Brigade consisted of the 29th Worcestershire, the 48th (1st Regular Battalion) and the 1st Battalion of Detachments (composite elements of Sir John Moore's army which had remained in Portugal after the retreat to Corunna).

27. The French regiments were, from left to right, the 24th, 9th and 96th.
28. The picquet of 7KGL was rallied by its company commander, Major Burger, and Adjutant Delius.
29. The Brunswick Oels had not joined the British service by the time of Talavera. Cooper met them later in the war.
30. Daniel Gardiner of the 43rd Foot had just under five years' service.
31. Captain Clement Hill of the Royal Horse Guards, commissioned lieutenant in March 1806, was 27 at Talavera. He served throughout the Peninsular War as ADC to Hill, but returned to the Blues for Waterloo, and was severely wounded. Hill needed an experienced senior ADC to deal with senior officers, hence the presence of Captain Edward Currie.
32. Edward Currie, although the newer ADC to General Hill, had been serving as a captain in the 90th Foot (Perthshire Volunteers, later 2nd Battalion, The Cameronians) since December 1802 (Army List, 1809).
33. The Blood Hospital at Talavera is behind the western slopes of the Medellín. It is long derelict and unlikely to stand for long. The wounded Captain Charles Boothby, who kept a graphic journal, was taken there before being evacuated next day to the town, where his leg was amputated – which he describes with no details spared. He was later a prisoner at Verdun. His direct descendent, Dr Christopher Boothby, visited the Blood Hospital on 1 October 1990 before the unveiling of the Talavera Memorial, and is now the possessor of the key of the building.
34. Joseph Bonaparte, King of French-occupied Spain, was Napoleon's elder brother. He lacked the Emperor's drive and military skills. Nicknamed 'Pepe Botella' ('Joe Bottle'), he remains a much-reviled king in Spanish tradition.
35. The 48th, later the Northamptonshire Regiment, proudly wore as a cap badge the battle honour TALAVERA beneath the Sphynx awarded for Egypt in 1801. It remains a proud honour of the Royal Anglian Regiment.
36. Major (later Major General) George Middlemore took command when Sir William Myers was wounded at Talavera, but left the Peninsula in April 1810, having taken command of the 8th Garrison Battalion in October 1809. His conduct at Talavera resulted in the award of a gold medal. He had previously served with a company of the 86th as Marines in HMS *Brunswick* with Lord Howe and Admiral Duncan in the North Sea. He accompanied a force from India under Sir David Baird to Egypt in 1801. He transferred to the 48th as a major in September 1804. In 1819 he was promoted colonel, and major general in 1830. He then became first Lieutenant Governor of Granada from 1833 to 1835, and was appointed the first Governor of St Helena in 1836 after its handover from the Honourable East India Company. He oversaw the repatriation of Napoleon's remains to France. He died at Tunbridge Wells in 1850.
37. The total Foot Guards casualties at Talavera were 567: 1st Coldstream, 272; 1st/3rd Guards 295.
38. The statistics remain much debated. Fusilier Cooper, in keeping with many others, says it was 60 miles in 24 hours. Oman calls the march one of unexampled severity, being 43 miles in 22 hours. The precise distance is unimportant; it was an astounding achievement by these three battalions, which had been through the retreat to Corunna under Moore, with Craufurd. These soldiers shone throughout the war. Some of those who marched to Talavera were at Waterloo in 1815, having fought and marched over 5,000 miles in the meantime.
39. 'English' wounded are officially recorded as 3,072.
40. Anonymous serjeant, 1st Bn, Coldstream Guards.
41. P.H. Stanhope, *Notes of conversations with the Duke of Wellington, 1831–1851*, entry for 26 October 1833.

Chapter 10: The Retirement to Badajoz, Portugal and Capture
(August 1809–September 1810)

1. Wellington (as he was by then) approached the Spanish Junta at Cadiz in November to try to arrange an exchange for General Franceschi, but was unsuccessful. Gurwood (ed.), *Wellington Dispatches* (1838), vol. 5, p. 271, concerning 7 November 1809.

2. The bridge was built in the fourteenth century for use by pilgrims going to Guadalupe. It was not repaired for more than thirty years. Today there are no towers.

3. Wellington was delighted with the good conduct of the troops and wrote to Colonel Stopford, who commanded the Brigade of Guards which led the march, praising their 'orderly and regular behaviour' which 'set the example to the other troops'. As a reward he asked for the name of a worthy sergeant from each battalion of the Guards who he would recommend for a vacant ensigncy in the army. (Wellington to Stopford, 13 January 1810; Maurice, *History of the Scots Guards*, vol. 1, p. 313.)

4. Cooper mistakenly refers to this as Nostra Senora de Tobo (*sic.*). He is probably referring to a hermitage some 12 miles north of Badajoz, which the local people say was damaged in the Peninsular War and which was rebuilt in the nineteenth century. Our Lady of Botoa is a local patron.

5. The footnote in Wellington's dispatches (Gurwood (ed.), *Wellington Dispatches* (1838), vol. 5, p. 156) states: 'The notification of Sir Arthur Wellesley's elevation to the Peerage was received on the 16 September; dated 26 August 1809, by the titles of Baron Douro of Wellesley, and Viscount Wellington of Talavera.'

6. This period at Badajoz enabled Wellesley to become familiar with the fortress. This proved helpful when he besieged it in April 1812.

7. Captain Victor de Thévenon was ADC to Brigadier General Braifer. He was sent under flag of truce with a letter from Marshal Mortier for Wellington about the British wounded left at Talavera. He arrived at the Spanish forward posts near Almaraz. It was necessary to establish the position about a cartel before Wellington could reply. Unbeknown to Wellington, the Spaniards detained de Thévenon and sent him to Seville. Wellington then received an entirely reasonable complaint from Mortier. The Spaniards by such means made it impossible to arrange for any exchange of prisoners left behind at Talavera. Gurwood (ed.), *Wellington Dispatches* (1838), vol. 5, p. 224.

8. Wellington's dispatch of 5 October 1809 from Badajoz, reporting the situation of Captain de Thévenon to the Marquis Wellesley at Cadiz, gives a flavour of his irritation. Gurwood (ed.), *Wellington Dispatches* (1838), vol. 5, p. 205.

9. R. Muir (ed.), *At Wellington's Right Hand*, p. 159.

10. A league was approximately 3 miles. Gordon had therefore ridden 210 miles in 50 hours, thus averaging 10 or more miles per hour, assuming some rest. Whether he was accompanied by an orderly dragoon or two for escort he does not say. It seems unlikely that he would travel such distances alone.

11. Gordon was a highly effective intelligence officer. He discovered the complete command structure, locations and strengths of the French Army during this visit.

12. At a rate of 4*d* per day.

13. Olivenza remains disputed. Today it lies on the Spanish side of the border, and Portuguese may be neither spoken nor taught there. Nonetheless, the Portuguese claim it. A series of complicated treaties before and after the Napoleonic wars have never satisfactorily resolved the age-old rivalry over its possession.

14. Kellermann's ADC, Lieutenant de Turenne, had been taken by the Spaniards, and was held by them. Wellington was unable to secure his exchange for Cameron. Instead Lieutenant Véron de Farincourt was sent, with an escort provided by Beresford. No French officer

could travel safely alone or in a small group without imminent threat of ambush by Portuguese or Spanish guerrillas.

15. Thirty-seven Camerons served as officers in the Peninsular War. Only one is recorded as having been a prisoner, captured at Talavera with the 1st Battalion of Detachments. He escaped the same night. So it seems unlikely to have been him who was exchanged for de Farincourt. Of the thirty-seven Camerons in the Peninsula, twenty were in the same regiment: unsurprisingly, the 79th Cameron Highlanders. In October 1809 the 1st Battalion had gone home after Corunna, and had not returned to Spain. Wellington's dispatch of 27 January 1810 says this Cameron was captured at Talavera on 27 July 1809 and was sent into Portugal by General Kellermann from Valladolid. He does not appear on the Talavera casualty role. Sixteen officers called Cameron fought at Waterloo, of whom four were from the 79th Foot. Which Cameron was he?

16. Gurwood (ed.), *Wellington Dispatches* (1838), vol. 5, p. 268, 1 November 1809.

17. In 1808 Masséna was accidentally wounded by his old rival Marshal Berthier, Napoleon's Chief of Staff, at a shooting party with the Emperor. 'The Prince', as he was known, lost the sight of one eye.

18. Henriette Leberton, known as Madame Leberton, was a dancer at the opera in Paris. Her real name was Maria Anne Eugénie Renique. She was alleged to have been married to Major Leberton, ADC to Masséna, but her descendant, Eric de Roo, states they were never married. The corps commanders strongly disapproved of her wearing uniform and particularly the Legion of Honour. Napoleon Series Archive, 2011.

19. Pelet's most interesting 1,000-page account of the French Campaign in Portugal 1810–1811 is at Vincennes.

20. There is much unwarranted criticism of the Spanish Army. True, it did not manoeuvre nor administer with any expertise, but nonetheless the Spaniards showed noble stamina and tremendous fortitude when besieged.

21. There are three Marmoleiro villages, all improbable contenders at face value. 'Marmaliera', as Cooper calls it, has been identified through the unpublished journal of Captain Samuel Trench, Royal Engineers, whose visit on 2 April 1811 indicates its position. It was, and remains, a very isolated little village high above the Coa, '6 leagues from Celorico'. Water is piped through supposedly Roman stone channels to the village. Its population of approximately 300 is diminishing. There is an old school building where the Light Company could have been accommodated, and a fine church.

22. Percy exchanged with Acting Captain Francis Keogh, who moved to the 57th Foot, joining as a lieutenant on the battlefield of Albuera, 17 May 1811. Henry's old company was heavily involved at Albuera, so his transfer probably saved his life (Army Lists, 1810 and 1811).

23. The commanding officer, Lieutenant Colonel Hawker, had been sent to England wounded, after Talavera.

24. Lieutenant Colonel Neil Talbot came from Malahide, Co. Dublin, and was the brother of the Hon. Richard Wogan Talbot, MP for the County of Dublin. Talbot's gallant death is described in the *Gentleman's Magazine* of August 1810, and by Wellington, Brotherton and Simmons.

25. At Abrantes in June 1809 Captain George Scovell, a gifted graduate of the Royal Military College at Marlow, formed the Corps of Guides from British and Portuguese officers to gain intelligence and cartographic information on roads and defensive potential. He later became Wellington's chief code-breaker.

26. A worthy memorial to General Herrasti stands by the west door of the Cathedral at Ciudad Rodrigo.

27. *British Defence Doctrine*, published in 2011, places this principle above all others; so did Wellington. Clausewitz, the guru on these esoteric delights of Staff Colleges, burst into

indigestible print on the matter in 1812, by which time Wellington had been putting the principle into practice since his Indian campaigns. Clausewitz served as Chief of Staff of III Prussian Corps at Ligny in 1815.

28. The handwriting of this Alnwick letter is difficult. It looks like General Le Tibou but this name does not appear in the Napoleonic generals roll. On closer inspection it is apparent that the name is Le Febvre, meaning Lefèbvre-Desnouettes.

29. Gurwood (ed.), *Wellington Dispatches* (1838), vol. 6, p. 305.

30. Junot, Duke of Abrantes, must have known Alorna in Portugal in 1808. Junot's 'official mistress' was Alorna's daughter. The Duchess of Abrantes, who later took up residence at Ciudad Rodrigo, makes no mention of Alorna in her gossipy journal.

31. Now restored and converted into a 35-room luxury hotel in the most atmospheric setting of the ruined fortress near Aldea del Obispo, on the Spanish side of the border.

32. Local historians at Almeida believe the explosion was the largest till the Lochnagar Crater, near La Boiselle, was blown on 1 July 1916.

33. *The Memoirs of General the Baron de Marbot, late Lieutenant General in the French Army* (London: Longmans Green, 1903). He served in the Peninsula with Masséna and Lannes, as a successful cavalry officer in Russia, and commanded a brigade at Waterloo, where he was wounded.

34. *Worcestershire Journal*, 29 October 1810.

35. Percy's capture is confused in the *History of the 14th Light Dragoons*, which was written many years later. The dates disagree with other reliable sources. For example, Wellington's letter to Masséna was unquestionably dated 17 September, and refers to Henry being wounded and captured or killed 'yesterday' near Celorico. The 14th Light Dragoons' History states: 'On 25th September, Captain the Honourable H. Percy was taken prisoner whilst reconnoitring near the heights of Busaco. "On this occasion the regiment, together with the Royals, was employed to cover the retreat of the Light Division to the position of Busaco. Whilst performing this duty against the masses of the French army advancing on Busaco during the 25th and 26th September, the casualties of the 14th Light Dragoons were as follows: Killed 1 horse. Wounded 1 sergeant, 2 rank and file, 4 horses. Missing 3 rank and file, 7 horses."'

36. Gurwood (ed.), *Wellington Dispatches* (1838), vol. 6, p. 454, 18 and 20 September 1810; Oman, *History of the Peninsular War*, vol. III, p. 352.

Chapter 11: Prisoner of War (1810–1811)

1. Sir Stapleton Cotton (1773–1865), later Field Marshal the Viscount Combermere. He had a long and distinguished career in Europe and India. He was not in charge of the cavalry at Waterloo, as Wellington had requested, because the Duke of York insisted on the Earl of Uxbridge having command. When Uxbridge was wounded at Waterloo, Wellington asked Cotton to command the cavalry in the Army of Occupation.

2. Gurwood (ed.), *Wellington Dispatches* (1838), vol. 6, p. 446.

3. Postscript to the previous note.

4. Captain the Hon. Edward Charles Cocks, a fluent linguist and highly educated officer, was one of Wellington's most brilliant exploring and intelligence officers; he was killed at the siege of Burgos, 1812. He had been ADC to Sir Stapleton Cotton. Wellington deeply regretted his death. This exceptional officer, who was frequently the source of vital intelligence, gained at immense risk, left a collection of eleven volumes of a diary with detailed observations on his daring and exciting life in the Peninsula.

5. Gouvea is west of Celorico.

6. On 22 December Wellington attempted to resume the General Court Martial, but ran into legal difficulties, since 'Captain Percy of the 14th Light Dragoons, one of the members, was

taken prisoner' and Major Butler and Captain La Mottle had returned to England for health reasons. Wellington's plan, under which the evidence already heard was to be read to substitute members of the reconvened Court, was not approved by the Judge Advocate General, who advised that it would be illegal. Wellington, Second Duke (ed.), *Supplementary Despatches*, entry for Cartaxo, 22 December 1810.

7. To deny its use to the French.

8. Stores and ammunition had been prepositioned for the Portuguese in case the French opted for the southern route. Now their axis was clear. The stores must therefore be denied to the enemy.

9. Mr Percy in this case is Algernon. It is further evidence that the countess and her daughters were home by then. The omission of 14-year-old Charles Percy, who could not have been an official *détenu*, being under age for militia service, is further evidence that Charles would have returned to England with his mother and sisters had he been on the continental excursion which ended with their detention.

10. Brigadier General Antoine-François Brenier de Montmorand. Wellesley knew him. Wounded and captured at Vimeiro, he was sent to England but returned to France in 1809 (exchanged for Lieutenant General John Abercromby, a *détenu* since 1803) and served with the Army of Portugal in 1810. As Governor of Almeida, he achieved the garrison's brilliant night escape when Masséna failed to relieve him after Fuentes de Oñoro in 1811.

11. This was a forward headquarters on the southern route, southeast of Fornos, not far from Celorico. The majority of the French force had already passed this position on the northern route. Wellington's daring choice of this position enabled him to be certain there was no unexpected force aiming for the southern route which might outflank him. Once satisfied, he withdrew to Busaco via Lorvaõ.

12. Now a fine hotel. The ridge at Busaco is well worth visiting.

13. Fine words from a 23-year-old strategist. He had the advantage of being privy to Wellington's every move, and knew several of the French generals. 'Scrape': his master's voice, perhaps? Alexander Gordon to Aberdeen, 21 September 1810.

14. R. Muir (ed.), *At Wellington's Right Hand*, p. 155.

15. Wellington saw him with a bloody face caused by bursting shrapnel, but with no serious wound. Simon was very lucky. Shrapnel shells had at times wiped out whole companies of advancing French infantry clambering bravely up the heather-strewn rocky hill.

16. Female sutler or canteen-keeper of a French regiment.

17. At 2016 values, a cavalry captain of 1810 was paid £45.42 per day, or £16,573 annually. (In 2016 a captain with six years' service is paid £45,592.)

18. National Archives: Payroll 14th Light Dragoons, September 1810.

19. Brigadier General Charles Marie Robert de Sainte-Croix commanded the cavalry brigade of Junot's VIII Corps. A court martial acquitted him for shooting, in a duel, the commanding officer of his battalion, Mariolles, a cousin of the Empress Josephine. Sainte-Croix was killed a few days later by a direct hit from a round shot fired from a naval gunboat, while reconnoitring the eastern end of the Lines of Torres Vedras.

20. Brigadier General Pierre Soult was the younger brother of Marshal Soult. He commanded the cavalry brigade of Reynier's II Corps.

21. Brigadier General Eloi Charlemagne Taupin commanded the 2nd Infantry Brigade of Clausel's 1st Division of Junot's VIII Corps. He was killed at Toulouse three days after Napoleon's abdication.

22. On 20 August 1812 Lovaine wrote to the Duke of Feltre (Minister for War), this time seeking exchange for Henry. The (British) Naval Transport Office, responsible for prisoners, was supportive. Lovaine emphasized that the Percy family had behaved kindly to French prisoners, telling the Minister about Junot's journey to La Rochelle with Josceline.

Junot, he said, had repaid Josceline's hospitality with interest when Henry was captured. Lovaine said he had arranged repatriation for some French officer prisoners when in charge of them. (He commanded the Northumberland Militia at Norman Cross prisoner of war camp for a while.) There was no cartel for exchange, so Henry remained at Moulins.

23. Brigadier General Jean Francois, Baron Graindorge, commanded the 2nd Infantry Brigade in Merle's 1st Division of Rainier's II Corps. Merle was also wounded.

24. General D.E. Ainslie, *Historical Record of the First, or Royal Regiment of Dragoons 1661–1887* (London: Chapman & Hill, 1887), p. 112.

25. Commissioned on 13 April 1809, he was relatively inexperienced, his regiment having missed Talavera.

26. The Lionel Challis card index of Peninsular War officers shows Henry Carden as wounded near Pombal, the information presumably sourced from his regimental history. His National Archives file makes no mention of a wound because no British doctor had treated him. Having been captured, he was treated by a French surgeon.

27. The unfortunate Picot, alias Macarenhas, was hanged (by the Portuguese Government). Wellington to Charles Stewart, 1 October 1811. Gurwood (ed.), *Wellington Dispatches* (1838), vol. 8, p. 312.

28. Jean Jacques Pelet, *The French Campaign in Portugal 1810–1811*, edited, translated and annotated by Donald D. Horwood (Oxford: Oxford University Press, 1973), p. 209.

29. Gurwood (ed.), *Wellington Dispatches* (1838), vol. 8, p. 390.

30. Jean Jacques Pelet, *The French Campaign in Portugal 1810–1811*, edited, translated and annotated by Donald D. Horwood (Oxford: Oxford University Press, 1973), p. 263.

31. Visual signalling stations manned by the Royal Navy were set up in late 1809 to link Lisbon with Badajoz. These withdrew as Wellington retired towards Lisbon. Hains was captured near the easternmost link of the Torres Vedras chain when Junot's VIII Corps approached the Lines.

32. Midshipman William Hains became a lieutenant on 3 February 1815 (his service as a Midshipman is not recorded) and he is shown as having died (without further increase in rank) in 1837. Gareth Glover to the author, 2016. Press reports of naval prisoners of war in Verdun do not usually name midshipmen, although the majority of them were held there.

33. Gurwood (ed.), *Wellington Dispatches* (1838), vol. 7, pp. 23–4, concerning 2 December 1810.

34. General Stewart knew Henry and Lovaine from August 1808, when Lovaine had been a volunteer with him at Lisbon.

35. Supplementary Despatches, Correspondence and Memoranda, vol. XIII, item no. 880: 8 November 1810, p. 508.

36. *Bien grave*, perhaps, but he continued to command his corps. R. Muir (ed.), *At Wellington's Right Hand*, p. 159.

37. Now a comfortable Parador, it was the site of the French surrender, 19 January 1812.

38. Wellington, en route for Paris after Napoleon's departure for Elba in 1814, visited General Foy in hospital at Cahors. Foy remarked that Wellington's French was fluent, but tinged with a Belgian accent. Perhaps he picked it up during his year in Brussels before going to Angers.

39. The English press reprinted excerpts from the French propagandist English language newspaper *Le Moniteur*.

Chapter 12: Life on Parole at Moulins

1. France was divided into police divisions which corresponded with the Départements, in this case the Allier, in the Auvergne region. Moulins was the headquarters of the 21st Division of the Gendarmerie de l'Empire.

2. On 5 May 1811.

3. The cavalry barracks now houses the national theatrical costume museum.

4. 21 October 1805: Battle of Trafalgar.

5. The Revolutionary calendar date of his order was 19 Vendemiaire An 14. The revolutionary calendar was discontinued from 1 January 1806.

6. France overran Switzerland in 1798, replacing the Swiss Confederation with the Helvetic Republic, a client state of France, complete with occupying garrisons. In 1801, under the Treaty of Lunéville at the start of the Peace of Amiens, Swiss neutrality was to be restored. The British raised the matter in 1803, and on 10 May 1803 all British adult males in France and French client territories were detained, on grounds of their being liable for British militia service. On 18 May war resumed.

7. Nineteen wives of peers were detained in 1803. J.G. Alger, *Napoleon's British Visitors and Captives*, pp. 317–18.

8. Brigadier General Antoine Maurin. A cavalry brigadier in Portugal, he was captured by Portuguese partisans on 16 June 1808, handed over the Royal Navy and paroled at Cheltenham till his escape in 1812. He used the same escape network as Lefèbvre-Desnouettes. The following year General Maurin married Colonel Macleod's niece in Paris.

9. Colonel Macleod of Colbeck was the uncle of Lord Moira (who helped over Lefèbvre-Desnouettes' watch). Detained in France, he was released in 1810 but asked to settle in France, which was not allowed by the French. He was described by a French police bulletin as honest but weak-minded, and as having incurred unpleasantness in Scotland by his liking for France and his advocacy of peace. He lived at Charlton Kings near Cheltenham.

10. From J.G. Alger, *Napoleon's British Visitors and Captives*, p. 199.

11. Over 900 officers were paroled at Bridgnorth, with about 400 living there at a time. Money could be remitted to them through Perregaux bank in Paris to Hoare's or Coutts in London. French officers complained at being paid in English notes instead of coin. They claimed the agent charged extortionate rates; so did Beverley in France.

12. As a long shot, I tried to discover about young Dubois at Bridgnorth. A local historian, Mr Gwynne Chadwick, was able to produce the register of prisoners, with Dubois and the Duke of Arenberg's full details. Beverley was right. Adolph (as the English record show him) was indeed a prisoner of war at Bridgnorth. The record of prisoners shows him as arriving from London on 18 September 1811. Aged 25, he was a blue-eyed slender young man, 5ft 6in tall, with brown hair and a round face. We do not know if Lovaine had any friend to introduce. Dubois was moved to Alresford, Hampshire, on 23 March 1813 and repatriated in 1814. We do not know if he returned to Moulins.

13. In the bad winter of 1815/16 he wrote complaining of the cold and rain, adding in early April 'till the last two days I have scarce been out in my cabriolet'.

14. Curiously, in 1815, as we know, Henry attended the Duchess of Richmond's ball in Brussels before Waterloo. So did the Duke of Arenberg, which begs the question as to who drew up the guest list.

15. The Countess Stéphanie, née Rollier, fourteen years younger than Lefèbvre-Desnouettes, was the daughter of a first cousin of Napoleon's mother, Letizia Bonaparte, known as Madame Mère. As a wedding present Napoleon gave the couple the house on Rue Chantereine (now Rue de la Victoire) in Paris, in which he and Josephine had first lived after their marriage. He promoted Lefèbvre-Desnouettes to general. Napoleon arranged a special passport for Stéphanie to go to England. They lived on parole at 1 High Street, Cheltenham. Lefèbvre-Desnouettes, after his escape to France in 1812, 'insolently' claimed that the Prince Regent's failure to honour his word had absolved him from his parole of honour.

16. The Great Comet of 1811 was visible from September 1811 to January 1812. The comet was popularly thought to have portended Napoleon's invasion of Russia in 1812, even being

referred to there as 'Napoleon's Comet'. It excited comment from besiegers at Ciudad Rodrigo.

17. Lefèbvre-Desnouettes' ring can be seen in Cheltenham Museum. It is said to have been pawned and never redeemed.

18. Richard Tapper, a carrier from Devon, who had been involved in January 1811 in the escape of five French naval officers on parole at Moretonhampstead. Heading for France with two Vinnicombe smuggler brothers, their vessel ran aground off Exmouth and they were caught. Tapper and the Vinnicombes were tried at Devon Assizes in the summer of 1812, and sentenced to transportation for life (T. James, *Prisoners of War at Dartmoor*).

19. When Tapper was sentenced to transportation for the affair with the French naval officers, an agent named Waddle from Dymchurch was on £400 bail from Maidstone, in connection with his part in the escape of General Lefèbvre-Desnouettes. The exact relationship between Tapper and Waddle is uncertain, but it seems that Waddle was probably the agent for a ring of smugglers.

20. L.É. Saint-Denis, *Napoleon from the Tuileries to St Helena*, pp. 14–15.

21. Another curious coincidence. Perregaux was not Stéphanie's father, but may have been related. He was the Parisian banker whom Beverley, a customer of Hoare's Bank in London, used as recipient of transferred funds for the purchase of works of art. In due course Henry Percy used Perregaux Bank in Paris, neither knowing that M. Perregaux was a relation of General Lefèbvre-Desnouettes.

22. Sir Edward Paget, newly arrived second-in-command to Wellington, was captured by the French 2nd Hussars in the retreat from Burgos, while accompanied by a single Spanish dragoon. Having only one arm, he was unable to put up a fight. Lefèbvre-Desnouettes' sword was of the 2nd Hussars.

23. At Boulogne.

24. There is a Rembrandt crucifixion in the church at Le Mas D'Angenais in the Garonne region, which was also bought at auction early in the nineteenth century.

25. The comparative purchasing value today is £16,060, i.e. the sum paid multiplied by the percentage increase in the retail price index (RPI).

26. Thomas Richard Underwood (1765–1836), a watercolourist and scientist, was detained at Calais, and like several artists and scientists was allowed parole in Paris.

27. Henry Marion Durand's original birth certificate is still at the Mairie at Coulandon.

28. 'Mr Ponsonby' is difficult to identify. The letter does not survive. The two famous Ponsonbys do not fit. Neither dates nor locations are feasible for them to have written. There is, however, a brief reference to a Captain (James or) John Ponsonby who was in the 68th and then the 44th (July 1803). His commission is dated 1800 and he went on half-pay in 1814. This suggests Walcheren fever (Source: Sir John Ponsonby, 'The Ponsonby Family 1929', privately printed). The 68th had suffered badly at Walcheren, so perhaps he and Francis had met there. The position of the 44th was near Ciudad Rodrigo, which would explain how Ponsonby knew of Francis's death at Cuellar. Courtesy, John Morewood, author of *Waterloo General – The Life, Letters and Mysterious Death of Sir William Ponsonby*.

29. Francis had died on 23 August 1812, according to the *Gentleman's Magazine*, so the arrival of news at Moulins was very slow. It seems to have been a recurrence of the Walcheren fever which claimed many victims long after the expedition.

Chapter 13: Paris and the Hundred Days (1815)

1. The cavalry barracks at Hounslow were built in 1793, and are still in use after a major refurbishment in 2015.

2. Sir Charles Stewart (no relation to the general) was Ambassador to the Netherlands between February and May 1815. During the Hundred Days, he was in Brussels and Ghent.

He attended the Duchess of Richmond's Ball. After Waterloo he escorted Louis XVIII back to Paris, and was British Ambassador until 1824.

3. *Bell's Messenger*, 15 May 1814.
4. The sons must have been Lovaine and Algernon. Henry was at home by now, although we do not know his date of arrival.
5. Napoleon, having asked to be transported to Elba by a British ship, embarked in HMS *Undaunted*, Captain Usher, at Fréjus on 28 April 1814.
6. Another unlikely and unsubstantiated theory is that Junot escaped to America.
7. Henry's monthly allowance equated to £3,124 at 2016 values.
8. As a major of Light Dragoons, Henry's pay was 19*s* 3*d* daily (2016: £60.16 daily; annual salary £21,950). Officers were paid monthly. There were no increases in pay between 1808 and 1814.
9. Hugh's loan was the equivalent of £2,500 in 2016 money.
10. With a capacity of 5,000 prisoners, its highest number of inmates was over 6,000 in 1810.
11. FitzRoy Somerset, 26, married 21-year-old Emily Wellesley-Pole, Wellington's niece, on 6 August 1814 at 3 Savile Row, her father's home. Wellington returned briefly from Paris for the wedding.
12. G. Glover, *Wellington's Voice*, Fremantle letters.
13. *Windsor and Eton Express*, Sunday, 25 September 1814. See also Peter Snow, *When Britain Burned the White House, The 1814 Invasion of Washington* (London: John Murray, 2013).
14. Henry had known Henry Hardinge as a staff officer with Sir John Moore at Corunna. Hardinge was attached as liaison officer with the Prussians and was severely wounded at Ligny, when his hand was amputated, so he was not involved in the main battle of Waterloo.
15. There had been disquiet at the number of Napoleonic officials who remained in post as civil servants at the abdication.
16. Sebastiani was a Corsican, against whom Henry and several of the 'family' had fought at Talavera. He bought Henry's mare but did not pay him. During the Hundred Days Sebastiani disappeared from Paris to join the Emperor, and Henry never got his money. Sebastiani was not at Waterloo. After Napoleon's second abdication Sebastiani did not feature for several years, but, having been Minister of Marine, he ended as Ambassador to London (1835–1840) after Henry's death.
17. Lady FitzRoy's father, who must have been glad she was safely in Brussels. 'Mrs Pole' later went to Brussels to help Emily with her baby daughter, born on 16 May.
18. A courier often means a King's Messenger. A number of these gentlemen were attached to the army headquarters from time to time. Unfortunately, *The History of the King's Messengers* does not have details of those involved in the Waterloo campaign, although we know Henry was later accompanied by a King's Messenger for part of his journey to England. This individual had probably taken correspondence from London to King Louis XVIII at Ghent, and joined Percy there. See V. Wheeler-Holohan, *The History of the King's Messengers* (London: Grayson & Grayson, 1935).

Chapter 14: Waterloo, London, France (1815–1818)
1. Gordon's numerous letters to his brother Lord Aberdeen, published in R. Muir (ed.), *At Wellington's Right Hand*, gave Aberdeen a real insight into Wellington's character and thoughts. They must have provided useful background when Aberdeen met Wellington at the Congress of Vienna.
2. Killed at Inkerman in the Crimea (under the command of FitzRoy Somerset, who was by then Lord Raglan).

3. Which goes to show that being an ADC, even with two arms, was a most hazardous business, not just a social sinecure for well-connected young gentlemen, as it is sometimes perceived.

4. Moore-Smith, *The Life of John Colborne, Field Marshal Lord Seaton*, pp. 401–2.

5. Archives, Alnwick Castle.

6. The 46ft-long painting hangs in the Royal Gallery of the House of Lords. Henry is named, but the likeness is open to question.

7. Mrs Charles Bagot, *Links with the Past*.

8. Napoleon's carriage at Genappe was captured by a Prussian officer, Major von Keller. After a long and chequered series of exhibitions in England, it was finally destroyed in the fire at Madame Tussaud's in 1925. How Henry Percy came to be in possession of the bees is unknown, but it seems most unlikely that he could have removed them from the carriage at Genappe that evening. During the Peace of Amiens in 1802 Madame Tussaud visited London and was unable to return to France because of the renewal of the war which resulted in Beverley's detention in Switzerland.

9. Pozzo di Borgo went immediately to Brussels and wrote his note to the king at 5am. He gave the letter to a French royalist who took it to Louis, probably arriving at about 9.

10. Serjeant McRea was FitzRoy Somerset's clerk, a Coldstreamer who had been with Wellington from his days in Portugal and was with the family in Paris.

11. Another guest at the Duchess of Richmond's Ball.

12. B.E. Hill, *Recollections of an Artillery Officer*, vol. 2, pp. 110–11.

13. Eagle House, Broadstairs, complete with an eagle on its roof, commemorates the historic landing. After 200 years to the day, the landing was re-enacted by sailors from HMS *Northumberland* (a happy choice of warship for a Percy) with actors taking the roles of Percy and Commander White.

14. P.H. Stanhope, *Notes of Conversations with the Duke of Wellington 1831–1851*, p. 173, entry for 6 October 1839.

15. The house was demolished, and a modern building now stands on the site.

16. Two of the engraved wine glasses reputedly used for the toast were auctioned by Bonhams in 2015.

17. Members of the Cabinet each received a Waterloo Medal, without experiencing so much as a whiff of powder in their nostrils.

18. Alexander Davison, Nelson's by now disgraced Prize Agent, had temporarily employed Henry before he was commissioned. In 1816 the bank in Pall Mall where Henry had worked ceased trading. If Davison was at home that midsummer night in 1815 he might have been surprised to see the former 'gap-year' lad playing such a key role.

19. It is said that Henry found a musket ball lodged in his shoe when he was going to bed. It was put into a ring, which was later stolen. It seems odd that he had not noticed it before.

20. Report by Surgeon D. O'Flaherty on Lieutenant Colonel Percy's Illness, Brighton, 28 August 1820. Alnwick Archives, DP-D5-1-1.

Epilogue

1. Joseph Napoleon, former King of Spain, was an émigré living quietly in New York.

2. *Weekly Register*, 14 September 1822.

3. L. Beamish, *History of the King's German Legion: Extract from the Deposition of Johann Bergmann, late private of the fifth troop of the third hussars of the king's German Legion, made before the amt at Osterholtz, 8th March 1830*. Translated from the German.

4. Stephen Lewis to the author, 2015.

5. The street directory of Penrith shows no public house of that name in his lifetime.

6. The Durand family recognize their descent from Henry Percy and Marion Durand, both of whose names are used to this day. The early generations were very distinguished in India and Nepal, and a baronetcy was granted to Henry Durand's son Edward Law Durand. Marion's name is well remembered and so is the Percy connection.

7. The Reverend Stella, Lady Durand to the author, 2014.

8. When Henry's father, the Earl of Beverley, died in France in 1830, his body was brought back to London and interred in the crypt at St Marylebone. Algernon, who had been at Moulins with Henry, died in 1833, and he joined Henry in the crypt of St Marylebone. Likewise, George Lovaine's wife Louisa (by then Countess of Beverley) was buried there in 1848. But time moves on, and materialism conquers all. Now the crypt, as with so many London churches, has been cleared and converted to a cafeteria. Its previous occupants have been buried in a named mass grave at Brookwood cemetery in Surrey. It was reported that Henry Percy was, most unusually, buried in his military uniform, which may explain why the whereabouts of his Waterloo Medal, his CB and his Russian Order of St Anne are unknown.

9. Letter from Colonel C.W. Pasley to Lord FitzRoy Somerset, 6 September 1829.

10. Marion's Bible has not been found, and none of the present Durand family has ever seen it.

Select Bibliography

Alger, John Goldsworth, *Napoleon's British Visitors and Captives* (London: Archibald Constable & Co. Ltd, 1904)

An Officer of the Staff, *Operations of the British Army in Spain: Involving Broad Hints to the Commissariat, and Board of Transports: with Anecdotes Illustrative of the Spanish Character* (London: Sherwood Neeley & Jones, 1809)

Anglesey, Henry Paget, Seventh Marquess of, *One Leg: The Life and Letters of Henry William Paget, First Marquess of Anglesey* (London: Jonathan Cape, 1961)

Bagot, Mrs Charles, *Links with the Past* (London: Edward Arnold, 1902)

Beamish, North Ludlow, *A History of the King's German Legion* (London: Thomas & William Boone, 1832)

Beverley, 1st Earl, 'Letters of 1st Earl of Beverley, while detained in France to his son George, Lord Lovaine 1812–1821', Alnwick Archives, DNA: F/39/2-9

Blaney, Major General Lord, *Narrative of a forced journey through Spain and France as a prisoner of war in the Years 1810 to 1814*, vol. 1 (of 2) (London: E. Kerby, 1814)

Boothby, Charles, *A Prisoner of France: The Memoires and Correspondence of Charles Boothby, Captain Royal Engineers, During his last Campaign* (London: Adam & Charles Black, 1898)

Bromley, Janet and David, *Wellington's Men Remembered*, 2 vols (Barnsley: Pen & Sword/ Praetorian Press, 2015)

Brotherton, Major Thomas William, 'The account of Major Thomas William Brotherton, 14th Light Dragoons' (National Army Museum, 1986-11-33)

Bury, J.T.P. and Barry J.C. (eds), *An Englishman in Paris: 1803. The Journal of Bertie Greatheed* (London: Geoffrey Bles, 1953)

Cathcart, Brian, *The News from Waterloo, the Race to Tell Britain of Wellington's Victory* (London: Faber & Faber, 2015)

Charmilly, Colonel Venault de, 'Narrative of his transactions in Spain with the Rt. Hon. John Hookham Frere' (London: Political pamphlet, 1810)

Colby, Reginald, *The Waterloo Despatch* (London: HMSO, 1965)

Cooper, John Spencer, *Rough Notes of Seven Campaigns in Portugal, Spain, France and America during the years 1809–15* (London: John Russell Smith and Carlisle: Geo Coward, 1869. Reprinted Staplehurst: Spellmount Ltd, 1996)

Corrigan, Gordon, *Wellington, A Military Life* (Hambledon & London, 2001)

Dalton, Edward, *The Waterloo Roll Call*, 2nd edn (London: Eyre & Spottiswood, 1904)

Downer, Martyn, *Nelson's Purse* (London: Bantam Press, 2004)

Durand, Algernon, *The Making of a Frontier* (London: John Murray, 1899)

Durand, Henry Mortimer, *The Life of Sir Henry Marion Durand* (London: W.H. Allen & Co., 1883 (Nabu Public Domain Reprints))

Flanegan, James, Paymaster 14th Light Dragoons, 'Payroll June to September 1810, showing Henry Percy's payment by flag of truce' (National Archives, WO 12/1149, 1810)

Fortescue, Hon. J.W., *A History of the British Army, Volumes VI, VIII and IX* (London: Macmillan & Co., 1899–1930, 1906/1912)

Foy, Le Général Maximilien Sébastien, *History of the War in the Peninsula*, 2 vols (London: Treutel & Wurtz, 1827)

Fraser, Sir William, Bt, *The Waterloo Ball* (London: F. Harvey, 1897)

Gentleman's Magazine, Various

Gleig, Revd G.R., *The Story of the Battle of Waterloo* (London: John Murray, 1848)

Glover, Gareth (ed.), *Wellington's Voice. The candid letters of Lieutenant Colonel John Fremantle, Coldstream Guards 1818–1815* (Barnsley: Pen & Sword/Frontline Books, 2012)

Glover, Gareth (ed.), *Eyewitness to the Peninsular War and the Battle of Waterloo, Letters and Journals of Lt Col Hon. James Stanhope, 1803–1825* (Barnsley: Pen & Sword, Military, 2010)

Glover, Gareth (ed.), *The Waterloo Archive*, Vols 1, 3 and 4: British Sources (Barnsley: Pen & Sword/Frontline Books, 2010/2011/2012)

Government of India, 'Telegrams and papers relating to the death of Major General Sir Henry Durand, Lieut Governor of the Punjab 1871' (Alnwick Archives, DNM: H/2/56-58, 1871)

Gurwood, Lt Col John (ed.), *The Dispatches of Field Marshal The Duke of Wellington 1799 to 1818*, 12 volumes (London: John Murray, 1834–39)

Gurwood, Lt Col John (ed.), *General Orders of Field Marshal The Duke of Wellington KG, etc in Portugal, Spain and France 1809–1814 and in the Low Countries and France in 1815, and in France, Army of Occupation* (London: W. Clowes & Sons, 1837 (British Library, Historical Print Editions))

Harris, Benjamin Randell, *Recollections of Rifleman Harris (Old 95th)*, edited Henry Curling Esq (Half-Pay 52nd Foot) (London: H. Hurst, 1848)

Hawker, Lt Col. Peter, *Journal of a Regimental Officer during the Recent Campaign in Portugal and Spain (14th Light Dragoons)* (London: Johnson, 1810)

Haythornthwaite, Philip, *Corunna 1809* (Oxford: Osprey, Campaign Series, 2001)

Hibbert, Christopher, *Corunna* (London: Batsford, 1961)

Hill, Benson Earle, *Recollections of an Artillery Officer, Including Scenes and Adventures in Ireland, America, Flanders and France* (London: Richard Bentley, 1836)

Hope, Sir John, 'Report to Gen Sir David Baird aboard HMS *Ville de Paris*, on operations at the Battle of Corunna' (National Archives, WO1/236, 1809)

Howard, Donald (ed.), *The French Campaign in Portugal 1810–1811, An account by Jean Jacques Pelet* (translated from the original at Vincennes) (Minneapolis: University of Minneapolis Press, 1973)

James, Trevor, *Prisoners of War at Dartmoor: American and French Soldiers and Sailors in an English Prison During the Napoleonic Wars and the War of 1812* (Jefferson North Carolina and London: McFarland & Company, Inc., 1934)

Junot, Laura, Duchess of Abrantes, *Memoirs of Madame Junot, Duchess of Abrantes*, 4 vols (London: Richard Bentley & Son, 1893)

Lejeune, Baron, *Memoirs of Baron Lejeune, Aide de Camp to Marshals Berthier, Davout and Oudinot*, translated and edited by Mrs A. Bell (London: Longmans, Green & Co., 1897)

Lloyd, Clive L., *History of Napoleonic and American Prisoners of War 1756–1816, Hulk, Depot and Parole* (Woodbridge, Suffolk: Antique Collectors Club, 2007)

London Gazette Extraordinary, no. 17028, *The Waterloo Dispatch, 23 June 1815* (London, 1815; Alnwick Archives, Acc 271. RT/BR/10/A/1, George Clark)

Lord Frederick Fitzclarence's interview, *Your Most Obedient Servant, James Thornton, Cook to the Duke of Wellington*. Introduction by Elizabeth Longford (Exeter: Webb & Bower Ltd, 1985)

Marbot, Baron, *The Memoirs of Baron de Marbot, Late Lieutenant General in the French Army*, translated from the French by Arthur John Butler (London: Longmans, Green & Co., 1903)

Marshall Cornwall, James, *Masséna, L'enfant Cheri de la Victoire* (Paris: Librairie Plon, 1967)

Maurice, Maj. Gen. Sir Frederick, *History of the Scots Guards*, vol. 1 (London: Chatto & Windus, 1934)

Moore, James Carrick, *Narrative of the Campaigns of the British Army in Spain commanded by H.E. Sir John Moore* (London: Joseph Johnson, 1809)

Moore, John Frederick, *The Diary of Sir John Moore*, vol. 2 (London: Edward Arnold, 1834)

Moore-Smith, George Charles, *The Life of John Colborne, Field Marshal Lord Seaton. GCB, GCH, GCMG, KTS, KStG, KMT* (London: J. Murray, 1903)

Muir, Rory, *Wellington. The Path to Victory 1769–1814* (London: Yale University Press, 2013)

Muir, Rory (ed.), *At Wellington's Right Hand, Letters of Lieutenant Colonel Sir Alexander Gordon* (Stroud: Sutton Publishing; Army Records Society, vol. 21, 2003)

Oman, Carola, *Sir John Moore* (London: Hodder & Stoughton, 1953)

Oman, Charles, *A History of the Peninsular War*, vols I–VII (Oxford: Clarendon Press, 1902)

Oman, Sir Charles, *Wellington's Army 1809–1814* (London: Edward Arnold, 1913; reprinted Greenhill Books, Lionel Leventhal Ltd, 1986)

Paget, Sir Julian, *Wellington's Peninsular War* (London: Leo Cooper, 1990)

Percy, Algernon, *A Bearskin's Crimea, Colonel Henry Percy VC and his Brother Officers* (Barnsley: Leo Cooper, 2005)

Percy, Capt. Hon. Henry, 'Military Notebook, Messina, Sicily 1807' (Alnwick Archives, DP/D1/III/5, 1807)

Percy, Capt. Hon. Henry, 'Military Notebook, Messina, Sicily, and Alexandria, Egypt 1807 (Alnwick Archives, DP/D1/III/6, 1807)

Percy, Lt Col. Hon. Henry, 'Pocket notebook inscribed Hon Capt Gordon. Col Percy's Account of the Retreat to Corunna 1808–9' (Alnwick Archives, Acc 224/1-2, 1816?)

Percy, Lt Col. Hon. Henry, 'Transcript of account of Retreat to Corunna' (Alnwick Archives, DNP:MS 803, date unknown)

Perrett, Bryan (ed.), *A Hawk at War: Peninsular Reminiscences of General Sir Thomas Brotherton, CB* (Chippenham: Picton Publishing, 1986, for 14th/20th King's Hussars Regimental Association)

Saint-Denis, Louis Étienne, *Napoleon from the Tuileries to St Helena*, translated by Frank Hunter Potter (New York and London: Harper & Brothers, 1922)

Schaumann, August Ludolf Friedrich, *On the Road with Wellington: The Diary of a War Commissary in the Peninsular Campaigns* (London: William Heinemann Ltd, 1924)

Shepherd, Revd William, *Paris in Eighteen Hundred and Two and Eighteen Hundred and Fourteen* (London: Longman, Hurst, Rees, Orme & Brown, 1814)

Smith, Winston, *Days of Exile: The Story of the Vine and Olive Colony in Alabama* (Tuscaloosa, Alabama: W.B. Drake & Son, 1967)

Souchère Deléry, Simone de la, *Napoleon's Soldiers in America* (Gretna, Louisiana: Le Cercle du livre de France, Ltée; reprinted by Pelican Publishing Inc., 1950)

Stanhope, Philip Henry, *Notes of Conversations with the Duke of Wellington 1831–1851* (London: John Murray, 1889)

Story, William, *A Journal kept in France During a Captivity of more than Nine Years, 1805–1814* (Sunderland: George Garbutt, 1815)

Stewart (later Vane), Lt Gen. Charles, Marquess of Londonderry, *Narrative of the Peninsular War from 1808 to 1813* (London: Henry Colburn, 1828)

Sweetman, John, *Raglan, From the Peninsula to the Crimea* (Barnsley: Pen & Sword, Military, 2010)

Treasure, Geoffrey, *Who's Who in History*, Vol V: Late Hanoverian Britain (London: Blackwell, 1974)

War Office, 'British and Portuguese Busaco Order of Battle' (National Archives, WO 78/5955, 1810)

Warre, William, *Letters from the Peninsula 1808–12* (London: John Murray, 1909)

Weller, Jac, *Wellington in the Peninsula 1808–1814* (Barnsley: Greenhill Books/Pen & Sword Books Ltd, 1992)

Wellesley, Sir Arthur, 'Oporto Dispatch to Lord Castlereagh, 12 May 1809' (National Archives, WO 1/238, 1809)

Wellington, First Duke, '5 Letters to Lt Col Hon. Henry Percy, from London, Calais, Menin, Liege, and Valenciennes, concerning despatches, fox hounds and letters Aug–Oct 1818' (Alnwick Archives, DNA: F/40/1-5, 1818)

Wellington, Second Duke (ed.), *Supplementary Despatches, Correspondence and Memoranda of Field Marshal the Duke of Wellington KG* (London: John Murray, 1860)

Index